P9-EDC-222

GUIDE TO
Moab, UT
Backroads &
4-Wheel Drive
Trails

By **CHARLES A. WELLS**

Easy • Moderate • Difficult
Backcountry Driving Adventures

FunTreks, Inc.

Published by FunTreks, Inc.
P.O. Box 3127, Monument, CO 80132-3127
Phone: Toll free (877) 222-7623, Fax: (719) 277-7411
E-mail: books@funtreks.com
Website: www.funtreks.com

Copyright © 2000 by FunTreks, Inc.

Edited by Shelley Mayer

Cover design, photography, maps, and production by Charles A.Wells

First Edition

Library of Congress Catalog Card Number 99-98311
ISBN 0-9664976-2-7

Printed in the United States of America

To order additional books, call toll-free 1-877-222-7623 or use order form in back
of this book. You may also order online at www.funtreks.com.

TRAIL UPDATES:
For latest trail updates and changes, check the *Trail Updates* page on our Web site
at www.funtreks.com.

GUARANTEE OF SATISFACTION:
If you are dissatisfied with this book in any way, regardless of where you bought it,
please call our toll-free number during business hours at 1-877-222-7623. We
promise to do whatever it takes to make you happy.

DISCLAIMER

Travel in the Moab backcountry is by its very nature potentially dangerous and could result in property damage, injury, or even death.
The scope of this book cannot predict every possible hazard you may
encounter. If you drive any of the trails in this book, you acknowledge
these risks and assume full responsibility. You are the final judge as to
whether a trail is safe to drive on any given day, whether your vehicle is
capable of the journey, and what supplies you should carry. The information contained herein cannot replace good judgment and proper prep-
aration on your part. The publisher and author of this book disclaim any
and all liability for bodily injury, death, or property damage that could
occur to you or any of your passengers.

ACKNOWLEDGMENTS

I am very much indebted to the following individuals and organizations for their help with this book:

Canyonlands National Park, Arches National Park, Bureau of Land Management, the U.S. Forest Service, and the Canyonlands Natural History Association. I worked with a long list of hard-working staffers whose courteous and professional advice, at every stage of this book's development, has helped ensure a safer and more enjoyable adventure for all readers.

Bob Wildmann and the El Jebel Jeep Patrol of Denver, CO. Bob lives part-time in Moab and, in addition to being president of the El Jebel club, is a member of the Red Rock 4-Wheelers. Bob and his wife, Mary, helped me in countless ways including inviting me on club runs, guiding me on virtually any trail I wished to drive, critiquing my book, and introducing me to some of the most knowledgeable four-wheelers in Moab.

Eric Steenburn and the Trailridge Runners of Longmont, CO. Eric coached me on GPS, gave me access to his extensive Moab map collection, and guided me on many trails. I had the privilege of joining the Trailridge Runners on several great runs, including difficult Pritchett Canyon.

Craig Stumbough and the Larimer County Mountaineers of Fort Collins, CO. A Moab run with this club is not complete until every detail is thoroughly discussed over a nightly campfire. Thanks, Craig, for letting me be a part of this close-knit club and for your personal help and support.

Ber Knight and the Red Rock 4-Wheelers. Ber has spent nearly two decades exploring and mapping Moab's backcountry. He is a highly respected authority on trails in the Moab area. He reviewed my book, offered suggestions, and guided me on several trails including Hell's Revenge, which he recently helped mark. I'd also like to thank Doug McElhaney for his personal tour of Poison Spider Mesa, as well as Hans Weibel and John Sensenbrenner for their advice. I thank all members and trip leaders of the Red Rock 4-Wheelers who volunteer countless hours annually to the Easter Jeep Safari.

My own club, the Colorado Four-Wheelers of Colorado Springs, CO, including Larry Leaveck, Neale Geis, Bob Niehoff, and Larry Miller, who first introduced me to Moab and have supported me over the years.

Dan Mick, Moab's most respected professional offroad guide and founder of bewildering Golden Spike. Dan reviewed my book, made trail suggestions and shared with me some of his unique perspective on the Moab area.

Rick Sparks, Steve Nantz, and Mike Bown of Moab Offroad, a team of hard-working, trustworthy mechanics who kept my Cherokee running smoothly throughout its long summer ordeal.

Shelley Mayer, a respected editor and writer in Colorado Springs, for her painstaking editing of this book.

Linda Meyer, expert in Macintosh graphics and digital prepress, continues to offer guidance and support whenever I need it.

Last but not least, my loving wife, Beverly, without whose support and assistance this book would not be possible.

White Rim (Trail #44) in Canyonlands National Park, rated Moderate.

Contents

Trails Listed by Area

Trail Locator Map

UTAH

Salt Lake City ✦

Area Detailed Below →

● Easy Trails
■ Moderate Trails
◆ Difficult Trails

See individual area maps for more detail.

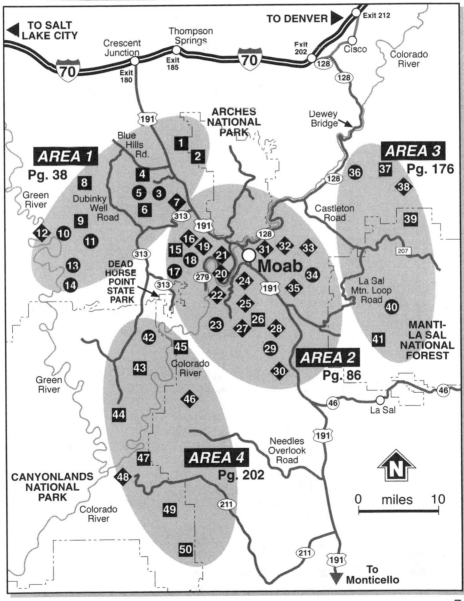

◄ TO SALT LAKE CITY

TO DENVER ► Exit 212

Crescent Junction

Thompson Springs

Exit 202

Cisco

Colorado River

Exit 180

Exit 185

70

70

128

128

191

ARCHES NATIONAL PARK

Dewey Bridge

AREA 1
Pg. 38

Blue Hills Rd.

1

2

4

AREA 3
Pg. 176

36

37

38

Green River

8

Dubinky Well Road

5 3

6

7

313

128

Castleton Road

39

9

16 19

15 18

21

31 32 33

191

128

12 10

11

207

13

DEAD HORSE POINT STATE PARK

17

313

20

279

24

Moab

34

35

La Sal Mtn. Loop Road

14

313

22

191

40

23

25

27 26

28

MANTI-LA SAL NATIONAL FOREST

42

29

41

45

43

Colorado River

30

AREA 2
Pg. 86

Green River

44

46

46

La Sal

47

48

AREA 4
Pg. 202

Needles Overlook Road

46

191

N

49

211

0   miles   10

CANYONLANDS NATIONAL PARK

Colorado River

50

211

191

To Monticello

7

Trails Listed by Difficulty

Easier

More Difficult

On this page, trails are ranked on a continuum from easiest to most difficult e.g., the last easy trail is more difficult than the first easy trail, etc.

Trail Ratings Defined

Trail ratings are very subjective. Conditions change for many reasons including weather and time of year. An easy trail can quickly become difficult when washed out by a rainstorm or blocked by a fallen rock. You must be the final judge of trail conditions on the day you drive the trail. If any part of a trail is difficult, the entire trail is rated difficult. You may be able to drive part of the trail before reaching a difficult spot. Read each trail description carefully for specific information.

Easy

Gravel, dirt, clay, sand, or mildly rocky road. Gentle grades. Water levels low except during periods of heavy runoff. Full-width single lane or wider with adequate room to pass most of the time. Where shelf conditions exist, road is wide and well-maintained with minor sideways tilt. Four-wheel drive recommended on most trails but some are suitable for two-wheel drive under dry conditions. Some clay surfaces may be impassable when wet.

Moderate

Rutted dirt or rocky road suitable for most sport utility vehicles. Some obstacles will require careful tire placement. Four-wheel drive, low range, and high ground clearance required. Standard factory skid plates and tow hooks recommended on many trails. Undercarriage may scrape occasionally. Some grades fairly steep but manageable if dry. Soft sand possible. Sections of sideways tilt will require caution. Narrow shelf roads possible. Backing may be necessary to pass. Water depths passable for stock high clearance vehicles except during periods of heavy runoff. Mud holes may be present especially in the spring. Brush may touch vehicle.

Difficult

Some trails suitable for more aggressive stock vehicles but most trails require vehicle modification. Lifts, differential lockers, aggressive articulation, and/or winches recommended in many cases. Skid plates and tow hooks required. Body damage possible. Grades can be steep with severe ground undulation. Sideways tilt can be extreme. Deep water crossings possible. Shelf roads extremely narrow; use caution in full-size vehicle. Read trail description carefully. Passing may be difficult with backing required for long distances. Brush may scratch sides of vehicle.

Trails Listed Alphabetically

*Author's favorite trails are shown
in boldface type.*

INTRODUCTION

Colorado River, Fisher Towers, and La Sal Mountains seen from Hwy. 128 heading to Moab.

Introduction

Visitors from all over the world are drawn to Moab's unusual and beautiful backcountry. They soon discover, however, that traversing these lands by foot, mountain bike, or motorized vehicle can be a bewildering experience. Twisting river valleys, sheer cliffs, and blind canyons make route-finding a significant challenge. Even those who have driven a particular road or trail before may have trouble finding it a second time. Fold-out maps provide necessary topographic information, but often don't provide enough detail about spur roads and trail difficulty.

This guide book does not attempt to describe every square foot of Moab's backcountry. Instead, it focuses on the most popular trails and covers them in extensive detail. Photographs show trail conditions as well as scenic features. Directions are straightforward and specific. Maps are simplified and easy to understand. The author has driven every trail himself and never relies on secondhand information. Although GPS (Global Positioning System) waypoints are provided, most routes can be driven without them.

If you're a new sport utility owner or new to backcountry driving, start with an easy trail. Learn the basics like how to use low range, how to place your tires on rocks rather than straddle them, and how to be environmentally responsible. Gradually, as you learn what your vehicle can and can't do, you'll develop more confidence. You'll find it's possible to have fun without worrying. Before long, you'll be ready to try more moderate trails. You may decide to add skid plates and tow points if you don't already have them. Many stock vehicles come with these features. If you're like most newcomers to backcountry driving, you'll find today's modern four-wheel-drive vehicles very capable, certainly good enough to take you almost anywhere you want to go.

If you're a hard-core four-wheeler, this book will be a real treat. For the first time ever, most of the popular Easter Jeep Safari trails are accurately documented. Some of the trails were driven during the safari; others were driven on separate trips guided by local experts. Most of the best-known trails like Hell's Revenge, Poison Spider Mesa, Golden Spike, etc. are presented in their entirety. Some trails like Flat Iron Mesa and Fins & Things have been shortened just a bit. Others like Secret Spire and Porcupine Rim have been significantly cropped. One trail (called the 3-D trail in the Safari) has been broken into three parts: Hidden Canyon, Hidden Canyon Overlook, and Bartlett Overlook. These changes were made to facilitate easier route-finding, to emphasize the best parts of each trail, or to separate difficulty levels. You should find these changes logical and beneficial.

Have fun but please remember to stay on designated roads and trails at all times. Needless tracking destroys the scenery that everyone has come to see. When other users see this abuse, it gives all off-highway drivers a bad name. Continued abuse often leads to trail closures, which disappoints everyone who enjoys driving in the backcountry. Make sure you know your responsibilities, which are discussed starting on page 23.

Please stay on the road at all times.

HOW TO USE THIS BOOK

This book has been designed for quick and easy use. Trails are grouped by area. First use the Trail Locator Map on page 7 to determine the big picture, then turn to each area map for more detail. Each trail is shown with photos and a map. All maps are to scale and oriented with north at the top. Scale is indicated using an overall grid. Check the size of the grid at the bottom of each map. A small legend or "Mini Key" is included on each map for quick reference. Find the full map legend on page 36.

The shaded portion of the trail is described in the text. Other roads are for reference only and should be traveled at your own risk. Water crossing and bridge symbols show major stream locations. Most trails are described in one direction; a few, however, are described both ways.

Trails are listed three ways for your convenience: in numerical order by area on page 6, by difficulty on page 8, and alphabetically on page 10. Geometric shapes are used to indicate difficulty. A circle indicates easy, a square moderate, and a diamond difficult. Trail ratings are described in detail on page 9.

The text for each trail includes: general location, difficulty, special features, length and driving time, how to get to the trail, a detailed trail description, how to get home, location of nearest services, and other maps.

Mileage readings can vary because of vehicle differences and driving habits. Readings were rounded to the nearest tenth of a mile. The author's odometers were calibrated for accuracy.

The appendix of this book includes a map of downtown Moab with services directory, helpful information on GPS, waypoint data, a glossary, a list of references and recommended reading, helpful addresses and phone numbers, an index, and information about the author.

SELECTING THE RIGHT TRAIL FOR YOUR VEHICLE

Today's modern sport utility vehicles are amazingly well designed for off-highway travel. Modern technology is making the backcountry accessible to ever more capable stock vehicles. More and more people are buying sport utilities and setting out to discover the fun that other SUV owners are having. Sometimes, however, beginners think that once they buy a four-wheel-drive vehicle, it will go anywhere. They soon learn that this is not the case. The following will help you decide which trails are right for your vehicle.

Easy: Suitable for all stock four-wheel-drive sport utility vehicles with high ground clearance and low range. Some trails can be driven in two-wheel drive without low range in dry weather. A few trails, under ideal conditions, are suitable for passenger cars.

Moderate: Suitable for most stock sport utility vehicles with high ground clearance and low range. For the toughest moderate trails, factory skid plates, tow points, and all-terrain tires are recommended. These options are available from your dealer or local four-wheel-drive shop.

Difficult: Suitable for some stock sport utility vehicles with very high ground clearance, excellent articulation, tow hooks, and a full skid plate package. All-terrain tires as a minimum, mud terrains preferred. A winch or differential lockers are recommended for the most difficult trails. Drivers who spend a great deal of time on extreme trails find it necessary to modify their vehicles with higher ground clearance, oversized tires, and heavy duty accessories. A trail is rated difficult if any spot on the trail is difficult. You may be able to enjoy much of a trail before running into the difficult portion. Read the trail description carefully.

MOAB AND ITS BACKCOUNTRY

Town Map: On page 242 you'll find a map of downtown Moab showing locations of basic needs, e.g., supermarkets, restaurants, campgrounds, hospital, churches, auto parts stores, etc. It is very easy to find your way around town. The Visitor Information Center is located in the middle of town at the intersection of Main Street and Center Street.

Lodging and Camping: For a small town, Moab has quite a few hotels, motels and campgrounds; however; the best ones fill up quickly, especially on weekends. Play it safe; make advance reservations. For the week of Easter Jeep Safari, call ahead several months. There are campgrounds at many points on the outskirts of town and along major highways. These are available on a first-come, first-served basis. Restrictions apply. Read and obey all regulations. Most in-town campgrounds offer full RV hookups; some provide showers to non-guests for a fee.

Town Etiquette: Moab is a very friendly town but some residents have had their fill of inconsiderate tourists. Be a good neighbor, show common courtesy, and remember you're a guest.

Looking for a group to go wheeling with? Stop by the City Market parking lot on weekend mornings. (See map on page 242.) It's a popular place for four-wheel-drive groups to gather before heading out.

Weather: Spring and fall are the best seasons to be in Moab. The average daytime temperatures range from 64 degrees in March to 84 in May.

14

June through August average highs are near 100 degrees with maximum highs reaching 110 in July. September's average high temperature is in the mid 80s while October is perfect at 77 degrees. The wettest months are April, July, and October, with the worst month, October, averaging 1.6 inches of precipitation. When it rains, it can come all at once. Flash floods are a major concern in canyon country. Weather is usually great for the Easter Jeep Safari but in 1999 four inches of snow fell on Big Saturday. Be prepared for anything.

Town History: Moab experienced several boom and bust economic periods during the 20th century. The most significant was the uranium mining period during the 1950s. Following World War II, demand for uranium ore was high. The town quickly grew as mining operations shot up everywhere. Many of the four-wheel-drive trails are remnants of these mining days. You can still see bulldozer tracks and rock cuts on many trails such as Poison Spider Mesa and Sevenmile Rim. In places, core drilling holes remain exposed in the slickrock. Demand for uranium died during the 1960s spelling near-disaster for the town. Many jobs were replaced by underground potash mining operations until 18 miners were killed in an underground explosion in 1964. The operation was quickly converted to automated solution mining requiring far fewer workers. Meanwhile, Hollywood discovered Moab's backcountry was a great place to shoot western movies. Over the years, dozens of movies have been shot in the area, including *Indiana Jones* in 1988, *Thelma and Louise* in 1990, and *Geronimo* in 1993. Today, tourism is Moab's biggest industry, driven primarily by the establishment of two National Parks and the growing popularity of mountain biking and four-wheeling.

Arches National Monument was dedicated in 1929 and became a National Park in 1971, seven years after Canyonlands National Park. The two parks record nearly 1.5 million visits each year.

The Slickrock Bike Trail started first as a motorcycle trail in 1969. Today it is predominantly used for mountain biking but motorcyclists still use the trail. People come from all over the world to ride the demanding trail.

The first Jeep Safari was held in 1967. What started as a one-day event now takes nine days. Sponsored by the Red Rock 4-Wheelers (Moab's local club) and the Moab Chamber of Commerce, the safari is held the week prior to Easter every year. Participants can sign up for over 30 different trail runs. Many stock vehicles participate on the easier rated trails. The event is so popular that a lottery system must be used to assign trails. On Big Saturday, Main Street is lined with people to watch the controlled "big bang" departure of some 1,000 vehicles.

Slickrock Bike Trail.

15

Geology: One cannot cross these lands without some curiosity as to how they were formed. In the area around Moab, the Colorado and Green Rivers have exposed 300 million years of geologic history. The process was extremely complex, with oceans covering the land, leaving deposits, and then retreating. Ten million years ago, the earth's crust was pushed up, forming an area called the Colorado Plateau. Waters flowing off the land formed into streams and rivers which quickly (in geologic time) cut through this high plateau, exposing layers thousands of feet below. Harder layers, like White Rim Sandstone, resist longer than softer layers, resulting in the varying stair-step effect that is prominently seen in the canyonlands. Spires and needles are the result of the more resistant layers that form a protective cap as erosion continues underneath.

The formation of arches started with the massive salt beds under the rock layers described above. This unstable base allowed the overlaying rock to shift and buckle, which formed domes. Cracks formed, slicing the domes like bread. Erosion then rounded the slices into fins. When softer spots on the sides of the fins broke away, pockets were created. Water and ice working on the pockets finally wore through the fin, creating a hole or window. Eventually, as the windows enlarged, only a small part of the fin remained, leaving an arch. As arches age, they become thinner and more dramatic. Eventually arches wear thin and collapse. Some arches are formed from the top down and start as potholes. Most of the arches in Arches National Park are formed in a salmon-colored layer of rock called Entrada Sandstone.

Fins and domes, especially prominent in the Behind the Rocks area, began as larger desert dunes that solidified into Navajo Sandstone. Surface erosion carved the dunes into smaller, rounded mounds, often called petrified dunes. Continued erosion created more vertical domes. Cracks in the domes allowed erosion to continue until narrower fins formed.

Many people are curious about desert varnish. This is a thin coating on hard rock surfaces that is red to black in color. The thin coating is created from a chemical/oxidation process involving microorganisms. The process takes thousands of years and is often darker where water flows over the rock surface. Desert varnish is typically seen on vertical surfaces of Wingate Sandstone.

Petroglyphs and Pictographs:
Petroglyphs are Indian motifs that have been scratched, pecked, or otherwise abraded into hard rock surfaces, often in desert varnish which provides a contrasting background color. Pictographs are paintings or drawings on rock surfaces using mineral pigments and plant dyes. Petroglyphs are more likely to be seen

Petroglyphs at Newspaper Rock.

today simply because they have lasted longer than pictographs. It's a federal crime to damage or deface petroglyphs or pictographs, commonly called rock art or Indian writings. Rock art should not be touched; oil from your hands can be damaging. If you see vandalism taking place, report it to authorities immediately. For information on where to find rock art around Moab, pick-up a free brochure called "Moab Area Rock Art Auto Tour" at the Moab Information Center and other government locations around Moab.

SAFETY TIPS

File a Flight Plan. Determine where you are going and when you plan to return. Be as specific as possible. Inform a friend or relative and call them when you return. If something goes wrong, you'll have the comfort of knowing that at least someone knows where you are and that you could be in trouble.

Travel with another vehicle. Your chances of getting stuck in the back-country are immensely reduced with two vehicles. If one vehicle breaks down, you have a back-up. This could also save you an enormous towing charge. On a trail like the White Rim or Lockhart Basin, it might take all day to reach you. Towing rates start at $50 per hour. Some places charge $150 per hour depending upon circumstances.

Carry extra maps and a compass. The maps in this book will clearly direct you along the trail. However, if you get lost or decide to venture down a spur road, you'll need additional maps with topographic information. Carry a compass so you can orient yourself. At the end of each trail description, I have listed several maps that I found useful. Make sure you have at least one.

The greatest amount of detail is shown on 7.5 minute U.S. Geological Survey Maps; however; each map covers a small area and many maps are required. Since I carry a laptop computer, I buy 7.5 minute maps on CDs. They are extremely economical and easy to use in this format, but they would be useless if something happened to my computer. I use them because they provide maximum detail for GPS tracking. I always carry other maps.

You must carry a fold-out map of some kind with topographic information. My favorites are the Moab East and Moab West Mountain Biking and Recreation Maps published by Latitude 40°, Inc. They have great topographic detail and show many of the trails in this book. They are made of durable, waterproof plastic. Although they are slanted toward mountain biking, many of the trails are the same as or similar to the four-wheel-drive trails. The two maps are available almost anywhere in Moab.

Trails Illustrated Maps are always good. There's one for Canyonlands National Park (Needles and Island in the Sky Districts #210) and one for Arches National Park (#211).

For anyone serious about exploring Moab's backcountry, you can't beat the maps and books of F.A. Barnes. He has spent decades exploring Moab's backcountry and his numerous publications provide ultimate authoritative detail. Besides directions to every corner of Moab's wildlands, he provides in-depth analysis of geography, geology, archaeology, history, and much more. He covers an array of topics including off-highway driving, hiking, biking, backpacking, climbing, and even hang-gliding.

Whatever map you choose, spend time looking it over before you head out. Familiarize yourself as much as possible with the map and the area.

Changing conditions. Moab's backcountry is fragile and under constant assault by forces of nature and man. Rock slides can occur or an entire road can be washed away from a single heavy rainstorm. A trail may be closed without notice. Directional signs may be removed or vandalized. New roads can literally spring up overnight from various forms of construction and mineral search activity. For these reasons, always question information on a map or in a guidebook. Use common sense when discrepancies occur.

High water, flash floods. Many of Moab's backroads cross or follow dry washes, small streams, and narrow canyons. Heavy rains can turn these places into raging torrents of water in minutes. Check weather forecasts

Kane Creek after a storm. Photo by Matt Peterson

and keep an eye on the sky. Be conservative and don't take chances. Cut your trip short if necessary. Don't attempt to cross a fast flowing stream unless you've done it before and know what your vehicle can do. Wait if necessary; water levels usually go down quickly after a single rain shower. If you're in a narrow canyon and water begins to rise, drive perpendicularly out of the canyon if possible. If this is not possible, get out of your vehicle and climb to higher ground. Most people who die in flash floods attempt to outrun the rising water in their vehicles.

Clay surfaced roads. A few roads around Moab, like the Blue Hills Road in the northwest area, are composed of clay. They are easy when dry but after a rain become impassable. Even a four-wheel-drive vehicle with good tires can't get through. Since most roads are crowned in the middle, you may slide to the side. If there's a ditch, you could slide into it. If the road is on a hill, like the switchbacks of Mineral Bottom Road, wet conditions can be downright dangerous. Your only recourse is to turn around or wait for the surface to dry. This usually doesn't take long after it stops raining.

Inspect your vehicle carefully. Before you start into the backcountry, make sure your vehicle is in top operating condition. If you have a mechanic do the work, make sure he is reliable and understands four-wheeling. Tell him where you plan to take your vehicle. Pay particular attention to fluids, hoses, belts, battery, brakes, steering linkage, suspension system, driveline, and anything exposed under the vehicle. Tighten anything that may be loose. Inspect your tires carefully for potential weak spots and tread wear.

Wear your seat belt. You might think that because you're driving slowly, it's not necessary to wear your seat belt or use child restraints. I've learned through experience that you are much safer with a seat belt than without. Buckle up at all times.

Keep heads, arms, and legs inside moving vehicle. Many trails are narrow. Brush, tree limbs, and rock overhangs may come very close to your vehicle. The driver must make it clear to every passenger to stay inside the vehicle at all times. Children, in particular, must not be allowed to stick their heads, arms, or legs out the windows.

Cliff edges. Watch children and be extremely careful around cliff edges. Hand rails are rarely provided. Watch for loose rock and stay away from these areas when it's wet, icy, or getting dark. If you climb up slickrock, remember it's harder to get down than to climb up.

Lightning. During a storm, stay away from lone trees, cliff edges, and high points. Stay low to the ground or in your vehicle. Lightning can strike from a distant storm even when it's clear overhead.

Altitude sickness. Some people may experience altitude sickness in the mountains. Geyser and La Sal Passes are near 10,000 ft. Symptoms include nausea, dizziness, headaches, or weakness the first time at high altitude. This condition usually improves over time. To minimize symptoms, give yourself time to acclimate, drink plenty of fluids, decrease salt intake, reduce alcohol and caffeine, eat foods high in carbohydrates, and try not to exert yourself.

Mines, tunnels, and old structures. Be careful around old mine buildings. Stay out of mines and tunnels. Don't let children play in these areas.

DESERT SURVIVAL

Self-reliance. Most of us live in populated areas and are accustomed to having other people around when things go wrong. In Moab's remote backcountry, you must be self-reliant. Don't count on anyone else's help. Try to anticipate what can go wrong and prepare accordingly.

Water, water, and more water. I can't stress enough the importance of carrying and drinking plenty of water—at least one gallon per person per day plus extra water for your vehicle. When I'm in Moab, I leave a five gallon container in my vehicle at all times and take more when I'm out on a trail. A canteen is handy if you have to walk out. Running out of water under certain circumstances can be a fatal mistake.

First Aid. Always carry a good first-aid kit. Take a first-aid course and learn the basics. Make sure the kit contains a good first-aid book.

What to do if you have mechanical problems or you get lost. Stay with your vehicle. There's always a chance that someone will come along if you stay near the road. Your vehicle is easier to see than you are. Your car can provide shelter from wind, rain, and cold. The desert can get very cold at night, especially if you get wet. You won't be able to stay in your car during the heat of the day. Seek shade. You're more likely to find a rock overhang than a shady tree. Don't sit on the hot ground. Dig down to cooler sand below. Create your own shade with blankets or tarp attached to your car or build a lean-to. If necessary, dig a depression under your car and crawl underneath after exhaust pipes and engine have cooled. If you don't have a shovel, dig with a hub cap. Work slowly; don't overexert yourself. Rest as much as possible. Drink plenty of water; don't wait until you're thirsty. Wear light-colored, loose-fitting clothing that covers as much of your skin as possible. Wear a hat and use sunscreen. Collect firewood before dark. Build a fire before you need it. If you get lost or separated from your group, stay in one place.

If you're familiar with the area and know exactly how far it is to hike out and are absolutely sure you can make it, consider walking out as a last resort. Cover up with loose clothing, take plenty of water, food, and rain protection to stay dry. Travel at night when it's cooler if the terrain is not too treacherous. Make sure you can see where you're walking.

Try to draw attention to yourself. Make noise anyway you can— whistles, horns, whatever you have. Don't run down your car battery. Build a smoky fire. Three fires in a triangle 150 feet apart are an international distress signal. Use flares if you have them. Some are designed for day use, others for night. Use a reflective mirror if you see an airplane or anyone in the distance.

If you have a cell phone, try to find a point where you can get a signal and call for help. Often you can reach Moab if you can see the La Sal Mountains. If you have a medical emergency, call 911. For mechanical problems, there are towing services available but charges can be exorbitant. You're better off to call a four-wheel-drive shop. I recommend Moab Offroad (see appendix). I know from experience that they charge fairly. They might even be able to advise you over the phone so that you can fix the problem yourself. If you're lost, try to reach Dan Mick of Dan Mick's Guided Tours (see appendix). Nobody knows the Moab area better than he. If you describe to him where you are, he may be able to figure out your location and tell you how to get out. He'll also come and get you. He's an excellent mechanic and has helped many people over the years. His fees are reasonable. It's a good idea to get to know a few people in town in case you need help. Visit a few places before heading into the backcountry.

If you have a CB radio, broadcast on channel 19 or emergency channel 9.

Continue intermittently even if no one responds. Make sure you give your location.

Hyperthermia. When your body overheats it's called hyperthermia. Symptoms include dry, flushed skin, inability to sweat, rapid heartbeat, and a rising body temperature. Hyperthermia is often preceded by cramps. They may not go away by drinking water alone. You may need food or salt. If hyperthermia is allowed to progress you could collapse from heatstroke which is extremely serious and can be fatal if not treated quickly.

To prevent hyperthermia, stay in the shade, don't overexert yourself, wear loose-fitting clothing, and drink plenty of water. If work is required to find or make shade, conserve your energy as best as possible.

Dehydration. As your body sweats to cool itself, it dehydrates. You may be drinking water but not enough. Eating may make you nauseous. You won't want to eat or drink. As symptoms get worse, your mouth will become dry, you may become dizzy, develop a headache, and become short of breath. At some point, you may not be able to walk or care for yourself.

You must prevent dehydration before it happens. Drink more than just to quench your thirst. If you must conserve water, rest as much as possible, try not to sweat, and don't eat a lot. Digestion requires body fluids. If you have plenty of water, drink it.

Hypothermia. It gets cold in the desert after the sun goes down. If it rains and gets windy, you could find yourself shivering in no time, especially if you've worked up a sweat during the day. Your hands and feet will become stiff. You may not be able to hold a match and start a fire.

Again, prevention is the key. Put on a jacket before you begin to get cold. Stay dry. Change clothes if necessary. If you get too cold, blankets may not be enough to warm you. Build a fire, drink hot liquids, or cuddle up with someone else. Your car is a great shelter—use it.

CHECKLIST. No single list can be all inclusive. You must be the final judge of what you need. Here's a list of basic items:

- WATER, WATER, WATER. At least one gallon per person per day. It's also wise to carry extra water for your vehicle.
- Food for normal eating and high-energy foods for emergencies. Energy bars, dried fruit, and hard candy store well.
- Loose-fitting, light-colored clothing, sun hats, shoes, socks, coats, and boots. Wool clothing keeps you warm when you're wet.
- Sleeping bags in case you get stuck overnight even if you're not planning to camp.
- A good first-aid kit including a first-aid book. Other important items include: sunscreen, insect repellent, water purification tablets, safety pins, needles and thread, tweezers, pocket knife or all-purpose tool.
- Candles, matches, fire starter, and a lighter.

- An extra set of keys and glasses.
- Toilet paper, paper towels, wet wipes, and trash bags.
- A large plastic sheet or tarp.
- Rain gear, small tent or tarp, nylon cords.
- Detailed maps, compass, watch, and a knife.
- If you plan to make a fire, carry your own firewood. (Wood fires are not permitted in Canyonlands National Park.)
- A heavy-duty tow strap. (The kind without metal hooks on the ends.)
- A fire extinguisher. Make sure you can reach it quickly.
- Jumper cables, extra fan belts, stop-leak for radiator.
- Replacement fuses and electrical tape.
- Flashlight and extra batteries.
- Flares, signal mirror, police whistle.
- Extra oil and other engine fluids.
- A full tank of gas. If you carry extra gas, make sure it's in an approved container and properly stored.
- A good set of tools, work gloves, and a complete service manual for your vehicle.
- Baling wire and duct tape.
- An assortment of hoses, clamps, nuts, bolts, and washers.
- A full-size spare tire.
- A tire pressure gauge, electric tire pump that will plug into your cigarette lighter, and a can of nonflammable tire sealant.
- A jack that will lift your vehicle fairly high off the ground. Take a small board to place under the jack. Carry a high-lift jack if you can, especially on more difficult trails. Test your jack before you leave home.
- Shovel and axe. Folding shovels work great.
- Tire chains for late and early season mountain travel. They can also help if you get stuck in the mud.
- CB radio and/or cellular phone.
- Portable toilet.
- If you have a winch, carry a tree strap, clevis, and snatch block.

Store these items in tote bags or large plastic containers so they can be easily loaded into your vehicle when it's time to go. Some things can be left in your vehicle all the time if you have room. Make sure you tie everything down thoroughly so it doesn't bounce around or shift.

Maintenance. Backroad travel puts your vehicle under greater stress than normal highway driving. Follow maintenance directions in your owner's manual for severe driving conditions. This usually calls for changing oil, oil filter, and air filter more frequently as well as more frequent fluid checks and lubrications. Inspect your tires carefully; they take a lot of extra abuse. After your trip, make sure you wash your vehicle. Use a high pressure spray to thoroughly clean the underside and wheel wells. Automatic car washes usually are not adequate. Do it yourself, if you want your vehicle in good shape for the next trip.

YOUR RESPONSIBILITIES AS A BACKCOUNTRY DRIVER

As you venture into the backcountry, make sure you understand the rules of backcountry travel and practice them at all times. Although much damage is done by deliberate violators, some is done by well-intentioned drivers who fail to learn the rules.

Stay on the trail. This is the single most important rule of backcountry driving. Leaving the trail causes unnecessary erosion, kills vegetation, and spoils the beauty of the land. Scars remain for years. Don't widen the trail by driving around rocks and muddy spots and don't short cut switchbacks. When you have to pass another vehicle, do so at designated pull-overs. Sometimes the edge of the trail is defined by a line of rocks. Don't move the rocks or cross over them. Drivers who leave existing trails risk fines and cause trails to be closed. Practice diligently to leave no trace of your passage.

Wilderness and Wilderness Study Areas. It is a serious offense to drive in a designated wilderness area or wilderness study area. Even mountain bikes are prohibited. These areas are usually well marked and clearly shown on maps.

Private Property. Many roads cross private property. Pass through quietly and stay on the road at all times. Don't disturb livestock. Leave gates the way you find them unless posted otherwise.

Ruins and archaeological sites. It is a federal crime to disturb archaeological sites. Don't touch them or climb inside. Since damage is often done unintentionally, I recommend people stay at least ten feet away at all times. Keep an eye on the kids. Do not remove or touch historical artifacts. Report any illegal activity to a ranger. A reward is offered for convicted violators.

Don't camp or picnic near an archaeological site.

Cryptobiotic crust. The black jagged crust you see everywhere in the desert is called cryptobiotic crust. It forms a base for future plant growth and is nature's first step to controlling erosion and reclaiming the land. In its early stages, it's nearly invisible. It is extremely delicate and takes decades to form. Never walk, ride, or drive on it.

Stay off cryptobiotic crust.

Pets. Dogs and other pets are prohibited in the backcountry of Canyonlands National Park. This includes transporting in your vehicle. Pets on leashes are allowed in developed areas, i.e., paved roads, parking lots, picnic areas, and at the Squaw Flat and Willow Flat Campgrounds. Arches National Park allows leashed pets near paved roads, parking areas, established picnic areas, and in Devils Garden Campground; however, they are not allowed in the backcountry. You may not leave a pet unattended in the car or tied up outside and you must clean up after your pet. It is dangerous and cruel to leave a pet in a hot car. On other public lands, it is best to keep your pet on a leash to stop it from chasing wildlife and disturbing cryptobiotic soil. Generally, you'll find that having a pet along is a big hassle. It's best to leave them at home.

Trash disposal and litter. Carry plastic trash bags and pack out your own trash, including cigarette butts. Where waste receptacles are provided, use them. When possible, clean up after others. Keep a litter bag handy and pick up trash along the trail.

When nature calls. The disposal of solid human waste and toilet paper is becoming a big problem as more visitors head into the backcountry. The arid climate does not decompose these materials as fast as they are being left behind. Canyonlands National Park provides an adequate number of vault toilets within its boundaries, but in other locations you're on your own. The best solution is to carry a portable toilet. Some places like the Maze District of Canyonlands National Park require you carry a cleanable, reusable toilet system. Otherwise, keep a small shovel handy and bury feces 4 to 6 inches deep, away from trails, campsites and at least 300 feet from any water source, which includes dry washes. The best place is beneath a juniper or pinyon pine tree where cryptobiotic crust does not form. Seal toilet paper and feminine hygiene products in a small plastic bag and discard with your trash.

Campfires. Regulations vary somewhat throughout the region. Canyonlands National Park does not allow any wood-burning campfires except in the river corridor. Charcoal and propane are okay, but you must carry out your ashes and fire debris. Arches National Park restricts fires to designated sites and firepans. You must bring your own firewood and pack out your ashes. In other areas, use existing fire rings whenever possible. Carry out fire debris with your trash. A propane camping stove is very convenient for cooking and is environmentally preferred.

Washing, cleaning, and bathing. If you must use soap, use biodegradable soap but never around lakes or streams. Heat water without using soap to clean utensils whenever possible.

Potholes. Potholes come in all shapes and sizes. Some contain water and some remain dry most of the time. Dry potholes contain microscopic organisms that remain dormant for years then spring to life when filled with water. Never drive into or over a pothole. Never wash dishes, swim, or bathe in a pothole. This pollutes the water and destroys microscopic life.

Potholes come in all sizes.

CANYONLANDS NATIONAL PARK

Canyonlands National Park consists of 527 square miles of remote, incredibly beautiful backcountry. Only a small portion of the roads in the park are paved. To see the park and many of its outstanding features up-close requires a high-clearance, four-wheel-drive vehicle. Fortunately, the backroads are maintained well enough for stock vehicles. A few places can be very challenging, however, so don't treat your drive lightly. Read each trail description carefully.

The park is divided into three distinct land districts: Island in the Sky, the Needles, and the Maze District. These districts are divided by the Colorado and Green Rivers. No bridges cross these rivers inside the park so each district is isolated from the other. Two districts— Island in the Sky and Needles—can be easily accessed from Moab and are therefore subjects of this book. The Maze District is not included because it is not convenient to Moab. If you are interested in touring this district, pick up a copy of *Canyon Country OFF-ROAD VEHICLE TRAILS-Maze Area* by Jack Bickers and its accompanying map by F.A. Barnes (series numbers 18 and 19). The Maze District is significantly more remote than the other two and route-finding is more difficult.

When you visit the park, bring everything you need with you. Make sure you have a full tank of gas. There are no services inside the park although water is available at the Needles Visitor Center and Needles Squaw Flat Campground. Island in the Sky and Needles Districts have modern vault toilets conveniently spaced along the routes.

When you enter the park you'll pay a flat fee of $10 per vehicle, which is good for 7 days. (All fees subject to change without notice.) This allows you to drive all trails in the Island in the Sky and Needles Districts except Lavender Canyon and Salt Creek/Horse Canyon. These two trails require a special permit and an additional $5 fee. The number of vehicles on these trails is restricted so check on availability. I had no trouble getting a permit as a walk-in. Permits for these trails must be obtained at the Needles Visitor Center.

All of the Canyonlands National Park trails in this book can be driven in a single day leaving from and returning to Moab. The White Rim Trail, however, is extremely long and exhausting. It is best to plan two or three days for this trip. Driving the trail does not require a special permit, but a backcountry permit is needed to camp overnight. These permits go quickly and often reservations must be made 6 months or more in advance, especially if you want to camp at White Crack or Murphy Campsite. These campsites are near the halfway point and reservations go quickly. Occasionally, permits are available to walk-ins when last-minute cancellations occur. Overnight camping permits for the White Rim cost $25 but are good for 3 vehicles for 14 days. Reservations must be made by mail or fax, **not** by phone. A reservation confirmation is not a permit. You must obtain your permit from the visitor center in the district where your trip starts. It is best to check in anyway so that you can find out about the latest trail conditions.

For complete details, call, write, or fax the reservation office. They'll send you a free *Canyonlands National Park Trip Planner*. The complete address is: Canyonlands National Park Reservation Office, 2282 S. West Resource Blvd., Moab, Utah 84532. Phone: (435) 259-4351, Fax: (435) 259-4285, Website: www.nps.gov/cany

The time required to plan ahead for these trips is well worth it. There are so few people in the far corners of the backcountry that you'll think the entire park was reserved just for you. Campsites are spaced a long way apart, each with a nearby modern vault toilet. For less than the cost of a nice dinner out, you can experience the trip of a lifetime.

As mentioned earlier, no pets are allowed in the backcountry, not even in vehicles. A list of kennels is available from the park information office. No wood fires are permitted except along the river corridors. Charcoal is okay at vehicle campsites but you must provide your own firepan and pack out all ashes. No hunting or firearms are allowed in the park.

ARCHES NATIONAL PARK

Arches National Park is much smaller than Canyonlands National Park but has more visitors. Most people visiting the park stay on paved roads. The park can become quite congested on weekends and anytime during the busy spring and fall seasons. Almost all of the main features in the park are within a short hike of the main road; consequently, much can be seen in a day or two. Many features can be seen without leaving your car. The park itself is absolutely incredible with more than 2,000 arches. Make sure you see the main features in the park before heading into its backcountry. At the time of this writing, the park entry fee was $10 per vehicle.

The most popular backroad trip in the park is to Tower Arch entering via Salt Valley Road and exiting via the Four Wheel Drive Road. It's the only trip within the park described in this book and is one of my favorites. The scenery is spectacular and the terrain is challenging but suitable for stock high-clearance four-wheel-drive vehicles. There's a turnaround loop near Tower Arch that's a great place to stop, eat lunch, or take a short hike to the arch. It makes a wonderful day trip for the whole family.

Pets are allowed on park roads, parking lots, and in the Devils Garden Campground. They must be leashed at all times and are not allowed on hiking trails or anywhere in the backcountry. For your pet's comfort, it's best to leave it at home. Fires are allowed but you must bring your own fuel and remove all ashes. No hunting or firearms are allowed in the park. There are 52 campsites available for tents and trailers in the Devils Garden Campground that are available on a first-come, first-served basis.

NATIONAL FOREST SERVICE
& BUREAU OF LAND MANAGEMENT

The National Forest Service and the Bureau of Land Management both have offices in Moab and welcome visitors. (See appendix for addresses and phone numbers.) The Forest Service provides helpful information and has maps available for the Manti-La Sal National Forest. The BLM has dozens of different free brochures available on a variety of topics, including the Slickrock Bike Trail, movie locations, Dinosaur footprints, rock art, hiking trails, the Sand Flats Recreation Area, Fisher Towers Recreation Area, local history, etc. A visit to both locations is sure to enhance your stay in Moab.

Staffs of both agencies work hard to protect our public lands so that all of us can enjoy them for generations to come. One of the most critical challenges facing both agencies is users straying from backcountry roads and trails. This results in ugly scars, spoils the scenery, kills vegetation and accelerates erosion. Please stay on the trail at all times and learn as much as possible about minimum impact practices.

ROUTE-FINDING TIPS

Route-finding in Moab's backcountry can be extremely challenging. Many times, you'll need to be a detective to figure out your location. You'll be surprised how proficient you can become if you take time to notice little things. Study your topographic maps carefully for clues of your position. Use a compass and look for landmarks. Realize that maps can be wrong. Roads can be closed without warning and new roads can be created overnight.

Don't depend on directional signs. They are often removed or vandalized. Keep track of your mileage as best you can; don't guess. Even when a trail is marked with painted symbols, the markings may be faint. Look

Cairns mark the trail.

carefully for small signs of paint. Watch for cairns (small stacks of rocks) that often mark the trail. They may be knocked over, but you can still recognize them if you pay attention. Cairns are often widely spaced so look far ahead in all directions. Sometimes colored ribbons are tied to tree limbs or bushes to mark the trail. Look for tire marks and oil drippings on the rock. Some trails still show bulldozer tracks made when the trail was created. Tire marks show up well on steep surfaces but are often washed off flat areas. Sometimes the trail makes a

27

sharp turn reversing direction. Look behind or to the side.

If you've driven very far without seeing signs of the trail, you've probably gotten off track. Get out of your vehicle and walk in a circle looking for clues. Bend down and look closely for any clues in the sand. Sometimes small patches of sand on top of the slickrock show faint tire marks. If you think you've lost the trail, retrace your steps back to a point you recognize. Relook for signs of the trail. You may see a cairn that you missed the first time. Even with GPS, these techniques will be necessary to stay on the trail between waypoints.

BACKCOUNTRY DRIVING LESSONS

Trail Etiquette. A little common courtesy goes a long way in making everyone's travel in the backcountry more enjoyable. After all, we're all out to have fun. Take your time and be considerate of others. If you see someone approaching from behind, look for a wide spot on the trail, pull over and let him pass. Conversely, if you get behind a slowpoke, back off or look for a scenic spot to pull over for a while. Stretch your legs and take a few pictures. Slow down when approaching blind curves. Assume someone is coming around the corner. When you're out of your vehicle, pick a wide spot where you can pull over so others can get by. A horn is rarely needed in the backcountry. When one is heard, it's a foreign sound that disturbs people and wildlife. The same is true of a loud radio. When you see bikers, pull over and let them pass. Give them plenty of room. Exchange courtesies. Ask if they have enough water. Share some of yours if you have plenty. Many bikers underestimate their water requirements and are extremely grateful when you offer. If you have problems later, they might be able to help you. Who knows, one might be a mechanic. I've found most bikers to be very friendly. Control your pets at all times. Don't let them bark or chase wildlife.

The basics. If you have never shifted into low range, grab your owner's manual now and start practicing. Read the rest of this book, then try some of the easy trails. Gradually you'll become more proficient and eventually you'll be ready to move up in difficulty.

Low and slow. Your vehicle was designed to go over rocky and bumpy terrain but only at slow speed. Get used to driving slowly in first gear low range. This will allow you to idle over obstacles without stalling. You don't need to shift back and forth constantly. Get into a low gear and stay there as much as possible so your engine can operate at high RPM and at maximum power. If you have a standard transmission, your goal should be to use your clutch as little as possible. As you encounter resistance on an obstacle or an uphill grade, just give it a little gas. As you start downhill, allow the engine's resistance to act as a brake. If the engine alone will not stop you from accelerating, then help a little with the brake. When you need more power but not more speed, press on the gas and feather the brake a little at the same time. This takes a little practice, but you will be amazed at the control you have. This technique works equally well with automatic transmissions.

Rocks and other high points. Never attempt to straddle a rock that is large enough to strike your differentials, transfer case or other low-hanging parts of your undercarriage. Instead, drive over the highest point with your tire, which is designed to take the abuse. This will lift your undercarriage over the obstacle. As you enter a rocky area, look ahead to determine where the high points are, then make every effort to cross them with your tires. Learn the low points of your undercarriage.

Using a spotter. Sometimes there are so many rocks you get confused about which way to go. In this case, have someone get out and guide you. They should stand at a safe distance in front, watching your tires and undercarriage. With hand signals, they can direct you left or right. If you are alone, don't be embarrassed to spot for yourself by getting in and out of your vehicle several times.

Driving on slickrock. The name *slickrock* probably came from the days when wooden wagon wheels were used. Today's modern rubber tires get excellent traction most of the time, making it possible to ascend and descend extremely steep grades. I've had good luck on slickrock even when it's wet. There are exceptions, however. Be careful when there is a heavy coating of oil or grease on the rock. Also, if the rock has a slight greenish color, it may have moss growing on it. Both of these situations can be disastrous on a steep grade when you are expecting good traction. Remember to drive straight up and down; don't get sideways on the hill.

Those clunking sounds. Having made every attempt to avoid dragging bottom, you'll find it's not always possible. It is inevitable that a rock will contact your undercarriage eventually. The sound can be quite unnerving the first time it happens. If you are driving slowly and have proper skid plates, damage is unlikely. Look for a different line, back up and try again. If unsuccessful, see next paragraph.

Crossing large rocks. Sometimes a rock is too large to drive over or at such a steep angle your bumper hits the rock before your tire. Stack rocks on each side to form a ramp. Once over the obstacle, make sure you put the rocks back where you found them. The next driver to come along may prefer the challenge of crossing the rock in its more difficult state.

Getting high centered. You may drive over a large rock or into a rut, causing you to get lodged on the object. If this happens, don't panic. First ask your passengers to get out to see if less weight helps. Try rocking the vehicle. If this doesn't work, jack up your vehicle and place a few rocks under the tires so that when you let the jack down, you take the weight off the high point. Determine whether driving forward or reverse is best and try again. You may have to repeat this procedure several times if you are seriously high centered. Eventually you will learn what you can and cannot drive over.

Look in all directions. Unlike highway driving in which your primary need for attention is straight ahead, backcountry driving requires you to look in all directions. Objects can block your path from above, below, and from the sides. Trees fall, branches droop, and rocks slide, making the trail into an ever-changing obstacle course.

Scout ahead. If you are on an unfamiliar trail and are concerned that the trail is becoming too difficult, get out of your vehicle and walk the trail ahead of you. This gives you an opportunity to pick an easy place to turn around before you get into trouble. If you have to turn around, back up or pull ahead until you find a wide flat spot. Don't try to turn in a narrow confined area. This can damage the trail and perhaps tip over your vehicle.

Anticipate. Shift into four-wheel drive or low range before it is needed. If you wait until it is needed, conditions might be too difficult, e.g., halfway up a hillside.

Blind curves. When approaching blind curves, always assume that there is a speeding vehicle coming from the opposite direction. This will prepare you for the worst. Be aware that many people drive on the wrong side of the road to stay away from the outer edge of a trail. Whenever possible, keep your windows open and your radio off so that you can hear an approaching vehicle. You can usually hear motorcycles and ATVs. Quiet SUVs are the biggest problem. Collisions do occur, so be careful.

Driving uphill. Use extreme caution when attempting to climb a hill. The difficulty of hill climbing is often misjudged by the novice four-wheeler. You should have good tires, adequate power, and be shifted into four-wheel drive low. There are four factors that determine difficulty:

Length of the hill. If the hill is very long, it is less likely that momentum will carry you to the top. Short hills are easier.

Traction. Slickrock is easier to climb than dirt.

Bumpiness. If the road surface undulates to the point where all four tires do not stay on the ground at the same time, you will have great difficulty climbing even a moderately steep hill.

Steepness. This can be difficult to judge, so examine a hill carefully before you attempt it. Walk up the hill if necessary to make sure it is not steeper at the top. If you are not absolutely sure you can climb a hill, don't attempt it. Practice on smaller hills first.

If you attempt a hill, approach it straight on and stay that way all the way to the top. Do not turn sideways or try to drive across the hill. Do not use excessive speed but keep moving at a steady pace. Make sure no one is coming up from the other side. Position a spotter at the top of the hill if necessary. Do not spin your tires because this can turn you sideways to the hill. If you feel you are coming to a stop due to lack of traction, turn your steering wheel back and forth quickly. This will give you additional grip. If you stall, use your brake and restart your engine. You may also have to use your emergency brake. If you start to slide backwards even with your brake on, you may have to ease up on the brake enough to regain steering control. Don't allow your wheels to lock up. If you don't make it to the top of the hill, shift into reverse and back down slowly in a straight line. Try the hill again but only if you think you learned enough to make a difference. As you approach the top of the hill, ease off the gas so you are in control before starting down the other side.

Driving downhill. Make sure you are in four-wheel drive. Examine the hill carefully and determine the best route that will allow you to go straight down the hill. Do not turn sideways. Use the lowest gears possible, allowing the engine's compression to hold you back. Do not ride the clutch. Feather the brakes slightly if additional slowing is needed. Do not allow the wheels to lock up. This will cause loss of steering and possibly cause you to slide sideways. The natural reaction when you begin to slide is to press harder on the brakes. Try to stay off the brakes. If you continue to slide despite these efforts, turn in the direction of the slide as you would on ice or snow and accelerate slightly. This will help maintain steering control.

Parking on a steep hill. Put your vehicle in reverse gear if pointing downhill and in forward gear if pointing uphill. For automatic transmissions, shift to park. Set your emergency brake hard. For extra insurance, block your tires.

Tippy situations. No one can tell you how far your vehicle can safely lean. You must learn the limitations through practice. Remember that sport utility vehicles have a higher center of gravity and are less stable than a passenger car. However, don't get paranoid. Your vehicle will likely lean a lot more than you think. Drive slowly to avoid bouncing over. A good way to learn is to watch an experienced driver with a vehicle similar to yours. This is an advantage to traveling with a group. Once you see how far other vehicles can lean, you will become more comfortable in these situations. Remember, too, that you're likely to slide sideways before you tip over. This can be just as dangerous in certain situations. Use extreme caution if the road surface is slippery from loose gravel, mud, or wet clay. Turn around if necessary.

Crossing streams and water holes. You must know the high water point of your vehicle before entering any body of water. Several factors can determine this point, including the height of the air intake and the location of the computer module (newer vehicles). Water sucked into the air intake is a very serious matter. If you don't know where these items are located, check with your dealer or a good four-wheel drive shop. A low fan can throw water on the engine and cause it to stall. You may have to disconnect your fan belt. Water can be sucked into your differentials so check them regularly after crossing deep streams.

After you understand your vehicle's capabilities, you must assess the stream conditions. First determine the depth of the water. If you are with a group, let the most experienced driver cross first. Follow his line if he is successful. If you are alone, you might wait for someone else to come along. Sometimes you can use a long stick to check the depth of small streams or water holes. Check for deep holes, large obstacles, and muddy sections. If you can't determine the water depth, don't cross. A winch line or long tow strap can be used as a safety line to pull someone back if he gets into trouble, but it must be attached before entering the water. It must also be long enough for him to reach shallow water on the other side. Once in the water, drive slowly but steadily. This creates a small wake which helps form an air pocket around the engine. I've seen people put a piece of cardboard or canvas over the front of their vehicle to enhance the wake affect. This only works if you keep moving. After exiting a stream, test your brakes. You may have to ride them lightly for a short distance until they dry out.

Always cross streams at designated water crossings. Don't drive in the direction of the stream. Try to minimize disruption of the water habitat.

Mud. Don't make new mud holes or enlarge existing ones. Stay home if you have reason to believe the trail will be too wet. Some trails, however, have permanent mud holes that you must cross. Mud can build up suction around your tires and be very difficult to get through. Always check a mud hole carefully to see how deep it is. Take a stick and poke around. Check the other side. If there are no tracks coming out, don't go in. If you decide to cross, keep moving at a steady pace and, if necessary, turn the steering wheel back and forth quickly for additional traction. If you get stuck, dig around the tires to break the suction and place anything hard under the tires for traction. It may be necessary to back out. If you are with a friend, and you are doubtful if you can get through without help, attach a tow strap before you enter so that you can be pulled back. But beware, sometimes the mud can be so bad, even a friend can't pull you out. Your only protection against this happening is to use your head and not go in the mud in the first place. When I've seen people stuck this badly it is usually due to a total disregard for the obvious.

If you can't get though the mud, search for an alternate route but don't widen the trail. If there is no alternate route, turn around.

Ruts. If you get stuck in a rut and have no one to pull you out, dig a small trench from the rut to the right or left at a 45-degree angle. The dirt you remove from this trench should be used to fill the rut ahead of the turning point. If both tires are in parallel ruts, make sure the trenches are parallel. Drive out following the new rut. Repair any damage after you get out.

Gullies or washouts. If you are running parallel to a washed out section of the trail, straddle it. If it becomes too large to straddle, drive down the middle. The goal is to center your vehicle so you remain as level as possible. This may require that you drive on the outer edges of your tires, so drive slowly and watch for any sharp objects. If you begin to tilt too far in one direction, turn in the direction of the tilt until you level out again. Sometimes it helps to have a spotter. To cross a gully from one side to the other, approach at a 45-degree angle and let each tire walk over independently.

Ravines. Crossing a ravine is similar to crossing a gully. Approach on an angle and let each tire go through independently. If the ravine is large with steep sides, you may not be able to cross at an angle because it could cause a rollover. If you don't cross at an angle, two things can happen. You will drag the front or rear of your vehicle, or you will high center on the edge of the ravine. If this is the case, ask yourself if you really need to cross the ravine. If you must cross, your only solution is to stack rocks to lift the vehicle at critical points.

Sand. Dry sand is more difficult than wet sand (unless it's quicksand). In either case, keep moving so that your momentum helps carry you through. Stay in a higher gear and use a little extra power but don't use excessive power and spin your tires. If necessary, turn your steering wheel back and forth quickly to give your tires a fresh grip. Airing down your tires is often necessary. Experiment with different tire pressures. Make sure you have a way to air up after you get through the sand. If you do get stuck, wet the sand in front of your tires. Try rocking the vehicle. If necessary, use your floor mats under the tires.

Quicksand. Quicksand is sometimes found in streambeds or in wet, sandy spots where there is an underground water source. Moab's quicksand won't swallow a whole vehicle or even a person, but it can get you badly stuck. If you suspect you're in an area with quicksand, keep moving—don't stop. If you get stuck, don't spin your tires or try to drive out; it will only make matters worse. You'll need help from someone else to pull you out. It may take several vehicles to break the suction of the sand. Find something wide and flat to put under your jack to lift up your vehicle. You might be able to winch or pull one end of the vehicle sideways to break the suction before pulling it forward or backward. The stuck vehicle should never help with its own power. Once out, pull and clean your brake drums as soon as possible.

Washboard roads. Washboard roads are a natural part of backcountry travel. Vibration from these roads can be annoying. It is a problem for everybody so don't think there is something wrong with your vehicle. Experiment with different speeds to find the smoothest ride. Slowing down is usually best, but some conditions may be improved by speeding up a little. Be careful around curves where you could lose traction and slide. Check your tires to make sure they are not over inflated.

Airing down. There may be times when you need to let air out of your tires to get more traction or improve your ride, e.g., when driving through sand, going up a steep hill, or driving on washboard roads. It is usually safe to let air out of your tires until they bulge slightly, provided you are not traveling at high speed. If you let out too much air, your tires may come off the rims, or the sidewalls may become vulnerable to damage by sharp objects. Consider how or where you will reinflate. A small air pump that plugs into your cigarette lighter is handy for this purpose. Airing down on hard-core trails is essential. I've seen some wheelers with larger tires air down to as little as 3-5 lbs. A typical SUV can usually be aired down to 18 to 20 lbs. without noticeable handling difficulties at low speeds.

Winching. Next to tow points and skid plates, a winch is one of the best investments you can make. If you drive more difficult trails and you don't have a winch, travel with someone who does. I've known some hard-core wheelers who have gone for years without owning a winch but they always travel with a group. If you never intend to buy a winch, carry a high-lift jack or come-along. Although these tools are slow and inconvenient, they can get you out of difficulty when there is no other way.

If you own a winch, make sure you also have these five basic winch accessories:

1. Heavy-duty work gloves.

2. A tree strap - Looks like a tow strap but is shorter. It has a loop on each end.

3. A snatch block - A pulley that opens on the side so you can slip it over your winch cable.

4. A clevis - A heavy U-shaped device with a pin that screws across one end. This enables you to connect straps together and to your vehicle. It has many other uses.

5. A heavy-duty chain with grab hooks to wrap around rocks. It's also handy when trying to pull another vehicle that does not have tow points.

Winching tips:

• Your winch cable should be lined up straight with the pulling vehicle. If you can't pull straight, attach a snatch block to a large tree or rock to form an angle. This technique also works for pulling a fallen tree off the trail.

• If your winch cable bunches up at one end of the spool but there's still room for the cable, let it go and rewind the cable later.

• When winching from trees, attach to the largest tree possible using your tree strap and clevis. If no tree is large enough, wrap several smaller trees. The strap should be put as low as possible on the tree. Finding a decent size tree in the desert may be impossible.

• Keep your engine running while winching to provide maximum electrical power to the battery.

• Help the winch by driving the stuck vehicle slowly. Be in the lowest gear possible and go as slowly as possible without spinning your tires. Don't allow slack in the winch cable. This can start a jerking motion that could break the cable.

• If there is not enough power to pull the stuck vehicle, attach a snatch block to the stuck vehicle and double the winch cable back to the starting point. This block-and-tackle technique will double your pulling power.

• Set the emergency brake on the anchor vehicle and block the wheels if necessary. In some cases, you may have to connect the anchor vehicle to another vehicle or tree.

• Throw a blanket or heavy coat over the winch cable while pulling. This will slow the end of the winch cable if it breaks and snaps back.

• Make sure there are at least 5 wraps of the winch cable left on the spool.

• Never hook the winch cable to itself. Use a tree strap and clevis. Never allow the winch cable to kink. This creates a weak spot in the cable.

• If tow points are not available on the stuck vehicle, attach to the vehicle's frame not the bumper. Use your large chain to wrap around the frame. If you are helping a stranger, make sure he understands that you are not responsible for damage to his vehicle.

• Never straddle or stand close to the winch cable while it is under stress.

• If you are stuck alone with no place to attach your winch cable, bury your spare tire in the ground as an anchor point. When you are finished, repair any damage to the ground.

• When finished winching, don't let the end of the cable wind into the spool. It can become jammed and damage your winch. Attach the hook to some other part of your vehicle like a tow point.

OTHER ACTIVITIES

To make the trip more enjoyable for everyone, especially if children are along, plan frequent stops with a variety of activities including picnics, hiking, biking, camping, and rafting. Get out of your vehicle and hike in places like Lavender Canyon and Salt Creek/Horse Canyon. Indian ruins are often tucked away at the base of canyon walls. Go to the library before your trip and learn a little history about the area or stop at the museum in Moab. Take a ride on Moab's new chair lift to the top of Moab Rim or spend an afternoon at the water slide north of town. Share maps with the kids and let them trace your route. Carry binoculars to look for wildlife and distant landmarks.

FINAL COMMENTS

I've made every effort to make this book as accurate and as easy to use as possible. If you have ideas for improvements or find any significant errors, please write to me at FunTreks, Inc., P.O. Box 3127, Monument, CO 80132-3127. Or, send e-mail to: *books@funtreks.com*. Whether you're a novice or expert, I hope this book makes your backcountry experience safer, easier, and more fun.

Map Legend

Interstate		Public Toilet
Paved Road*		Gas, Service
Easy Trail*		Parking
Moderate Trail*		Picnic Area
Difficult Trail*		Camping Area
Other Road*		Mine
Described in text		Hiking Trailhead
Hiking Trail		Mountain Biking
Boundaries, & Divides		Arch
Cliff		Water Crossing
Area of Difficult Route-Finding		Bridge
Mountain Peak		Dinosaur Footprint
Lake		Scenic Point
Map Orientation		Rock Art
Interstate		Archaeological Site, Ruin
U.S. Highway		Major Obstacle
State & County Road		GPS Waypoint
Forest Service Road		
Starting point of trail		

Scale indicated
by grid

Scale is different
for each map;
check grid size at
bottom of map.

These items repeated on each map for your convenience. See Mini Key.

THE TRAILS

High Dive obstacle on Behind the Rocks (Trail #28), rated Difficult.

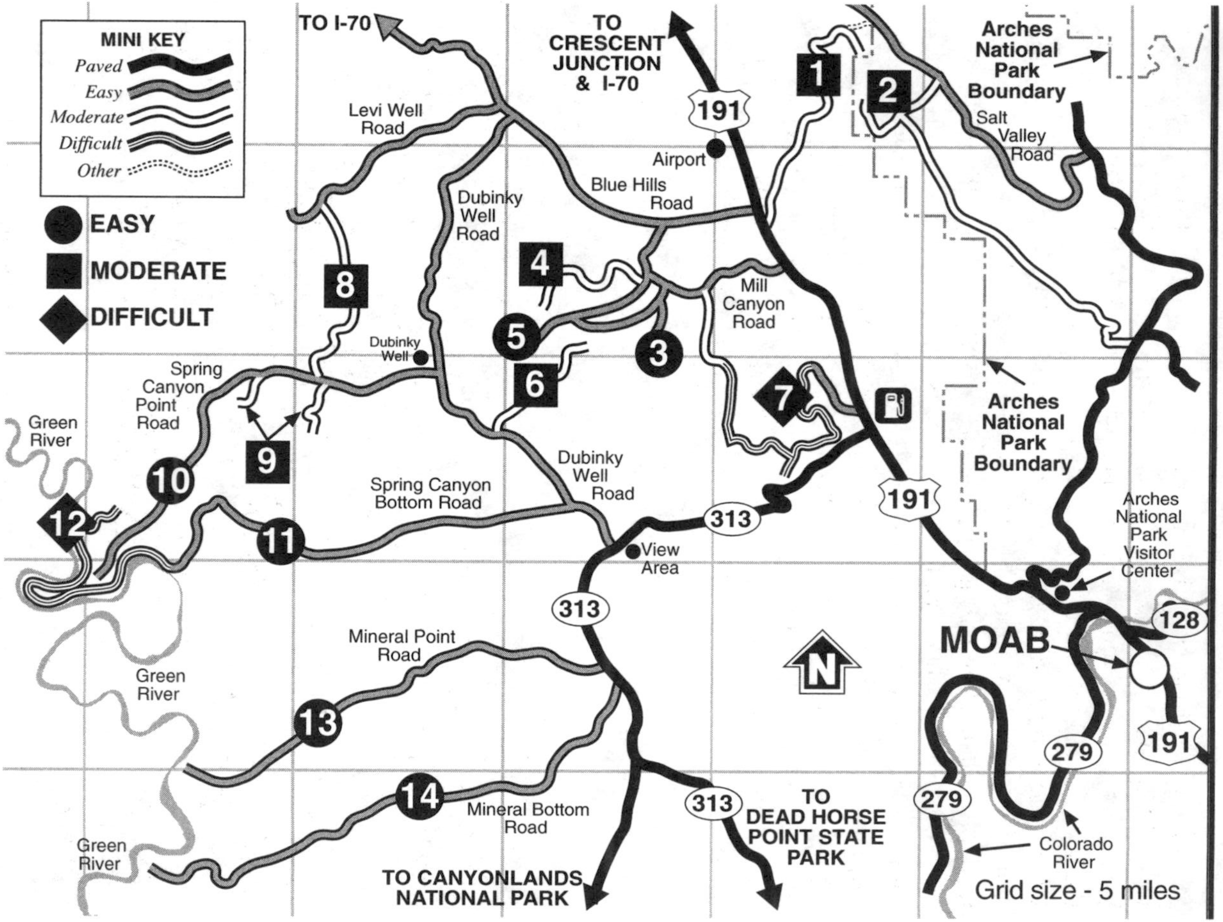

AREA 1

Northwest Moab & Arches National Park

1. Klondike Bluffs
2. Tower Arch
3. Tusher Tunnel
4. Hidden Canyon Overlook
5. Hidden Canyon
6. Bartlett Overlook
7. Sevenmile Rim
8. Rainbow Terrace
9. Secret Spire, Dellenbaugh Tunnel
10. Spring Canyon Point
11. Spring Canyon Bottom
12. Hey Joe Canyon
13. Mineral Point
14. Mineral Bottom

Northwest Moab & Arches National Park

Visitors to the Moab area often overlook the broad area of rangeland northwest of Highway 313. They assume that such flat land has little to offer backcountry drivers looking for excitement. What they fail to realize is that the land is anything but flat. It is actually deeply cut with dramatic canyons which extend north from Canyonlands National Park. Several trails take you to impressive overlooks along canyon rims and two go to canyon bottoms on descents that will get your blood pumping. Other trails take you to unusual rock formations, fun little tunnels, and sand dunes magically formed in the middle of nowhere. One trail takes you to a stunning view on the edge of Arches National Park while another takes you through the park's remote backcountry to features that can only be reached in a high-clearance, four-wheel-drive vehicle or by foot. And finally, if you own a stock sport utility vehicle, you'll appreciate the fact that most of the trails in this area are rated easy to moderate. Only 2 of 14 are rated difficult.

This stock sport utility vehicle makes its way to Tower Arch inside Arches National Park.

Klondike Bluffs in Arches National Park. Requires a short hike from end of trail.

Stock sport utilities can drive this trail, but careful tire placement is required in places.

Large expanses of slickrock like this make route-finding challenging in a few places.

Much of the trail is quite easy.

Watch for dinosaur footprints along the trail.

40

Klondike Bluffs

Location: Northwest of Moab between Highway 191 and the north end of Arches National Park.

Difficulty: Moderate. Much of the trail is easy when dry, but several rocky sections require stock sport utility vehicles be equipped with skid plates. Some experience is recommended. Parts of the trail become very muddy and slippery when wet. Intermittent sections of slickrock make route-finding difficult at times. In recent years, the trail has been painted with white dashes to mark the biking route, which is primarily the same as the four-wheel-drive route. Use the markings if they're there, but don't count on them.

Features: This trail crosses interesting, varied terrain and climbs to a high point overlooking Arches National Park and beautiful Klondike Bluffs. A short hike is necessary to see the bluffs because the trail ends at the park boundary. You'll also see relics of an old copper mine near the end of the trail. Along the slickrock portions of the trail, watch for fossils of dinosaur footprints often encircled with small rocks to make them easier to find. Watch for mountain bikers.

Time & Distance: The one-way trip up is about 7 miles and takes 1 1/2 to 2 hours. Add time for the return trip and a little hiking time.

To Get There: From the intersection of Highways 191 and 128, drive 14.0 miles north on Highway 191 and turn right soon after mile post 142 into a dirt parking area. The trail departs through a gate and is marked.

Trail Description: Reset your odometer when you turn right off 191 [01]. Go straight at 1.1 miles as a faint road goes right [02]. Use caution where the soil is a light green color. This soil is extremely slippery when wet. At 2.6 miles bear left on a lesser road [03]. At mile 3.2 follow the road left away from a creek bed. Bear right at a T intersection at 3.7 miles [04]. A right turn at 3.9 miles takes you up through a narrow rocky canyon. You'll soon find it necessary to shift into low range. You may have to use a spotter to negotiate increasingly larger rocks.

The first large expanse of slickrock is encountered at 4.4 miles. Watch for a nice dinosaur footprint on the left. (Please do not drive on the footprints.) The trail primarily goes up the left side of this first rock slab. Follow the flattest places between the boulders. Watch for logs, rock cairns, and painted white dashed lines to help guide you. Stay on the left side of the slab. You must cross a deep crack at 5.1 miles. Seek the shallowest spot to cross. You may still drag your rear bumper. At 5.2 miles bear more right as the trail heads in a northwesterly direction. You should begin climbing slightly uphill over a wide rock slab defined by short trees on each side. At 5.6 cross over to the adjacent rock slab on the right and continue to climb. At 5.8 the trail begins to alternate between dirt and rock. If you lose the trail, get out of your vehicle and scout ahead on foot for cairns or tire marks. Gradually, the road becomes more defined as you swing north.

A lesser road goes left at 6.2 miles. At 6.3 [05] bear right in a southeast direction toward the Klondike Bluffs. Left would take you up a rocky switchback and over to Salt Valley Road. The next fork is reached at 6.5 miles; turn left. You effectively reach the end of the trail at 6.9 miles (06). You'll see relics of an old copper mine to the right. There's a place to park and turn around at the mine. The trail actually goes up the hill a little farther but soon narrows to a hiking path before reaching the boundary to Arches National Park. There is no good place to turn around if you continue. I recommend you park near the mine and hike the rest of the way.

Return Trip: Return the way you came or take an alternate route over a ridge to Salt Valley Road. To do this, go back to the rocky switchback that you passed at 6.3 [05] miles and turn right up the hill. *Reset your odometer at this point.* At 0.2 miles turn left at a T intersection followed by an immediate right at another T at 0.3. Bear right at 0.4 past a collapsed building before beginning a steep descent through a narrow section. Several spots are tippy, so take your time. It soon flattens out. Bear right across a sandy two-track road before reaching Salt Valley Road at 1.2 miles. A left turn on Salt Valley Road takes you northwest towards Crescent Junction. A right on Salt Valley Road connects to the main paved road inside Arches National Park. You'll pay an entrance fee when you leave the park.

Services: There is a service station and campground just north of the intersection of Highway 191 and 313 about 5 miles south of where the trail begins.

Maps: Latitude 40°, Inc. *Moab West* Mountain Biking Map and USGS 7.5 minute maps Klondike Bluffs 38109-G6 and Merrimac Butte 38109-F6.

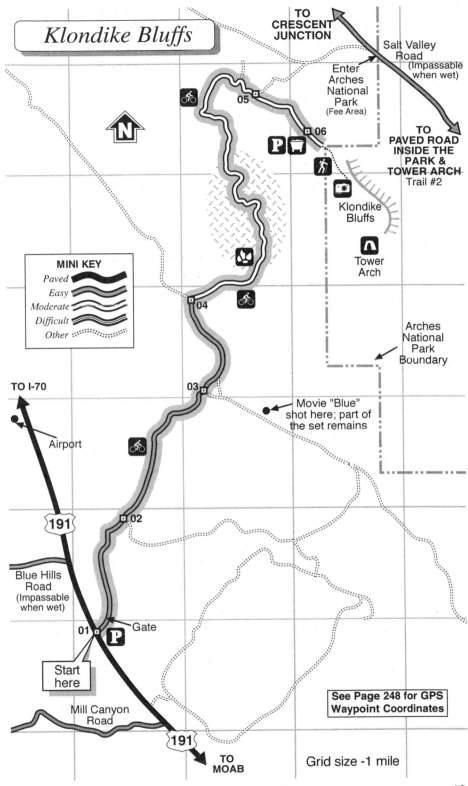

Klondike Bluffs

MINI KEY
Paved
Easy
Moderate
Difficult
Other

N

TO CRESCENT JUNCTION

Salt Valley Road
(Impassable when wet)

Enter Arches National Park
(Fee Area)

05

06

P

TO PAVED ROAD INSIDE THE PARK & TOWER ARCH
Trail #2

Klondike Bluffs

Tower Arch

Arches National Park Boundary

04

03

TO I-70

Airport

Movie "Blue" shot here; part of the set remains

191

02

Blue Hills Road
(Impassable when wet)

01   Gate
P

Start here

Mill Canyon Road

191

TO MOAB

See Page 248 for GPS Waypoint Coordinates

Grid size -1 mile

Tower Arch viewed from the turnaround.

Part of the "Four Wheel Drive Road".

A four-wheel-drive club enjoys lunch at the turnaround adjacent to Tower Arch.

West side view of "Eye-of-the-Whale" Arch.

This SUV has no trouble on this easy stretch.

44

Tower Arch 2

Location: North of Moab inside Arches National Park.

Difficulty: Moderate. Although much of the drive is easy, there are several challenging rocky sections. One of the hardest spots is at the beginning. You should have some backcountry driving experience and skid plates are recommended. Much of the drive is sandy so lower tire pressure if necessary to avoid getting stuck. Because of one steep sand hill, the National Park Service recommends travel as described here, north to south, only. Salt Valley Road can be impassable when wet. Route-finding is easy.

Features: The central paved corridor of the park, at times, can be quite congested. With a capable high-clearance four-wheel-drive vehicle, you have an opportunity to escape the crowds and visit far corners of a truly spectacular national park. The main features of this drive are Tower Arch, Marching Men, and Eye-of-the-Whale Arch.

Time & Distance: This 14.5 mile trip will take 2 to 3 hours. Add another hour to reach the start of the route from the main gate of the park. The drive on Salt Valley Road is not long, but the washboard surface can slow you to a crawl.

To Get There: From the intersection of Highways 191 and 128 north of Moab, take Highway 191 north 2.6 miles to the main entrance of Arches National Park on the right. When you pay your entry fee at the gate, you will be given a handy detailed map of the park. (Take a few minutes to stop at the Visitors Center to learn more about the park.) Follow the main paved road north past the 16-mile marker. Just after the Sand Dune Arch, turn left on Salt Valley Road. Drive about 7 miles and watch for two dirt roads on the left. Take the first road. The second road goes to a hiking trailhead to Tower Arch.

Trail Description: Reset your odometer when you turn off Salt Valley Road [01]. After less than a mile you'll encounter the hardest spot of the drive—a series of rock ledges that will challenge stock SUVs. With careful tire placement, you should get through just fine. Use a spotter if you feel uncomfortable. At 1.8 miles continue past a road that goes south to Balanced Rock [02]. (The official name of this road is *Four Wheel Drive Road*.) You'll return to it soon. The next 1.5 miles are pure driving joy as you wind your way to Tower Arch. To your right watch for Klondike Bluffs

45

and the unusual rock formations of Marching Men. At 3.3 miles you reach the turnaround area for Tower Arch [03]. This is a great spot to have lunch or perhaps take a short hike to the arch.

Return to Four Wheel Drive Road mentioned earlier and turn right. You'll head southeast through twisting washes, rolling sand hills, and rocky fun spots. A variety of colors and textures makes for great pictures. At 10.9 you descend a long sandy hill. It's easy going down, but difficult going back up. At 12. 6 miles stop and take a short hike for a close-up view of Eye-of-the-Whale Arch. Four Wheel Drive Road ends at Willow Flats Road at 14.5 miles [04].

Return Trip: Turn left at Willow Flats Road and drive 0.8 miles back to the main paved road inside the park. At Balanced Rock, turn right for the main gate.

Services: There are modern vault toilets at the end of the paved road at Devils Garden and on Willow Flats Road west of Balanced Rock. If you're heading north after leaving the park, there is one gas station at the intersection of Highway 313 and 191. Full services can be found in Moab.

Other Activities: Obviously, while you're in the park, you'll want to visit all the natural wonders it has to offer. Make sure you take the two paved side trips to the Windows Section and Delicate Arch. I enjoy the Devils Garden hiking trail that leads to many interesting arches, including the longest in the world—Landscape Arch. Devils Garden hiking trail also takes you to Pine Tree Arch, pictured on page 241. Stop at the Visitor Center for details of every aspect of the park.

When hiking and driving in the park, make sure you stay on designated roads. Never walk on the cryptobiotic crust described in detail in the introduction to this book. Take plenty of water—temperatures can reach 110 degrees in the summer. Pets must be leashed and are not allowed on trails or anywhere in the backcountry. It's best to leave your pet home.

Maps: The Arches National Park free brochure, Trails Illustrated's *Arches National Park,* Latitude 40°, Inc. *Moab West* biking map.

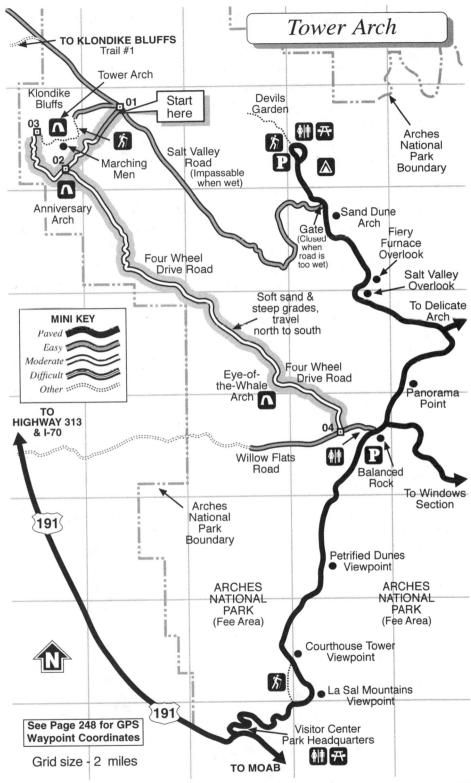

Tower Arch

TO KLONDIKE BLUFFS
Trail #1

Tower Arch

Klondike
Bluffs

01 Start here

03

02

Marching Men

Anniversary Arch

Salt Valley Road (Impassable when wet)

Four Wheel Drive Road

Devils Garden

Arches National Park Boundary

Gate (Closed when road is too wet)

Sand Dune Arch

Fiery Furnace Overlook

Salt Valley Overlook

To Delicate Arch

Soft sand & steep grades, travel north to south

Eye-of-the-Whale Arch

Four Wheel Drive Road

Panorama Point

MINI KEY
Paved
Easy
Moderate
Difficult
Other

TO HIGHWAY 313 & I-70

04

Willow Flats Road

Balanced Rock

To Windows Section

Arches National Park Boundary

191

Petrified Dunes Viewpoint

ARCHES NATIONAL PARK (Fee Area)

ARCHES NATIONAL PARK (Fee Area)

N

Courthouse Tower Viewpoint

La Sal Mountains Viewpoint

191

See Page 248 for GPS Waypoint Coordinates

Grid size - 2 miles

Visitor Center Park Headquarters

TO MOAB

Tunnel exit. Look for Indian petroglyphs near upper left corner of this photo.

Looking south from the tunnel exit.

An easy road leads to the tunnel.

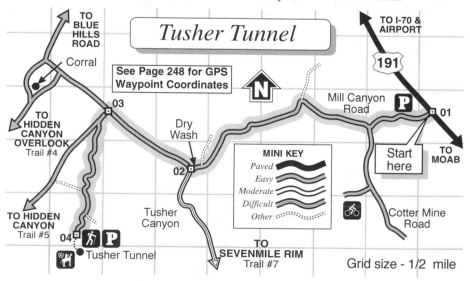

Tusher Tunnel

TO BLUE HILLS ROAD

TO I-70 & AIRPORT

191

Corral

See Page 248 for GPS Waypoint Coordinates

N

Mill Canyon Road

P

01

03

TO HIDDEN CANYON OVERLOOK
Trail #4

Dry Wash

02

Start here

TO MOAB

MINI KEY
Paved
Easy
Moderate
Difficult
Other

TO HIDDEN CANYON
Trail #5

04

P

Tusher Tunnel

Tusher Canyon

Cotter Mine Road

TO SEVENMILE RIM
Trail #7

Grid size - 1/2 mile

Tusher Tunnel ③

Location: Northwest of Moab, west of Highway 191, and south of the airport.

Difficulty: Easy. The road is mostly graded and consists of sand and gravel surfaces. Some spots can be slippery when wet. There is one small sandy wash to negotiate that is no problem when dry.

Features: A fun little adventure if you're short on time. At the end of a short drive, hike to the tunnel in about 3 minutes. You can stand up in the center of the tunnel most of the way but be careful not to bump your head. While inside, both ends of the tunnel are visible at all times. Great views on the other side.

Time & Distance: About 5 miles from Highway 191 to the tunnel. Allow about 1/2 hour each way under dry conditions.

To Get There: From the intersection of Highways 191 and 128, drive about 13.0 miles north on Highway 191 and turn left on Mill Canyon Road just north of mile post 141. It's easy to miss the small sign for the road.

Trail Description: Reset your odometer as you turn off 191 [01]. You immediately cross railroad tracks then pass a parking area just around the bend. At 0.7 bear right as Cotter Mine Road goes left. The road drops down into a wash at mile 2.6. If dry, turn left and follow the wash around the corner to another intersection at 2.7 [02]. A sign indicates a Jeep trail to the left—you go right up the hill. Turn left at 3.6 miles [03] and again, on a lesser road, at 3.7. Bear left again at 4.6 as the road climbs ahead. Turn right at the bottom of the hill (in a matter of several hundred yards) as a lesser road goes left. In about 0.2 miles, you reach a turnaround area [04]. Park here and hike a short distance up to the tunnel, following brown sign posts.

Return Trip: Return the way you came.

Services: Service station at the intersection of 191 and 313.

Maps: Mill Canyon Road is shown on the Latitude 40°, Inc. *Moab West* Biking Map. Some of this trail is shown on the USGS 7.5 minute maps Jug Rock 38109-F7 and Merrimac Butte 38109-F6. I'm not aware of any map that shows the road to Tusher Tunnel. I plotted the route using my own GPS equipment.

The road into Hidden Canyon (Trail #5) as seen from the overlook.

The trail is not very well defined after passing through these boulders. Watch for cairns.

The end of the trail provides plenty of space to park and turn around.

Hidden Canyon Overlook

Location: Northwest of Moab and west of Highway 191.

Difficulty: Moderate. The road up to the canyon rim is a little narrow and steep in places, but there are no narrow shelves. Careful tire placement is important for stock vehicles. Skid plates are helpful. Route-finding can be tricky across two large expanses of slickrock. You may have to occasionally scout ahead to find the trail. Watch for cairns in the distance. Blue Hills Road is extremely slippery when wet and is completely impassable after a prolonged period of heavy rain.

Features: A short but exciting drive across sometimes lunar-like terrain culminating in a gorgeous view of Hidden Canyon.

Time & Distance: Less than 8 miles from Highway 191 to the overlook. Allow 2 to 3 hours for the round trip. It could take longer depending upon how much additional time you need for scouting.

To Get There: From the intersection of Highways 191 and 128, drive 14.6 miles north on Highway 191 and turn left on Blue Hills Road just south of mile post 143. (Some maps show Blue Hills Road as Ten Mile Road.) You can see it stretching across the prairie before you get to the airport.

Trail Description: Reset your odometer as you turn off 191 [01]. Drive west 2.3 miles and turn left [02]. Continue straight at 3.1 miles as the road swings to the left and begins to climb. Bear right after passing a corral and continue uphill as the road narrows. At 3.9 miles turn right and head across the hill [03]. Bear to the right at 4.0 and 4.2. You'll head downhill before crossing a small sandy wash, then start climbing again. Bear left at 4.7 miles before reaching a gate. Close the gate after passing through and turn left uphill at 5.0 miles. You'll climb a short rocky section then start across slickrock. Stay on the flatter stretches as the trail weaves between boulders. The trail tends to hug the high ridge to the right.

At 5.7 miles [04] you'll round a bend as you continue to hug the right side of the ridge. Another trail comes over the ridge and joins the trail from the right. It is difficult to see. This alternate way passes through Lunar Canyon and is very confusing. Don't try it unless someone in your group has driven it before. (The Easter Jeep Safari uses this route as part of the 3D Trail.)

Still at 5.7 miles, continue straight along the right side of the slickrock. At 5.9 you'll pass between some large boulders (See center picture on previous page.) Continue hugging the right side after the boulders until 6.2 miles, at which time you'll turn left and head south across the slab. The trail is very difficult to see so pay close attention to details. Scout ahead and watch for cairns and other signs of the trail. You'll gradually swing right as trail definition improves.

At 6.9 miles, after crossing some challenging ledges, make a hard left as you begin to leave the slickrock portion of the trail [05]. Watch carefully here; the trail appears to go straight. This is one of the hardest turns to see even for people who have driven the trail before. After this turn, the trail becomes sandy again and well defined. You'll dip down into a steep ravine and climb back out. Bear left at 7.5 and continue on to the overlook at mile 7.7 [06].

If you intend to drive Hidden Canyon (Trail #5), study the road pattern from the overlook. This will make it easier to find your way later.

Return Trip: The easiest way out is to return the way you came. If you have someone with you who is familiar with the Lunar Canyon route, you could try this way. I've shown this route with dotted lines on the map.

Services: Service station at the intersection of Highways 191 and 313.

Maps: This trail is not shown on any map that I could find. I plotted the route, with the help of an experienced guide, using my own GPS equipment. The beginning part of the route is shown on the Latitude 40°, Inc. *Moab West* Biking Map. The area is shown on USGS 7.5 minute map Jug Rock 38109-F7.

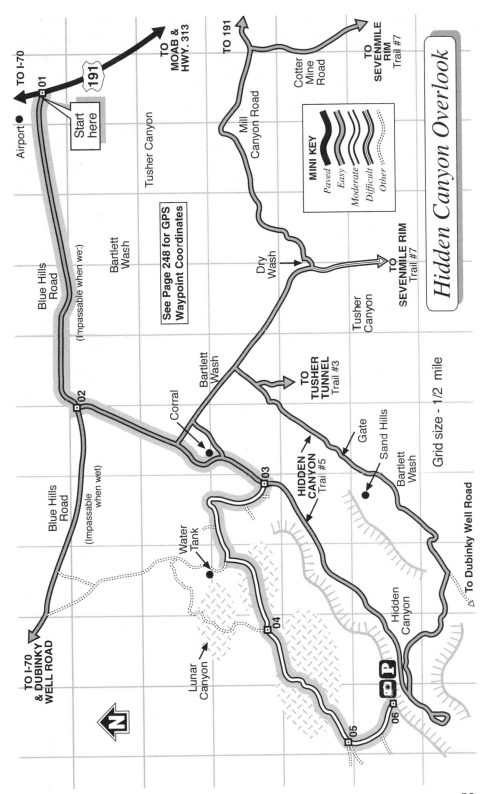

Hidden Canyon Overlook

MINI KEY
Paved
Easy
Moderate
Difficult
Other

Grid size - 1/2 mile

See Page 248 for GPS Waypoint Coordinates

Start here

Airport

TO I-70

191

TO MOAB & HWY. 313

TO 191

TO SEVENMILE RIM Trail #7

Cotter Mine Road

Mill Canyon Road

Tusher Canyon

Blue Hills Road

(Impassable when wet)

Bartlett Wash

Dry Wash

TO SEVENMILE RIM Trail #7

Tusher Canyon

Bartlett Wash

Corral

TO TUSHER TUNNEL Trail #3

Gate

Sand Hills

Bartlett Wash

HIDDEN CANYON Trail #5

Blue Hills Road

(Impassable when wet)

Water Tank

Lunar Canyon

Hidden Canyon

TO I-70 & DUBINKY WELL ROAD

To Dubinky Well Road

N

01

02

03

04

05

06

P

53

The trail coming into the canyon follows a dry wash and leaves on a well-defined road.

A few small challenges coming in.

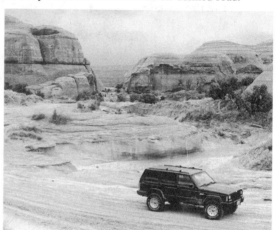

Be aware of the possibility of flash floods in the wash.

Heading northeast out of the canyon—the sandy road is easy and fun to drive.

Hidden Canyon ⑤

Location: Northwest of Moab and west of Highway 191.

Difficulty: Easy. Once you enter the canyon, most of the road is sandy wash bottom and fairly easy; however, conditions can change due to the fluid nature of the trail. Avoid this trip during periods of heavy rain and be aware of the possibility of flash floods. There is one steep sandy descent into the canyon that has the potential to wash out. It is difficult to drive up so plan to drive the trail in the direction described here. Route-finding may be a little confusing because there are often several choices available while in the wash. Fortunately, most choices lead to the same place. Mileage will vary based on the specific path you choose.

Features: This is a very pleasant trip as the trail softly winds its way into a picturesque and quiet canyon. The sandy nature of the trail allows for many fun choices without doing damage to the environment. A great place to take the kids, have a picnic, and play in the sand.

To extend the trip, but still keep it easy, add a short side trip to Tusher Tunnel (Trail #3). See directions within the Trail Description below.

If you are looking for a little more challenge after completing Hidden Canyon, consider adding Hidden Canyon Overlook (Trail #4). You pass by the turn-off point for this trail as you come out of Hidden Canyon. All three of the above trails can be driven in a single day.

Time & Distance: The entire loop from Highway 191 and back is about 14 miles and takes 1 to 2 hours.

To Get There: From the intersection of Highways 191 and 128, drive 14.6 miles north on Highway 191 and turn left on Blue Hills Road just south of mile post 143. You can see Blue Hills Road stretching across the prairie before you get to the airport.

Trail Description: Reset your odometer as you turn off 191 [01]. Drive west 2.3 miles and turn left [02]. At the next major intersection, turn left [03]. Continue on a wide road. After passing through Bartlett Wash, turn right at mile 3.8 [04]. Within 0.2 miles the road to Tusher Tunnel (Trail #3) goes to the left. You may wish to add this short but interesting side trip. If not, continue straight. Pass through a gate at 4.9 miles. Close the gate behind you.

After the gate, you'll pass a series of sand hills on the right. Please stay out of this area. The sand hills do not need any further damage from vehicles as you will see. As you continue, the trail splits in several directions. I prefer the right side as it meanders in the wash; however, turn left out of the wash at 5.5 miles and rejoin the trail. If you stay in the wash too long, it becomes very difficult.

Make an important right turn down into a wash at mile 6.2 [05]. Sometimes there's a cairn marking this turn. This is the entrance to Hidden Canyon. If you miss this turn, you'll find yourself on a long sandy trek to Dubinky Well Road. Before you turn down into the wash, inspect the trail to make sure it is in good condition. It is fairly steep and is susceptible to damage from heavy rain. It is also difficult to drive back up this hill so make sure it is dry at the bottom. Once in the wash, you pass through a section with high walls on both sides. Avoid getting close to any wall that is undercut. Don't let children play in this area. You'll pass through a barbed wire gate—leave it as you find it. After passing through this narrow section, the wash widens with various choices. Choose a path with which you feel most comfortable. At 7.5 miles the trail merges with the exit trail. Bear left and continue into the canyon a short distance until you reach the turnaround [06]. This is a good place to stop for lunch and explore the area.

As you head back out of the canyon, bear left at the point the trails merged and stay on a well-defined sandy road. You'll soon head into another wash—this one with trees. Resist the urge to climb out of the wash as spur trails head uphill to the right. Stay in the wash until it becomes a defined road again. Go straight at 10.4 miles as you pass the turn for Hidden Canyon Overlook (Trail #4). Bear left at the corral and head back out to Blue Hills Road where a right turn will take you back to Highway 191 at 14.1 miles.

Return Trip: Turn right at 191 to go back to Moab.

Services: Service station at the intersection of 191 and 313.

Maps: Part of this trail is shown on USGS 7.5 minute map Jug Rock 38109-F7. I plotted the remainder of the route using my own GPS equipment. The beginning part of the route is shown on the Latitude 40°, Inc. *Moab West* Biking Map.

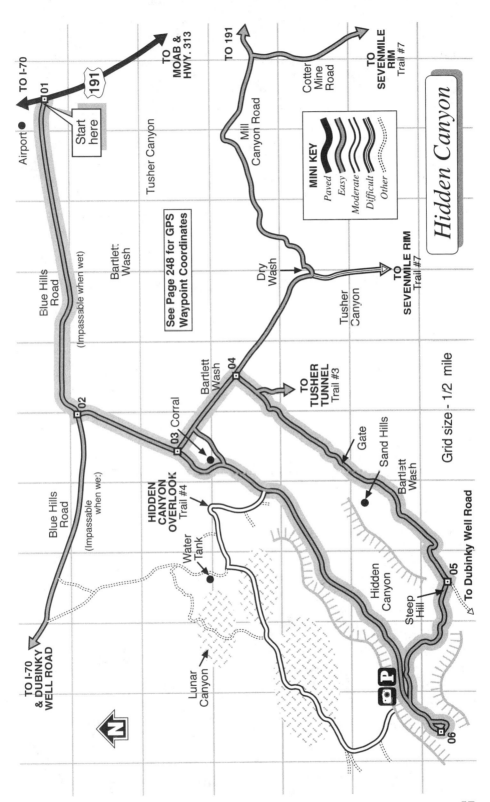

Hidden Canyon

Grid size - 1/2 mile

MINI KEY
Paved
Easy
Moderate
Difficult
Other

See Page 248 for GPS Waypoint Coordinates

TO I-70

TO MOAB & HWY. 313

191

Airport

Start here

01

Blue Hills Road

(Impassable when wet)

Tusher Canyon

Bartlet Wash

TO 191

Mill Canyon Road

Cotter Mine Road

TO SEVENMILE RIM Trail #7

Dry Wash

Tusher Canyon

TO SEVENMILE RIM Trail #7

02

Blue Hills Road

(Impassable when wet)

TO I-70 & DUBINKY WELL ROAD

N

Lunar Canyon

Water Tank

HIDDEN CANYON OVERLOOK Trail #4

03 Corral

Bartlett Wash

04

TO TUSHER TUNNEL Trail #3

Gate

Sand Hills

Bartlett Wash

To Dubinky Well Road

05

Steep Hill

Hidden Canyon

P

06

57

Looking north at Hidden Canyon from Bartlett Overlook as storm approaches.

This is the toughest spot on the trail.

A stock pick-up truck negotiates steep turn.

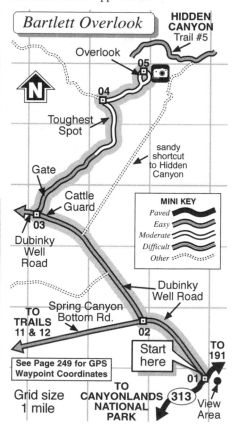

Bartlett Overlook

HIDDEN CANYON Trail #5

Overlook

05

04

Toughest Spot

Gate

Cattle Guard

03

Dubinky Well Road

sandy shortcut to Hidden Canyon

MINI KEY
Paved
Easy
Moderate
Difficult
Other

Dubinky Well Road

Spring Canyon Bottom Rd.

TO TRAILS 11 & 12

02

Start here

TO 191

See Page 249 for GPS Waypoint Coordinates

01

313

View Area

Grid size 1 mile

TO CANYONLANDS NATIONAL PARK

58

Bartlett Overlook

Location: Northwest of Moab and Highway 313.

Difficulty: Moderate. Starts easy but gradually becomes more difficult near the overlook. Passable but challenging for stock vehicles. Skid plates recommended.

Features: If you're ready to graduate from easy to moderate, this trail is a good one. The challenging portion of the trail is rather short and provides a taste of difficulty without being overwhelming. Culminates at a great view.

Time & Distance: Less than 8 miles from Highway 313 to the overlook. Allow about 1 to 1 1/2 hours for the round trip.

To Get There: Drive north from Moab on Highway 191 to Highway 313. Turn left following signs to Canyonlands National Park and Dead Horse Point State Park. Just after a view area on the left at 8.5 miles, turn right on a good quality wide gravel road. This is Dubinky Well Road. (Not marked.)

Trail Description: Reset your odometer as you turn off 313 [01]. Head northwest and turn right at 1.5 miles as Spring Canyon Bottom Road goes straight [02]. At 4.1 miles [03], just after a cattle guard, turn right on a lesser road. Within a short distance, you'll pass through a gate that must be opened and closed. The road stays easy for a while but at 6.4 miles you'll encounter a steep angled rock. This is the toughest spot on the trail and there is no way around it. (See photo opposite page.) Stock vehicles may scrape bottom here even with careful tire placement. Use a spotter if necessary. Turn right at mile 6.7 [04]. There's another tough spot at 7.5 before the road forks again. You can go either way; this is a loop for the overlook just ahead [05].

Return Trip: The quickest way out is to return the way you came in. However, an alternate route goes north from Waypoint 04. It is confusing with quite a few spurs, but if you head predominately west, you'll eventually get back to Dubinky Well Road.

Services: Service station at the intersection of 191 and 313.

Maps: Some of this trail is shown on the USGS 7.5 minute map Jug Rock 38109-F7. I plotted the last mile of this route using my own GPS equipment.

On this day, haze from California fires obscures distant view of Arches National Park.

This tippy spot heading down to the bottom of Uranium Arch can be avoided.

Uranium Arch as seen from above.

Monitor (left) and Merrimac Buttes.

Sevenmile Rim ◀ 7 ▶

Location: Northwest of Moab, immediately west of Highway 191 and 313.

Difficulty: Difficult. Most of the trail is moderate with just a few difficult spots. Some stock vehicles with very high ground clearance and good artic-ulation can manage this trail. A tough section down to Uranium Arch can be avoided by simply viewing the arch from above. One spot near Merrimac Butte tilts sideways to an extreme degree. The trail can be made much more difficult by driving optional Wipe Out Hill which requires lockers or a winch to get back up.

    The exact trail described here is sometimes difficult to find, but because it follows a well-defined rim, you can't stray too far off course. Monitor and Merrimac Buttes are excellent landmarks and are usually vis-ible across this open area. A network of connecting roads provides many alternate routes and exit points but also adds to the confusion of route-finding.

Features: Many beautiful overlooks and interesting rock formations includ-ing Corral Canyon, Monitor and Merrimac Buttes, Determination Towers, Uranium Arch, and Courthouse Rock. The drive itself is interesting as the terrain changes from slickrock to sagebrush to wash bottom.

Time & Distance: The loop described here is about 20 miles including side trips to Uranium Arch and the Sevenmile Canyon Overlook. Allow about 5 hours driving time plus stops.

To Get There: Drive north from Moab on Highway 191. Continue 0.6 miles past Highway 313 and turn left on a wide gravel road.

Trail Description:
    From the start to Uranium Arch: *Reset your odometer as you turn off 191* [01]. Head north on Cotter Mine Road, gradually passing west of the power lines. Go straight at 0.7 then turn left uphill at 1.2 miles. At 2.0 miles [02] turn left, leaving the main road. Shift into low gear as the road steepens through rougher switchbacks. Stay right at 2.7 and ignore lesser spurs. At 3.1 [03] turn left downhill as an equal size road goes straight. Drop down a ledge into a wash at 3.6. Where the road goes straight at 3.9 [04], you turn left and descend a couple of steep ledges then make an immediate right turn. At 4.0 make a hard left at a four-way intersection then bear right. Make a left at 4.1 and another at 4.4. You should be heading downhill. An overlook to Corral Canyon is reached at 4.5 miles [05] just around the corner. Take a few minutes

The correct route passes by these two large slabs of rock that look like giant burnt toast.

This is not trick photography. You must cross this section of tilted slickrock.

Going down the upper portion of optional Wipe Out Hill. Coming back up is tough.

to look around. You can see why this canyon functioned well as a natural corral. Not a lot of fencing is necessary.

Bear right uphill in a southeast direction following cairns away from the overlook. At 5.0 turn left at a T and approach the rim. Stay along the rim until 5.6 miles [06] where a cairn marks a trail to the right. This is a short side trip to Uranium Arch. The rocky trail drops steeply along the south side of the arch then returns the same way. You can avoid the tough spots by viewing the arch from above.

From Uranium Arch to Sevenmile Canyon Overlook: *Reset your odometer when you get back to the rim above Uranium Arch* [06]. Continue south along the rim. Go straight at 0.1 as a lesser road goes right. At 0.5 [07] turn right and head downhill away from the rim, even though the trail appears to go straight. You'll soon swing left back towards the rim. It may take some detective work to find the trail through this area. Watch for cairns and tire tracks. After a long downhill section of slickrock at 0.9 miles [08], watch for a cairn on the left. Turn left at the cairn before the slickrock ends. You should be able to see Sevenmile Canyon to the south.

Gradually the trail becomes more defined as it swings southwest on a course roughly parallel with Highway 313. For a short distance it heads northwest. At 2.0 miles turn left where a lesser road goes right. Go straight at 2.1 [09] on what is now a well-defined sandy road. A right here would bypass the overlook. Bear right at 2.3, go straight at 2.6 [10], and left at 2.9 before reaching the overlook at 3.3 miles [11].

From Sevenmile Canyon Overlook to Wipe Out Hill: *Reset your odometer at the overlook* [11]. Drive out the same way you came in, then turn left at 0.7 miles [10]. At 1.1 [12] the road swings left and joins the bypass road mentioned above. Go straight through a four-way intersection at 1.4 and another cluster of roads at 1.5. Immediately turn left at a small tree [13] and follow a sandy road towards the opening between Monitor and Merrimac Buttes. A high ledge extends north from the base of Monitor Butte at 1.8. Swing north around the ledge even though tracks go up it. The trail is not obvious between the buttes. Curve right around the southwest side of Merrimac Butte. At 2.2 swing left through a narrow space between a high rock ledge and two large rocks standing on edge [14]. They look like two giant pieces of burnt toast (see photo). Follow around the base of Merrimac. At 2.4 you can stay high along the wall or drop down where it's not so tippy. You'll pass through a small sandy canyon then swing uphill again towards the base of the Merrimac. At 2.7 you can't avoid an extremely tilted section of slickrock (see photo). Study the slope carefully for the best line. I went high to the right then turned downhill before the steepest part. My tilt gauge measured 28 degrees.

At 2.8 miles [15] you reach a sign pointing ahead to Wipe Out Hill. It's just around the corner to the left. If you're looking for a tough challenge, this is an opportunity to drive down and up the obstacle without having to drive the entire Wipe Out Hill Trail (not covered in this book). I managed the obstacle successfully with the help of a good spotter and lockers in both axles. I must admit, driving up was quite a thrill.

From Wipe Out Hill to Highway 191: *Reset your odometer at the sign above Wipe Out Hill* [15]. Head north along the east side of Big Mesa. The road is mostly easy with an occasional rock ledge to make it interesting. Bear left at a fork at 0.8 miles [16]. The dramatic rock needles ahead are called Determination Towers and are very popular with rock climbers. At 1.2 miles the road goes straight but we went left across some slickrock to get a closer view of the towers. Turn left at a T intersection at 1.5 miles [17]. Right would take you into Mill Canyon. Pass through a fence at 1.9 and begin a gradual descent into Tusher Wash. Turn right at 2.7 [18] into the main wash. At 3.7 you'll pass through a narrow section. Notice that the rock is red on one side and white on the other. That's because this part of the trail follows a major fault line. The rocks have shifted, exposing different rock layers on each side of the trail.

You intersect with Mill Canyon Road at 4.6 miles [19]. Turn right following the wash. Just around the corner at 4.7 turn right out of the wash on a well-defined road. Bear left at 6.6 before reaching Highway 191 at 7.2 miles [20].

Return Trip: Turn right for Moab or left for Interstate 70.

Services: There's a campground and gas station just north of the intersection of Highways 191 and 313. Otherwise, return to Moab.

Maps: Some of this trail is shown on the USGS 7.5 minute maps Merrimac Butte 38109-F6 and Jug Rock 38109-F7. I plotted much of the route using my own GPS equipment.

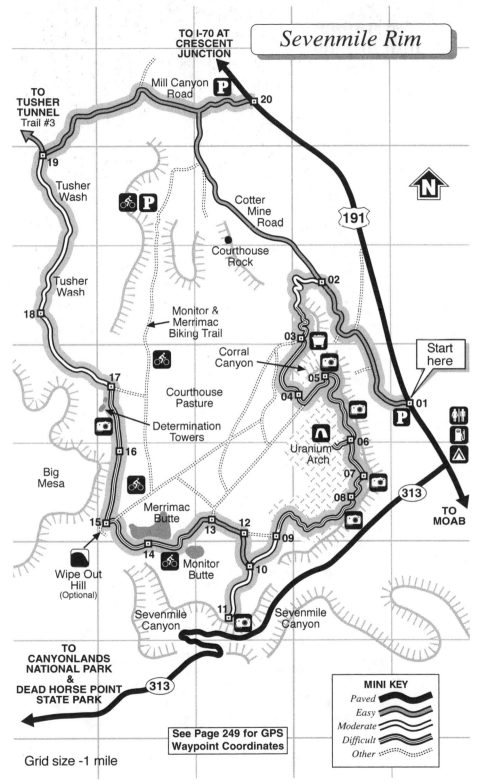

Sevenmile Rim

TO I-70 AT
CRESCENT
JUNCTION

Mill Canyon Road — P — 20

TO
TUSHER
TUNNEL
Trail #3

19

Tusher Wash

Cotter Mine Road

N

191

Tusher Wash

Courthouse Rock

18

Monitor & Merrimac Biking Trail

02

Corral Canyon

03

Start here

05

17

Courthouse Pasture

04

01

P

Determination Towers

16

06

Big Mesa

Uranium Arch

07

313

TO MOAB

Merrimac Butte

08

15

13   12

09

14

Monitor Butte

10

Wipe Out Hill
(Optional)

11

Sevenmile Canyon

Sevenmile Canyon

TO
CANYONLANDS
NATIONAL PARK
&
DEAD HORSE POINT
STATE PARK

313

MINI KEY
Paved
Easy
Moderate
Difficult
Other

See Page 249 for GPS Waypoint Coordinates

Grid size -1 mile

The trail begins across this sandy stretch then turns east and becomes rocky.

A left turn here takes you over the toughest spot on the trail.

This section of the trail follows a high ledge and passes between some large boulders.

Rainbow Terrace 8

Location: Northwest of Moab and Highway 313.

Difficulty: Moderate. Much of this trail is easy. The rocky moderate portion measures less than 2 miles and has one small challenge. Stock vehicles can get through with careful tire placement. One portion of the trail follows a dry creek bed where flash floods are possible but unlikely. Avoid the trail if heavy rains are expected.

Features: This little-known trail takes you across open rangeland but offers some very nice scenery as it follows along the backside of Rainbow Rocks. The dark purple color of the rock is unusual. You'll pass by some large sand dunes on the left as you head northeast on Levi Well Road.

Time & Distance: The trail is 12.6 miles including Levi Well Road. Allow 1 1/2 to 2 hours as described here plus transit time.

To Get There: Drive north from Moab on Highway 191 to Highway 313. Turn left following signs to Canyonlands National Park and Dead Horse Point State Park. Just after a view area on the left at 8.5 miles, turn right on a good quality wide gravel road. This is Dubinky Well Road (not marked). After about 1.5 miles bear right, staying on Dubinky Well Road as Spring Canyon Bottom Road goes straight. You're looking for Spring Canyon Point Road which is another 4.9 miles on the left. It is just before Dubinky Well. Its tall windmill can be seen from a distance. You must turn before you get to the well. Once on Spring Canyon Point Road, drive west 2.2 miles and turn right on a single-lane sandy road a short distance past a large rock formation called The Needles. Some maps call this Tombstone Rock, a more descriptive name, in my opinion. This rock, alongside the longer Rainbow Rock formation, is an easily recognizable landmark and is helpful to use as a reference point when driving other trails in the area.

Trail Description: Reset your odometer as you turn off Spring Canyon Point Road [01]. At first, you'll head northwest away from the rock formations on the right. Within 0.2 miles bear right at a fork [02]. Left appears to be an easier route but is not. After this fork, you'll swing back in a northeast direction towards Rainbow Rocks. Bear left at 1.2 miles as the road becomes rockier and more challenging. Route-finding also becomes more difficult so scout ahead when necessary. At 1.3 you'll head uphill across stratified purple-colored rock. At 1.6 miles turn left at a poorly defined T. This is the toughest

67

spot on the trail. Select a route from three uphill choices. Use a spotter if necessary.

After this tough spot, you'll begin climbing across a high terrace. Again, the trail is not always obvious. At 1.8 miles, pass to the right of a large boulder that, at first, appears to be blocking the trail. Gradually, you'll come down from the terrace back onto sandy terrain. At 2.4 miles [03] a lesser road comes in from the left as you go right. Continue straight again at 4.1 miles as a lesser road intersects. At mile 4.8 bear left at a fork. At 5.3 miles the road passes in and out of a dry creek bed until reaching Levi Well Road at 6.3 miles [04].

Turn right on Levi Well Road. It is well defined from here all the way to Blue Hills Road at 12.6 miles [05]. Like Blue Hills Road, parts of Levi Well Road can become impassable when extremely wet.

Return Trip: Turn right on Blue Hills Road to return to Highway 191 in about 7.4 miles. Bear left as several well-traveled roads go right. Hidden Canyon (Trail #5) is one of these roads. If you wish to return via Dubinky Well Road, turn right off Blue Hills Road about 0.2 miles south of Levi Well Road.

Services: Service station at the intersection of Highways 191 and 313.

Maps: USGS 7.5 minute maps Dubinky Wash 38109-F8 and Dee Pass 38109-G8. This trail is also faintly shown on the Latitude 40°, Inc. *Moab West* Biking Map.

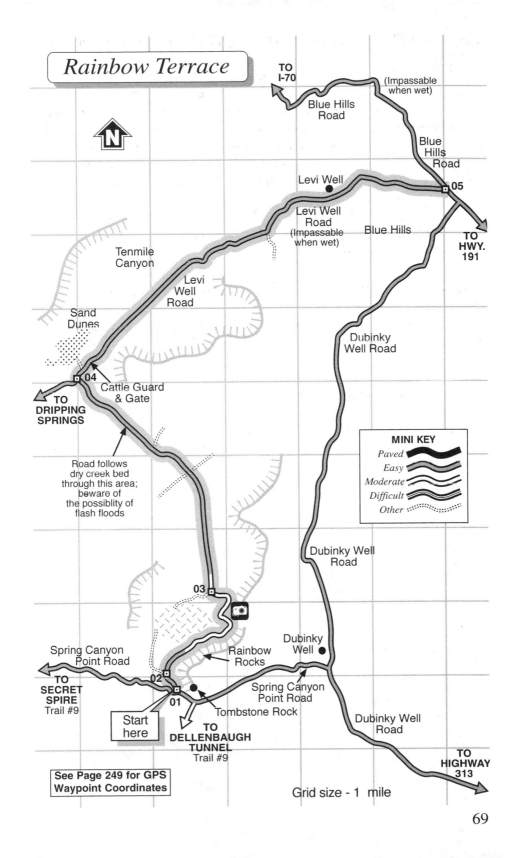

Rainbow Terrace

N

TO I-70

(Impassable when wet)

Blue Hills Road

Blue Hills Road

05

Levi Well

Levi Well Road (Impassable when wet)

Blue Hills

TO HWY. 191

Tenmile Canyon

Levi Well Road

Sand Dunes

Dubinky Well Road

04

Cattle Guard & Gate

TO DRIPPING SPRINGS

Road follows dry creek bed through this area; beware of the possiblity of flash floods

MINI KEY
Paved
Easy
Moderate
Difficult
Other

Dubinky Well Road

03

Spring Canyon Point Road

Rainbow Rocks

Dubinky Well

TO SECRET SPIRE Trail #9

02

Spring Canyon Point Road

01

Tombstone Rock

Start here

TO DELLENBAUGH TUNNEL Trail #9

Dubinky Well Road

See Page 249 for GPS Waypoint Coordinates

Grid size - 1 mile

TO HIGHWAY 313

Secret Spire up close.

The trail is a mixture of sand and slickrock.

There's just enough room to stand up on the short hike through Dellenbaugh Tunnel.

Bighorn sheep on a ridge near Secret Spire.

Water-carved rock formations.

Location: Northwest of Moab and Highway 313.

Difficulty: Moderate. A few rock challenges require careful tire placement. There is one smooth but steep descent on slickrock and some mildly tippy sections. Skid plates are helpful but not absolutely necessary. Suitable for stock high-clearance vehicles. Route-finding is a little confusing in a couple of places but, due to the shortness of the routes, you can't get too far off course.

Features: Dellenbaugh Tunnel is very short and not at all intimidating to walk through. The tunnel was formed over eons of time by water draining into Spring Canyon. It is unlikely that it could rain hard enough to be dangerous, but I'd stay out of the tunnel during a heavy rain as a precaution. There are other interesting water-carved features around the canyon rim (see photo at left). The hike through the tunnel leads to a hiking trail along the rim of the canyon which is deep with dangerous vertical walls. Children should be supervised.

Spring Canyon provides a beautiful photogenic backdrop for the strange-looking Secret Spire. Many hiking-accessible caves and water-formed features surround the canyon near the spire. You might get lucky, as I did, and catch a glimpse of bighorn sheep on the rock ledges nearby.

Time & Distance: The trip to Dellenbaugh Tunnel is 1.8 miles. The trip to Secret Spire measures 0.4 miles. Spring Canyon Point Road between the two trails is 2.6 miles. Allow 2 to 3 hours plus transit time. It takes less than an hour to reach the start of the trail from Moab.

To Get There: Drive north from Moab on Highway 191 to Highway 313. Turn left following signs to Canyonlands National Park and Dead Horse Point State Park. Just after a view area on the left at 8.5 miles, turn right on a good quality wide gravel road. This is Dubinky Well Road (not marked). After about 1.5 miles bear right, staying on Dubinky Well Road as Spring Canyon Bottom Road goes straight. You're looking for Spring Canyon Point Road which is another 4.9 miles on the left. It is just before Dubinky Well. Its windmill is visible from a distance. You must turn before you get to the well. Once on Spring Canyon Point Road, drive west 2.0 miles. When you reach Tombstone Rock (The Needles), turn left on a single-lane, sandy road to Dellenbaugh Tunnel.

Trail Description: *Reset your odometer as you turn off Spring Canyon Point Road* [01]. At 0.2 miles bear left and drop down a steep section of slickrock. Maneuver your vehicle through some tippy sections. Continue through the slickrock until you reach a dry wash at 0.8 miles. Turn right and follow the widest part of the wash before reaching more slickrock. At 1.2 miles you should reach the tip of Spring Canyon. To your right—you'll have to get out of your vehicle and search for it—you'll find the water-carved trench seen in the photo on page 70. It's on the very edge of the canyon cliff.

Bear left around the tip of the canyon then swing right. You may have to do a little scouting to find the trail in the sand. After several more twists and dips, the trail ends on a large dome of slickrock at 1.8 miles [02]. Hike about 100 feet downhill in a westerly direction. You'll see a deep hole. At the bottom is the narrow entrance to the Dellenbaugh Tunnel.

To reach the Secret Spire, retrace your route back to Spring Canyon Point Road [01], *reset your odometer* and turn left. Stay on the main road as lesser roads go right. Bear left at 1.6 miles before reaching a gate at 2.3 miles. Leave the gate the way you found it. Turn left off the main road at mile 2.6 [03]. Continue just 0.4 miles to a side road on the left [04]. Park here and take a short walk to the spire.

Return Trip: Retrace your route back to Spring Canyon Point Road. Turn right and drive back to Dubinky Well Road where another right will take you to Highway 313.

Services: Service station at the intersection of Highways 191 and 313.

Maps: I plotted these routes using my own GPS equipment. Spring Canyon Point Road is shown on USGS 7.5 minute map Dubinky Wash 38109-F8. The trail to Dellenbaugh Tunnel is shown on the Latitude 40°, Inc. *Moab West* Biking Map.

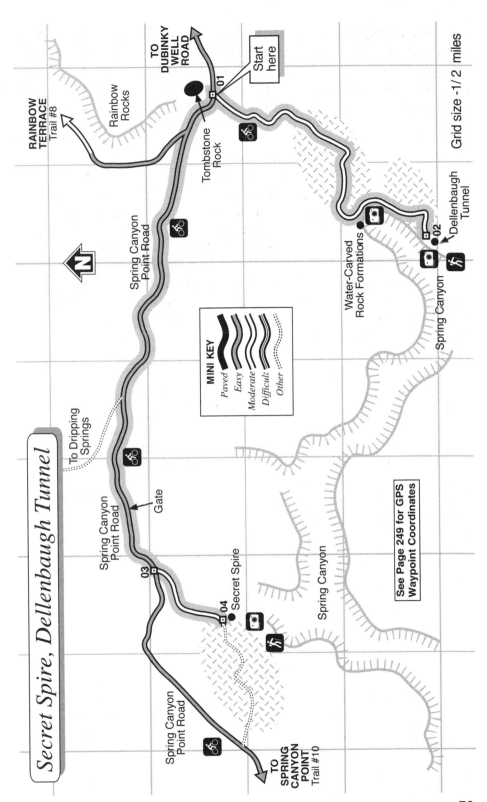

Secret Spire, Dellenbaugh Tunnel

TO DUBINKY WELL ROAD

Start here

01

Rainbow Rocks

RAINBOW TERRACE Trail #8

Tombstone Rock

Spring Canyon Point Road

N

To Dripping Springs

Gate

Spring Canyon Point Road

03

04

Secret Spire

Spring Canyon Point Road

TO SPRING CANYON POINT Trail #10

Spring Canyon

MINI KEY

Paved
Easy
Moderate
Difficult
Other

Water-Carved Rock Formations

02

Dellenbaugh Tunnel

Spring Canyon

See Page 249 for GPS Waypoint Coordinates

Grid size -1/2 miles

Heading west on Spring Canyon Point Road towards Tombstone and Rainbow Rocks.

One view at Spring Canyon Point.

Arch (Cliff Hanger Bridge) at end of spur before point.

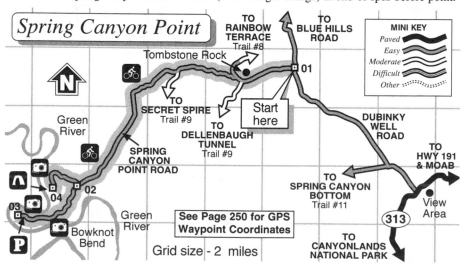

Spring Canyon Point

TO RAINBOW TERRACE Trail #8

TO BLUE HILLS ROAD

Tombstone Rock

01

MINI KEY
Paved
Easy
Moderate
Difficult
Other

TO SECRET SPIRE Trail #9

Start here

TO DELLENBAUGH TUNNEL Trail #9

DUBINKY WELL ROAD

Green River

SPRING CANYON POINT ROAD

TO HWY 191 & MOAB

TO SPRING CANYON BOTTOM Trail #11

02

04

03

Green River

View Area

Bowknot Bend

See Page 250 for GPS Waypoint Coordinates

313

Grid size - 2 miles

TO CANYONLANDS NATIONAL PARK

Spring Canyon Point ⑩

Location: Northwest of Moab and Highway 313.

Difficulty: Easy. A graded gravel road with intermittent sandy stretches. Heavy rains may cause a few ruts and an occasional washout is possible. The spur road prior to reaching the point is narrow and offers a few more challenges.

Features: A nice relaxing drive across open rangeland culminating in a spectacular view of the Green River at the bottom of Labyrinth Canyon.

Time & Distance: Spring Canyon Point Road is 13.6 miles long. Allow about 1 to 2 hours for the round trip starting from Dubinky Well Road. Add extra time to explore the spur road and to find the arch.

To Get There: Drive north from Moab on Highway 191 to Highway 313. Turn left following signs to Canyonlands National Park. Just after a view area on the left at 8.5 miles, turn right on Dubinky Well Road (not marked). At 1.5 miles bear right. Spring Canyon Point Road is another 4.9 miles on the left.

Trail Description: Reset your odometer as you turn off Dubinky Well Road [01]. Head west on Spring Canyon Point Road past Tombstone Rock (see photo opposite page). Stay on the main road as spur roads depart along the way. Bear left at 3.6 and 5.4 miles. At mile 10.6 the spur road to the arch goes right [02]. You'll come back here later. Continue straight to the end of the road at 13.6 miles [03]. There's plenty of room to park while you explore the area on foot. Be careful, there are many high, dangerous cliffs in the area.

If you're looking for a little more challenge, go back to the spur and turn left. *Reset your odometer.* Bear left at 0.1 as a lesser road goes right. The road becomes faint in places as it curves back to the south and ends at 1.7 miles [04]. The arch is west along the cliff edge and may take a while to find.

Return Trip: Return the way you came.

Services: Service station at the intersection of Highways 191 and 313.

Maps: This entire trail is shown on the Latitude 40°, Inc. *Moab West* Biking Map. Three USGS 7.5 minute maps are required: Dubinky Wash 38109-F8, Tenmile Point 38110-F1, and Bowknot Bend 38110-E1.

Starting the descent into Spring Canyon. Road looks scary but is wide all the way down.

Nearing the bottom of the canyon. The Green River is just ahead.

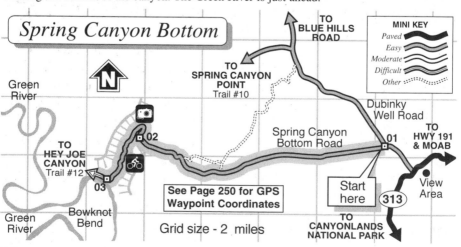

Spring Canyon Bottom

TO
BLUE HILLS
ROAD

MINI KEY
Paved
Easy
Moderate
Difficult
Other

Green
River

N

TO
SPRING CANYON
POINT
Trail #10

Dubinky
Well Road

TO
HEY JOE
CANYON
Trail #12

02

Spring Canyon
Bottom Road

01

TO
HWY 191
& MOAB

03

**See Page 250 for GPS
Waypoint Coordinates**

Start
here

313

View
Area

Green
River

Bowknot
Bend

Grid size - 2 miles

TO
CANYONLANDS
NATIONAL PARK

Spring Canyon Bottom (11)

Location: Northwest of Moab and Highway 313.

Difficulty: Easy (special caution if wet). A two-lane gravel road most of the way, including the ledge portion that drops into the canyon. Persons afraid of heights may find the ledge road disconcerting. This road can be dangerous when wet. Road damage possible after rains. Route-finding is easy.

Features: After an uneventful drive across open rangeland, you'll drop about 800 feet into rugged, tourist-forgotten Spring Canyon. Despite its spectacular beauty and easy access, you rarely see another vehicle.

Time & Distance: The first 9 miles go quickly as you proceed on a wide, frequently straight road. You'll slow significantly as you complete the last 3.7 miles to Green River. Allow about 3 hours for the round trip.

To Get There: Drive north from Moab on Highway 191 to Highway 313. Turn left following signs to Canyonlands National Park. Just after a view area on the left at 8.5 miles, turn right on Dubinky Well Road (not marked). After 1.5 miles Dubinky Well Road goes to the right; you go straight on Spring Canyon (Bottom) Road.

Trail Description: Reset your odometer where Spring Canyon Bottom Road begins [01]. After 4 miles you'll begin to see Hellroaring Canyon on the left. Bear left at 5.9 miles as a lesser road goes right. Curves tighten at 9.1 miles before the serious descent into Spring Canyon. At 9.4 the canyon makes itself known in a big way as you find yourself on a shelf road with a precipitous cliff on your left [02]. Even though the road is wide and well-graded, I recommend you shift into low range to minimize use of your brakes. At one point, the shelf is cut into the cliff edge and rock overhangs the road. The road levels out at 10.3 miles as you cross a small creek. There's a fork at 12.1 miles. You can turn around here or bear right on a lesser road to reach the river at 12.5 miles [03]. To continue, see Hey Joe Canyon (Trail #12).

Return Trip: Return the way you came.

Services: Service station at the intersection of Highways 191 and 313.

Maps: This road is shown on the Latitude 40°, Inc. *Moab West* Biking Map or use USGS 7.5 minute map Dubinky Wash 38109-F8.

The trail hugs the banks of the Green River until Hey Joe Canyon. Brush is dense in places.

Several places are a little tight and rocky.

Abandoned truck from the old mining days.

Erosion near the river may be a problem.

Entrances to Hey Joe Mine. Best to stay out.

Hey Joe Canyon ◆12◆

Location: Northwest of Moab and Highway 313.

Difficulty: Difficult. Most of this trail is easy to moderate but there are a few places that earn it a difficult rating. One small water crossing can be deep and muddy. Several rocky sections are narrow and require careful maneuvering to avoid body damage. Erosion along the river has cut into the trail in a few places. I question how long this trail will stay open before repairs are necessary. Check with the BLM for up-to-date conditions. Although a stock SUV can get through, I wouldn't take a shiny new vehicle on this trail. Heavy brush (called tamarisk) is extremely dense along the river banks and will make deep brush marks in your paint. The trail is dusty and dirty and very hot most of the time. Flies and mosquitoes can be nasty in the summer, so take along insect repellent. Route-finding is very easy.

Features: Despite all the negatives explained above, this trail is worth your time if you have the right vehicle. At the end of the trail, you'll climb high up into Hey Joe Canyon where an interesting abandoned uranium mine awaits. The mine is in excellent condition with several large, well-preserved pieces of mining equipment strewn about the entrance area, including the old truck pictured on the opposite page. Despite the good condition of the mine, stay out. Uranium mines have the added risk of radon and are very dangerous.

Time & Distance: From the starting point shown here, allow about 2 to 3 hours for the round trip. It is 8.6 miles, one way, to the mine. Add to that another 2 hours for the round trip of Spring Canyon Bottom (Trail #11) which you must complete before you reach the start of this trail. With transit time to Moab and stopping time along the way, this adventure can easily take all day.

To Get There: Follow all directions to the end of Spring Canyon Bottom (Trail #11). At the point where that trail ends, this one begins. When you reach the river, turn right and follow the narrow, single-lane road that parallels the river.

Trail Description: Reset your odometer as you turn right along the Green River [01]. You soon run into the tamarisk brush described earlier. This plant was brought to the West many years ago to help prevent erosion along the river banks. It has worked well for its intended purpose, but unfortunately

79

it consumes tremendous amounts of water, now a precious commodity. It has also displaced the native willows and cottonwoods that once lived along the riverbanks. The BLM would like to get rid of the pesky plant but can't figure out how. All you need to know, however, is that tamarisk is rough on paint.

At 0.7 miles a small tributary can become a nasty mud hole—fortunately, it's not wide. With a little momentum, you should get through okay. At 2.7 there's a small rock obstacle and at 5.5 watch for a sharp rock that juts out into the trail. It's hidden by the bushes on the left. In a few places, erosion has washed away the left edge of the trail. You must use your own judgment as to whether the trail is safe to continue.

At mile 8.0 [02] bear right at a rusty bulldozer and start uphill into Hey Joe Canyon. At 8.1 bear left to continue uphill. The trail is very rocky for the next half mile, but with careful tire placement it is passable by a stock high-clearance vehicle. You reach the mine at 8.6 miles [03]. There is adequate room for several vehicles to park. This is a good place for lunch. Under no circumstances should you remove any old equipment or artifacts from the mine site.

Return Trip: Return the way you came.

Services: Service station at the intersection of Highways 191 and 313.

Maps: This entire trail is shown on the Latitude 40°, Inc. *Moab West* Biking Map. Three USGS 7.5 minute maps are required: Dubinky Wash 38109-F8, Tenmile Point 38110-F1, and Bowknot Bend 38110-E1.

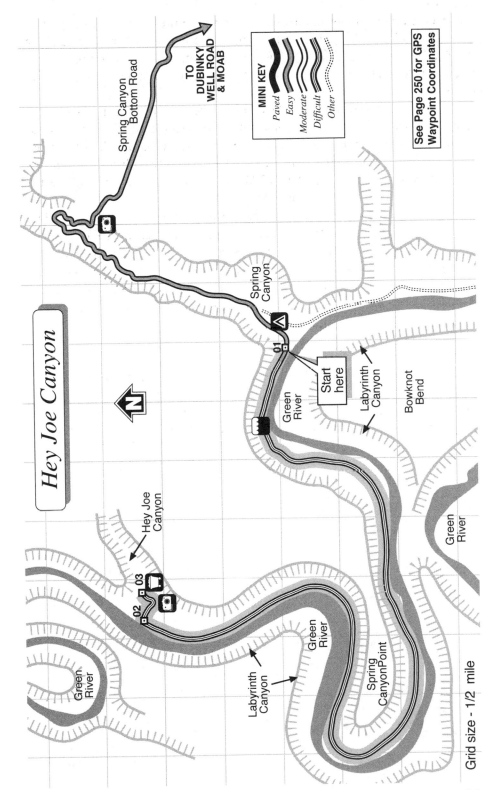

Hey Joe Canyon

N

Spring Canyon Bottom Road

TO DUBINKY WELL ROAD & MOAB

MINI KEY
- *Paved*
- *Easy*
- *Moderate*
- *Difficult*
- *Other*

See Page 250 for GPS Waypoint Coordinates

Spring Canyon

01

Start here

Green River

Labyrinth Canyon

Bowknot Bend

Green River

Hey Joe Canyon

03

02

Green River

Labyrinth Canyon

Green River

Spring Canyon Point

Green River

Grid size - 1/2 mile

81

Mineral Point is usually deserted except during the week of the Easter Jeep Safari.

Jeep Safari participants cluster at the Point.

Hellroaring Canyon top right.

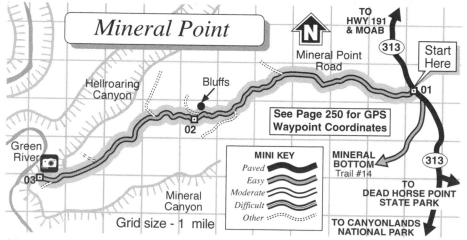

Mineral Point

N

TO
HWY 191
& MOAB

(313)

Start
Here

Mineral Point
Road

01

Bluffs

Hellroaring
Canyon

02

See Page 250 for GPS
Waypoint Coordinates

Green
River

03

MINERAL
BOTTOM
Trail #14

(313)

MINI KEY
Paved
Easy
Moderate
Difficult
Other

TO
DEAD HORSE POINT
STATE PARK

Mineral
Canyon

Grid size - 1 mile

TO CANYONLANDS
NATIONAL PARK

82

Location: West of Moab and Highway 313. Northwest of Dead Horse Point State Park.

Difficulty: Easy. A mixture of sand, gravel, and hard-rock surfaces with a few ruts and washed-out spots. The last half mile has some larger rock ledges but they are maneuverable with a stock high-clearance vehicle. Route-finding is easy.

Features: An easy drive with just a few bumps and turns to make it interesting. You'll enjoy the seclusion and incredible view at the end. Mineral Point is one of many stops on the Easter Jeep Safari Hellroaring Rim Trail.

Time & Distance: From Highway 313 to the point is 12.3 miles. Allow about 2 hours for the round trip.

To Get There: Drive north from Moab on Highway 191 to Highway 313. Turn left following signs to Canyonlands National Park. Drive 11.8 miles and turn right on what starts briefly as a paved road. Be careful—it is easy to confuse this road with Mineral Bottom Road (Horsethief Trail) which is just 0.3 miles farther south on 313.

Trail Description: *Reset your odometer when you turn off Highway 313* [01]. The pavement ends quickly but the main road remains well defined until 6.9 miles. As you pass a series of small bluffs on the right, the road appears to go straight. You should bear left here on a lesser road [02]. Watch for cairns. Bear left two more times at 8.3 and 10.8 miles. You must turn right at 11.9 miles or you will miss the best viewpoint. This last 0.4 miles has some rock ledges to negotiate. Stock vehicles can get through with a little patience, but if you feel uncomfortable, it's only a short walk to the end at 12.3 miles [03]. Watch for an old cable lying on the ground. It's not a road-closure cable but a remnant from a tram cable that once serviced a thriving uranium mine at the bottom of the canyon.

Return Trip: Return the way you came.

Services: Service station at the intersection of Highways 191 and 313.

Maps: This road is shown on the Latitude 40°, Inc. *Moab West* Biking Map and two USGS 7.5 minute maps: Mineral Canyon 38109-E8 and The Knoll 38109-E7. The last 0.4 miles are not shown on any map that I've found.

Stay off the switchbacks when wet.

Heading north along the Green River.

Bikers complete the White Rim Trail and begin the long climb out of the river valley.

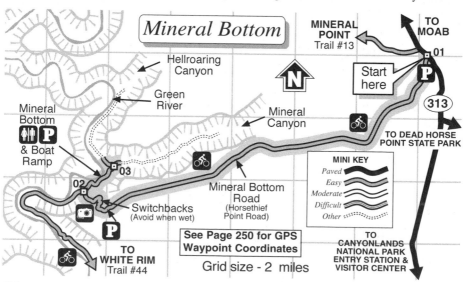

Mineral Bottom

MINERAL POINT
Trail #13

TO MOAB

01

P

Start here

313

TO DEAD HORSE POINT STATE PARK

Hellroaring Canyon

Green River

Mineral Canyon

N

Mineral Bottom
& Boat Ramp
P

03

02

Switchbacks
(Avoid when wet)

P

Mineral Bottom Road
(Horsethief Point Road)

MINI KEY
Paved
Easy
Moderate
Difficult
Other

TO WHITE RIM
Trail #44

See Page 250 for GPS Waypoint Coordinates

Grid size - 2 miles

TO CANYONLANDS NATIONAL PARK ENTRY STATION & VISITOR CENTER

Location: West of Moab and Highway 313. North of Canyonlands National Park.

Difficulty: Easy. Suitable for high-clearance two-wheel-drive vehicles when dry. When wet, however, the road can be impassable, especially on the switchbacks that descend into the river valley. Avoid this road if wet. If it rains while you're at the bottom, wait an hour or two until the road dries. Route-finding is extremely easy.

Features: A wide county road drops rapidly to the Green River on spectacular switchbacks to a pleasant drive along the river's edge. This road provides access to the western half of the White Rim Trail (#44) inside Canyonlands National Park. If you enter the park, first obtain an entry pass at the main park entrance south of paved road 313. It's also a good idea to check at the visitors center for road conditions in the park.

Time & Distance: From Highway 313 to the boat ramp is 15.5 miles. Allow 2 to 3 hours for the round trip. Allow extra time in case it rains.

To Get There: Drive north from Moab on Highway 191 to Highway 313. Turn left following signs to Canyonlands National Park. Drive 12.2 miles and turn right on a wide gravel road just after a cattle guard. Several signs mark the start. Mineral Bottom Road is also called Horsethief Point Road.

Trail Description: Reset your odometer when you turn off Highway 313 [01]. Follow a well-defined road west. The road is usually in excellent condition but may be rutted after a heavy rain. At 13.0 miles the road begins its descent down the switchbacks. Don't attempt if wet. Go straight at 14.5 miles [02]. (Left takes you into Canyonlands National Park in another 3.8 miles.) After a short winding section along the river, you'll go past the boat ramp. You can continue a short distance past a fork at 15.9 miles [03] before the road deteriorates into Mineral Canyon right and eventually Hellroaring Canyon left. You may wish to continue if you're equipped for more difficult terrain.

Return Trip: Return the way you came.

Services: Service station at the intersection of Highways 191 and 313. Modern vault toilets at the boat ramp.

Maps: This road is shown on the Latitude 40°, Inc. *Moab West* Biking Map.

AREA 2

Central Moab

15. Gemini Bridges
16. Metal Masher
17. Long Canyon
18. Bull Canyon
19. Gold Bar Rim
20. Poison Spider Mesa
21. Golden Spike
22. Cliff Hanger
23. Hurrah Pass
24. Moab Rim
25. Pritchett Canyon
26. Pritchett Arch
27. Kane Creek Canyon
28. Behind the Rocks
29. Picture Frame Arch
30. Flat Iron Mesa
31. Hell's Revenge
32. Fins & Things
33. Porcupine Rim
34. Sand Flats Road
35. Steel Bender

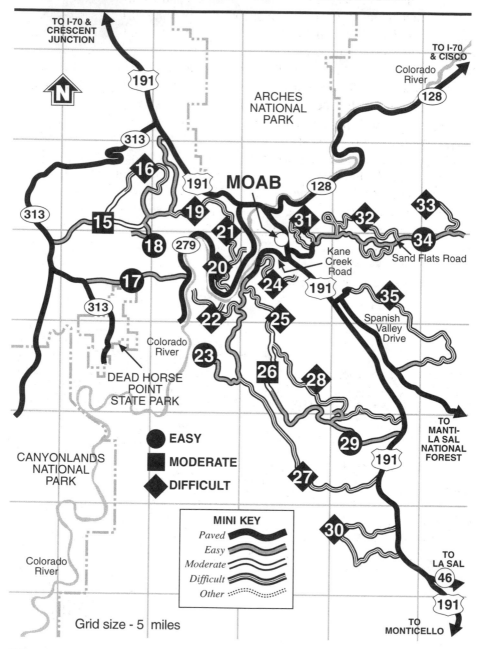

TO I-70 &
CRESCENT
JUNCTION

TO I-70
& CISCO

Colorado
River

N

191

313

128

ARCHES
NATIONAL
PARK

16

191

MOAB

128

313

15

19

33

31

32

18

279

21

34

17

20

Kane
Creek
Road

Sand Flats Road

313

24

191

35

22

Colorado
River

25

Spanish
Valley
Drive

23

DEAD HORSE
POINT
STATE PARK

26

28

● **EASY**

TO
MANTI-
LA SAL
NATIONAL
FOREST

CANYONLANDS
NATIONAL
PARK

■ **MODERATE**

29

191

◆ **DIFFICULT**

27

30

Colorado
River

MINI KEY
Paved
Easy
Moderate
Difficult
Other

TO
LA SAL

46

191

TO
MONTICELLO

Grid size - 5 miles

86

Central Moab

This area includes 5 easy trails, 2 moderate trails and 14 difficult trails. The latter include nationally known names like Poison Spider Mesa, Golden Spike, Moab Rim, Pritchett Canyon, Behind the Rocks, and Hell's Revenge. Obstacles include, among others, White Knuckle Hill, the Golden Crack, Double Whammy, and the Rock Pile. Many of the trails are featured in the popular Easter Jeep Safari sponsored annually by the Red Rock 4-Wheelers, Inc. and the Moab Chamber of Commerce. Where possible, trails match the routes driven during the safari. However, some routes have been shortened and feature only the best parts of the trails. Other routes have been divided to make route-finding simpler or to set apart easier portions of the trail. For example, the exit route from Pritchett Canyon features a moderate trail to Pritchett Arch and an easy trail to Picture Frame Arch. Some routes like Golden Spike and Metal Masher cross nearly featureless terrain and, frankly, defy description. Here the use of GPS is necessary for those who have never driven the trail, and waypoints are closely spaced to better define the trail. Without GPS or some previous experience on these trails, a professional guide is recommended.

Looking back at the Colorado River from the start of Moab Rim (Trail #24).

View from shelf road at the start—La Sal Mountains in distance, Highway 191 below.

Landmark Gooney Bird Rock.

Gemini Bridges (Second bridge hidden in this photo).

This brand new sport utility vehicle tested its skid plates in several places along the trail.

Gemini Bridges

Location: West of Moab and Highway 191. South of Highway 313.

Difficulty: Moderate. The trail begins on a high, two-lane shelf road. Although easy, use extra caution when wet. Parts of the trail are rocky but suitable for stock high-clearance vehicles with skid plates. The last 0.2 miles before Gemini Bridges are the toughest. It is recommended that you walk this section. Because this trail is a heavily used biking route, it is well marked with painted white dashed lines; consequently, route-finding is fairly easy.

Features: One of the most popular biking and four-wheel-drive routes in Moab. The east side approach has dramatic views of the La Sal Mountains and Arches National Park. The Gemini Bridges are really two large arches, side by side, several hundred feet high. This is not immediately apparent because you approach them from the top looking down. Be careful walking around until you get your bearings. Don't let children play by themselves in this area. To view the arches from below, see Bull Canyon (Trail #18).

Time & Distance: It is 7.7 miles to Gemini Bridges from the east side and 5.6 from the west side—a total of 13.3 miles. Allow about 3 hours for the whole trip plus return time on Highway 313.

To Get There: From the intersection of Highways 191 and 128, drive 7.3 miles north on Highway 191 and turn left into a parking area. This turn is 1.3 miles south of Highway 313.

Trail Description: Reset your odometer when you turn off Highway 191 [01]. Pass through the parking area, cross a set of railroad tracks and bear left following a wide dirt road which parallels 191. Soon the road turns west and starts to climb. At the high point along this ledge road, don't be distracted by the outstanding view. Pay close attention to traffic which can be heavy at times. This road accesses many trails in the area and is extremely popular. Continue south as the road descends and swings a little right through a wide valley. After passing Gooney Bird Rock (see photo at left), spur roads head in various directions but the main road is well traveled. At 4.7 miles [02], turn right at a T and climb a steep hill. Turn right at 5.1 and again at 5.3 miles [03] as a sign indicates Bull Canyon (Trail #18) to the left. You may wish to come back here later and see Gemini Bridges from the bottom.

Make an important left turn at 6.1 miles [04]. Soon you begin crossing slickrock marked with painted white dashed lines. At 7.0 bear right as a lesser road goes left. At 7.3 bear left [05]. A larger road comes in from the right at 7.5. You will exit on this road later. It is recommended that you park here and walk downhill from this point. The trail gets tougher with some good sized ledges. Skid plates are definitely recommended. Follow the white dashed lines as you continue the last 0.2 miles to the bridges at 7.7 miles [06]. When exploring around the bridges, be very careful. You are hundreds of feet above the valley below.

You may return the way you came or continue west to Highway 313. To reach 313, go back 0.2 miles to the wider road you passed before you turned downhill. *Reset your odometer at this point.* Head north 0.1 miles and turn left on a single lane road. At 1.0 bear right [07]. You'll pass under a power line before reaching a major intersection at 1.7 miles [08]. Turn left and follow this wide gravel road all the way to Highway 313 at 5.6 miles [09].

Return Trip: Turn right on Highway 313. You'll reach Highway 191 in a little more than 13 miles. From there, turn right for Moab or left for Interstate 70. To reach Canyonlands National Park and Dead Horse Point State Park, turn left on Highway 313.

Services: There is a service station near the intersection of Highways 191 and 313. There are no services, other than vault toilets, at the parks.

Maps: This road is shown on the Latitude 40°, Inc. *Moab West* Biking Map and two USGS 7.5 minute maps: Gold Bar Canyon 38109-E6 and The Knoll 38109-E7.

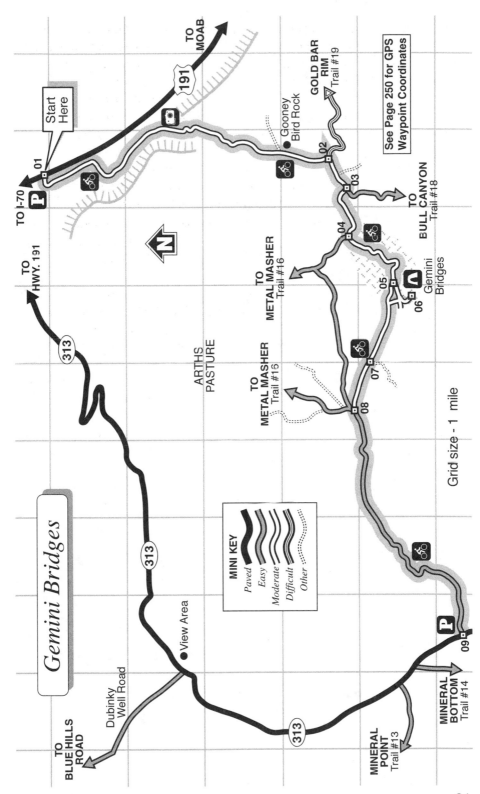

Gemini Bridges

MINI KEY

Paved
Easy
Moderate
Difficult
Other

Grid size - 1 mile

See Page 250 for GPS Waypoint Coordinates

N

Start Here

TO MOAB
191
TO I-70
TO HWY. 191

01

GOLD BAR RIM
Trail #19

Gooney Bird Rock

02

03

TO BULL CANYON
Trail #18

04

TO METAL MASHER
Trail #16

05

06
Gemini Bridges

07

TO METAL MASHER
Trail #16

ARTHS PASTURE

08

313

313

313

View Area

Dubinky Well Road

TO BLUE HILLS ROAD

MINERAL POINT
Trail #13

MINERAL BOTTOM
Trail #14

P
09

91

Attempts of Rock Chucker Hill usually draw a crowd during the Easter Jeep Safari.

The beginning of difficult Mirror Gulch.

Location: Northwest of Moab, west of Hwy. 191, and south of Hwy. 313.

Difficulty: Difficult. Many high rock ledges with tight maneuvering required in several places. While some of the most difficult obstacles can be bypassed, the remaining ones are still difficult. I've seen stock vehicles get through but not without the help of an occasional tow strap or winch. In these cases, body damage is common. Vehicle modifications and lockers are recommended.

Route-finding is easy most of the way but a two mile stretch of slickrock is extremely confusing. Even with this guidebook you will likely make some wrong turns unless someone in your group has driven this trail before. Scouting ahead for signs of the trail will likely be necessary. Cairns and colored ribbons tied to shrubs often help although you can't count on them. It helps to understand the geography of this trail. Much of it follows a ridgeline around the outside of Arths Rim. Several roads lead to an easy area back to the center where route-finding is easier. Officials at the BLM office tell me this trail may someday be painted with white dashed lines which would be immensely helpful.

Features: This trail features two well-known obstacles—Rock Chucker and Widowmaker. Rock Chucker is a side obstacle and is entirely optional. During the Easter Jeep Safari that I attended, only 4 out of 25 vehicles attempted it. Widowmaker is somewhat easier. Most vehicles got up but some needed tow-strap assistance. In addition to tough challenges, the scenery along the northwest ridgeline is outstanding.

Time & Distance: As described here, from Highway 191 to 313 is a total distance of just under 22 miles. If you have a big group, allow all day to complete this trip. A well-equipped, smaller group, with infrequent stops, could probably complete the trip in 4 to 5 hours.

To Get There: From the intersection of Highways 191 and 128, drive 7.3 miles north on 191 and turn left into a parking area. This turn is 1.3 miles south of Highway 313.

Trail Description:

From the start to Rock Chucker: Reset your odometer when you turn off highway 191 [01]. Pass through the parking area and follow a wide gravel road south. It turns uphill and crosses a high shelf. Watch for bikers.

You will drive around this deep canyon just before arriving at Rock Chucker.

Starting back down from the highest point of the trail. Great views from along this ridge.

Vehicles from the Easter Jeep Safari line up below Widowmaker.

The first ledge at Widowmaker is a big one. Excellent driving skills are required.

At 2.3 miles the road swings right and heads inland. Continue south past Gooney Bird Rock (see photo page 88) to a T intersection at 4.7 miles [02]. Turn right and head up a steep hill. Bear right at 5.1 and again at 5.3 miles where Bull Canyon goes left [03]. At 6.1 miles Gemini Bridges goes left; you go right [04]. Make right turns at 6.9 [05] and 7.3 miles [06]. At mile 8.3 cross a dry sand wash. Continue straight, do not follow the wash. Bear left at 8.7. Turn left off the main road at 8.8 [07] onto a much lesser road. This is an easy turn to miss but it is very important. At 9.1 bear right as a lesser road goes left.

There's a confusing area of slickrock at 9.3 miles [08]. A faint road appears to go left up a ridge but you'll make a right up a series of ledges, some of which are difficult. At 10.1 you'll find yourself crossing a large slab of slickrock [09]. Head generally in a northeast direction. Watch for cairns, colored ribbons tied to shrubs, and faint tire marks anywhere you can find them. Learn to recognize cairns even when they are knocked over. If you go very far without seeing some sign of the trail, you've probably gotten off line. Back up to the last point you were sure you were on the trail and restudy your choices. There are always signs—you just have to look harder. Bear somewhat left over the slab at 10.3 miles. You should pass to the left of a deep canyon (see photo) before rounding a corner to the right where you'll see Rock Chucker on the right at 10.5 miles [10]. It's a short series of big steps over some large boulders. Everyone I watched during the Safari turned around and came back down Rock Chucker.

From Rock Chucker to Widowmaker: *Reset your odometer at Rock Chucker.* The trail does not go up Rock Chucker. Instead it turns left and circles around in the opposite direction and heads downhill. After crossing a shallow ravine and climbing over a 5 ft. high rounded-off ledge, bear right. Soon the trail appears to dead end in a small canyon; however, if you look closely, you'll see a narrow V-shaped gulch to the right at 0.2 miles. This is Mirror Gulch [11]. The narrowness of the gulch adds to the difficulty of a series of high ledges. The trail appears to end at a drop-off at 0.3 miles, but it continues directly behind you at what is really a very tight switchback. Gradually the road becomes more apparent as you reach the top of the bluff at 0.5 miles. This is a great place for lunch, with incredible views.

Continue northwest across this high ridge on a well-defined road. Ignore lesser roads that go left at the top. Bear left at 1.9 miles as a lesser road goes right [12]. At 2.8 miles a good road goes straight [13]. This is the quickest way out but bypasses the entire second half of the trail. Turn right and continue towards Widowmaker. At 2.9 miles the bypass of Widowmaker goes left. (See bypass directions on next page.) Turn right for Widowmaker. At 3.9 miles bear left uphill on a steep, narrow road. There is a tippy spot at the top of this first hill next to a steel post. Stay well left here even though it gets tippy. The soil on the right is soft and will not support a vehicle. After that, bear left and you will see Widowmaker on the right [14].

I was able to get up Widowmaker on the first try in my modified Cherokee with 32-inch tires, a lift, and lockers front and rear. I aired down to 10 lbs. Conditions of the trail can make a big difference. If it is dry and windy, sand gets on the rock and adds to the difficulty. After a rain, it is easier.

Above Widowmaker, the trail curves to the left then turns uphill to the right (south). *Reset your odometer at this point.*

From Widowmaker to Highway 313: Head south after completing Widowmaker. Drop down a big ledge at 0.4. Continue straight at 0.7 miles as a road comes in on the left [15]. At 1.6 miles drop down two more ledges [16] after which a road joins on the left. A rocky section at 1.9 miles has several choices but all come back to the trail. After a long stretch of sandy road, at 2.7 miles curve around to the left then back to the right to go around Mother-in-Law Hill [17]. After Mother-in-Law Hill, bear left at 3.0 at a 4-way intersection then right at 3.6 miles. At 3.8 miles join a wide gravel road [18]. Follow this road west all the way to Highway 313 at 7.6 miles.

How to bypass Widowmaker: *Reset your odometer when you make a left turn 1.0 miles before Widowmaker.* After a steep hill, bear right at a patch of slickrock at 0.5. Bear left at 1.1. When you reach a 4-way intersection at 1.2, bear right. The trail fades but you can only go one way. Turn right at 1.4 before reaching a point above Widowmaker. Walk downhill to the left and Widowmaker will be on the right.

Return Trip: Turn right on Highway 313 to get back to 191 in about 13 miles. A right turn at 191 takes you back to Moab; left takes you to Interstate 70 at Crescent Junction.

Services: There is a service station at the intersection of Highways 191 and 313. Otherwise return to Moab.

Maps: The Latitude 40°, Inc. *Moab West* Biking Map roughly shows this trail. I used more detailed USGS 7.5 minute maps Merrimac Butte 38109-F6, Gold Bar Canyon 38109-E6, and The Knoll 38109-E7. Even these maps are not complete; consequently, I had to fill in gaps using my own GPS equipment.

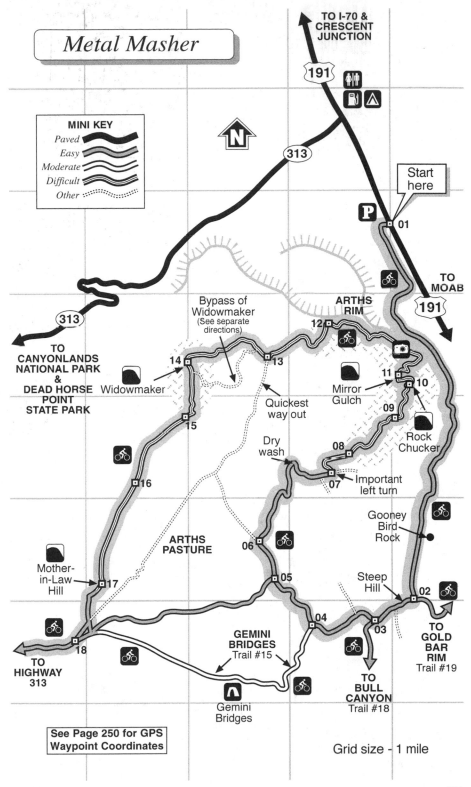

Metal Masher

MINI KEY
Paved
Easy
Moderate
Difficult
Other

N

TO I-70 &
CRESCENT
JUNCTION

191

313

Start
here

P

01

TO
MOAB

191

ARTHS
RIM

Bypass of
Widowmaker
(See separate
directions)

12

13

14

Widowmaker

11

Mirror
Gulch

10

09

Quickest
way out

15

Dry
wash

08

Rock
Chucker

TO
CANYONLANDS
NATIONAL PARK
&
DEAD HORSE
POINT
STATE PARK

313

16

07

Important
left turn

Gooney
Bird
Rock

Mother-
in-Law
Hill

17

ARTHS
PASTURE

06

05

Steep
Hill

02

TO
GOLD
BAR
RIM
Trail #19

18

TO
HIGHWAY
313

04

03

TO
BULL
CANYON
Trail #18

GEMINI
BRIDGES
Trail #15

Gemini
Bridges

**See Page 250 for GPS
Waypoint Coordinates**

Grid size - 1 mile

This trail is a scenic shortcut from Canyonlands National Park to Moab.

You pass under this massive fallen rock.

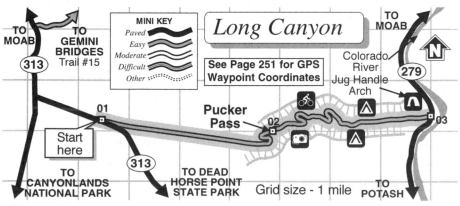

Pucker Pass when damaged–rarely this bad.

Long Canyon

MINI KEY
Paved
Easy
Moderate
Difficult
Other

See Page 251 for GPS
Waypoint Coordinates

TO
MOAB
313

TO
GEMINI
BRIDGES
Trail #15

TO
MOAB

Colorado
River
Jug Handle
Arch

N

279

**Pucker
Pass**

01

Start
here

313

02

03

TO
CANYONLANDS
NATIONAL PARK

TO DEAD
HORSE POINT
STATE PARK

Grid size - 1 mile

TO
POTASH

Long Canyon 🔟⑦

Location: Southwest of Moab between Highways 313 and 279. North of Canyonlands National Park and Dead Horse Point State Park.

Difficulty: Easy. A wide gravel road except through Pucker Pass where it is narrow and steep. Except when damaged by heavy rain, or when wet, this road can often be driven in 2-wheel drive. Route-finding is easy.

Features: Outstanding views from top to bottom. A great short cut when returning to Moab from Dead Horse Point State Park or Canyonlands National Park.

Time & Distance: 7.5 miles from Highway 313 to 279. Allow 1 hour.

To Get There: This trail is described downhill, assuming you are returning to Moab from Canyonlands National Park or Dead Horse Point State Park. The trail starts from Highway 313 at a point 1.6 miles east of the intersection where the road to Canyonlands National Park departs south from 313.

Trail Description: Reset your odometer as you turn off 313 [01]. Follow a wide gravel road east, ignoring all side roads. After about 3 miles the road curves left and starts downhill. At 3.3 miles [02], after a tight switchback, the road narrows significantly as you drop steeply through Pucker Pass. This section is usually quite easy when dry. The picture of Pucker Pass at left was taken after a nasty rainstorm. Since then, the county road department has done major work to repair the road and is confident conditions this bad are unlikely to occur again. But use caution just in case damage does occur. You pass under a giant fallen rock at 3.5 miles. After this point, the road widens and is very easy all the way to Highway 279 at 7.5 miles [03]. Don't let the fantastic views distract the driver. As you near 279, look for Jug Handle Arch on the left.

Return Trip: A left turn on Highway 279 takes you back to Highway 191, where a right turn takes you back to Moab.

Services: Return to Moab.

Maps: The Latitude 40°, Inc. *Moab West* Biking Map is adequate for this road. For more detail, use USGS 7.5 minute maps Gold Bar Canyon 38109-E6 and The Knoll 38109-E7.

Heading into the upper end of Bull Canyon. Gemini Bridges are just around the corner.

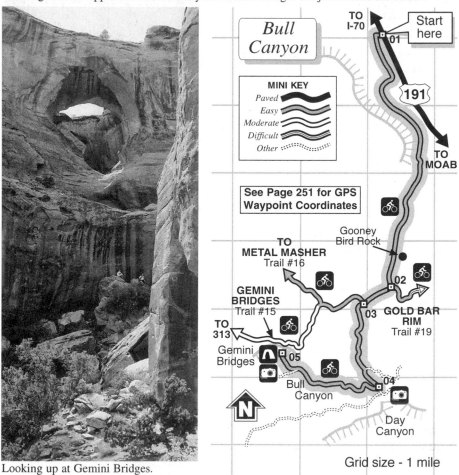

Bull Canyon

TO I-70

Start here

01

191

TO MOAB

MINI KEY
Paved
Easy
Moderate
Difficult
Other

See Page 251 for GPS Waypoint Coordinates

Gooney Bird Rock

TO METAL MASHER
Trail #16

GEMINI BRIDGES
Trail #15

02

03

GOLD BAR RIM
Trail #19

TO 313

Gemini Bridges

05

Bull Canyon

04

Day Canyon

N

Grid size - 1 mile

Looking up at Gemini Bridges.

Bull Canyon 18

Location: West of Moab and Highway 191. South of Highway 313.

Difficulty: Easy. Much of this trail follows a dry creek bed; consequently, the rating of the trail can change quickly. When I drove the trail it was easily passable by a stock high-clearance vehicle. Walk a rough section of several hundred feet just before Gemini Bridges.

Features: A short but exciting trip to the bottom of the Gemini Bridges. Sheer canyon walls form an interesting, photogenic backdrop. Several other spur roads in the area may be explored, including a beautiful overlook of Day Canyon 0.6 miles southeast of Waypoint 04.

Time & Distance: About 8.7 miles from Highway 191. Allow about an hour to reach Gemini Bridges.

To Get There: From the intersection of Highways 191 and 128, drive 7.3 miles north on Highway 191 and turn left into a parking area.

Trail Description: *Reset your odometer as you turn off 191* [01]. Pass through the parking area and follow a wide gravel road south. It turns uphill and crosses a high shelf. Watch for bikers. Continue south past Gooney Bird Rock (see photo page 88) to a T intersection at 4.7 miles [02]. Turn right and head up a steep hill. Bear left at 5.3 miles at a sign for Bull Canyon [03]. After a gradual descent, turn right at 6.8 miles [04]. The road follows a dry creek bed through a narrow, rocky ravine. It splits at various points but comes back together. Bear right at 8.1 miles, continuing to follow the creek bed. Bear right again at 8.4 staying on a sandy road. At 8.7 there's a small turnaround area [05]. Stop here and walk the rest of the way to the base of the Gemini Bridges.

Return Trip: Return the way you came or exit to Highway 313 via moderate Gemini Bridges (Trail #15) or difficult Metal Masher (Trail # 16).

Services: There's a service station near the intersection of Highways 191 and 313. Otherwise, head back to Moab.

Maps: The Latitude 40°, Inc. *Moab West* Biking Map is adequate for this road or use USGS 7.5 minute map Gold Bar Canyon 38109-E6.

Gold Bar Canyon. Butte top center contains Jeep Arch. Use butte as landmark.

First obstacle begins difficult portion of trail. Stock vehicles risk body damage at this point.

Looking south from the overlook. Note bridge that crosses Colorado River north of Moab.

Location: West of Moab and Highway 191. South of Highway 313.

Difficulty: Difficult. This trail starts easy but gradually becomes more difficult as it gains altitude. Stock high-clearance vehicles can negotiate the first two miles before reaching a challenging obstacle. Large tires, excellent articulation and/or lockers are recommended to reach the end of the trail.

Route-finding is extremely difficult on the upper portion of this trail. Watch for cairns and scout ahead when in doubt. If you get off course, backtrack to a familiar point and try again. The first time you drive this trail, try to go with someone who has driven it at least once. GPS is highly recommended. You should always carry a compass and a detailed map.

Features: The first two miles end at an impressive overlook of Gold Bar Canyon, making this a worthwhile trip for stock vehicles especially if combined with other easy and moderate trails in the area. The hard-core portion leads to a bird's-eye view of the area east of Highway 191, which includes Arches National Park. This trail is commonly driven in the other direction as part three of the popular Poison Spider Mesa/Golden Spike/Gold Bar Rim combination trail. The hard-core crowd often hurries through this trail to beat the setting sun. Gold Bar Rim is better appreciated if driven independently. I recommend you drive it first as described here. Later it will be less confusing if you choose to add it to Golden Spike (Trail #21).

Time & Distance: The trail, as described here, is 3.8 miles and takes 1 to 2 hours each way, not allowing for wrong turns. Add to that 4.7 miles of easy road to get from Highway 191 to the start.

To Get There: From the intersection of Highways 191 and 128, drive 7.3 miles north on Highway 191 and turn left. Pass through a parking area and follow a wide gravel road south. It turns uphill and crosses a high shelf. Watch for bikers. Continue south past Gooney Bird Rock (see photo page 88) to a T intersection in another 4.7 miles.

Trail Description (Uphill): Reset your odometer at the T intersection [01]. A sign here indicates Gold Bar Canyon left and Gemini Bridges right. You'll pass through a sandy area with roads running in many directions. Go straight at 0.2 miles, left at 0.3, and left again at 0.4. Shift into low gear as the trail becomes more difficult. At 1.0 miles, turn left at another T [02]. Right heads back to Bull Canyon (Trail #18). Bear left at mile 1.5 [03] as an equal size road goes right. This road leads to a prominent butte that contains Jeep Arch (Gold Bar Arch). You can't see the arch from Gold Bar Trail but the butte makes a great landmark. At 2.1 miles there's a large slab of slick-rock that overlooks Gold Bar Canyon [04]. Stock vehicles should stop here.

To continue, bear left at the overlook then swing right down a steep rocky trail. The first significant obstacle is encountered at 2.2 miles. At 2.6 cross over a wide crack. At 2.8 cross a large undefined area of slickrock [05]. Soon you should be able to see the trail in the distance as you continue north. Gold Bar Canyon should be on your right. At 3.3 miles [06] bear left as the trail appears to go straight. After a tough spot, make a hard right downhill. The trail heads southeast for a short distance before turning north again. At 3.8 miles, avoid a steep ledge to the right. This is the connecting point to Golden Spike (Trail #21). Bear left where the trail ends at a small, hard-to-see loop [07]. Park here and walk several hundred feet north to a high overlook of Arches National Park.

Trail Description (Downhill): *Reset your odometer at the top of Gold Bar Rim* [07]. If you're driving this trail as a continuation of Golden Spike, Gold Bar Rim starts about 0.2 miles above Double Whammy where you reach the top and start down. The trail heads south for a short distance and then swings back uphill in a northwest direction. Bear left at 0.3 miles and head south again. Bear left of a big mushroom rock at 0.5 and head downhill [06]. You should be able to see Gold Bar Canyon on the left. At mile 1.0 the trail swings away from the canyon edge and heads more southwest [05]. Cross over a wide crack at 1.2 miles. Swing right and circle left around a small canyon. About 1.4 miles, you'll zig-zag uphill over several challenging ledges. At the top of this section there's a wide slab of slickrock that overlooks the canyon [04]. Bear right here continuing downhill. At 2.2 bear right as an equal size road goes left [03]. Make a sharp right at 2.7 miles as the road gets sandier [02]. Turn right again at 3.3 and 3.4. Go straight at 3.6. You reach the start of the trail at 3.8 miles [01] before a steep hill starts up to Gemini Bridges. Turn right for Highway 191.

Return Trip: From the top of the trail follow the downhill directions back to the starting point. From there, turn right and drive north 4.7 miles back to Highway 191 where another right takes you back to Moab.

Services: There's a service station at the intersection of Highways 191 and 313. Otherwise, head back to Moab.

Maps: USGS 7.5 minute map Gold Bar Canyon 38109-E6 has the best detail although the upper portion of the trail is not shown. I plotted this portion with my own GPS equipment.

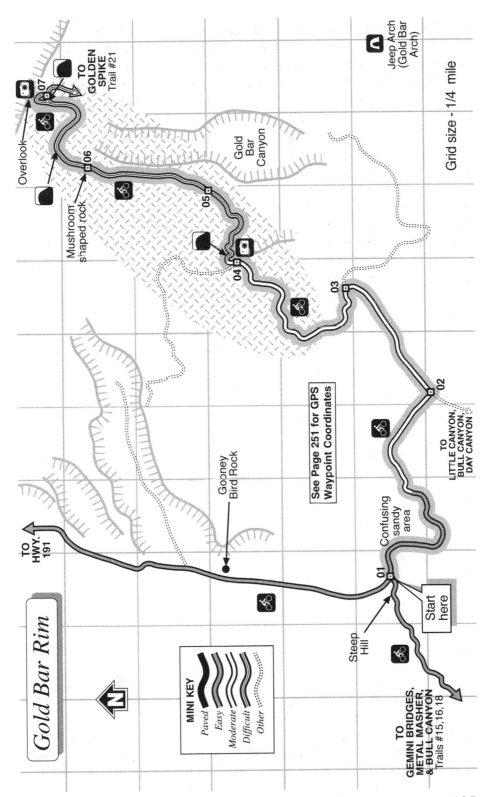

Gold Bar Rim

N

Jeep Arch (Gold Bar Arch)

Grid size - 1/4 mile

Gold Bar Canyon

07

TO GOLDEN SPIKE Trail #21

Overlook

Mushroom shaped rock

06

05

04

03

02

TO LITTLE CANYON, BULL CANYON, DAY CANYON

See Page 251 for GPS Waypoint Coordinates

Gooney Bird Rock

Confusing sandy area

01

Steep Hill

Start here

TO HWY. 191

MINI KEY

Paved
Easy
Moderate
Difficult
Other

TO GEMINI BRIDGES, METAL MASHER, & BULL CANYON
Trails #15,16,18

105

At 2.8 miles stop for this great view of Behind the Rocks and the La Sal Mountains.

Painted Jeep symbols mark the trail.

This Jeep's about to get a Wedgy.

Beware of Poison Spiders.

Giving directions and helping each other out is important.

Poison Spider Mesa ◆20▶

Location: Southwest of Moab off Highway 279.

Difficulty: Difficult. A classic hard-core trail with many challenging obstacles including tight switchbacks, high irregular ledges, steep slickrock climbs, and several tippy spots. Few stock vehicles can complete this trail without body damage. Vehicle modifications including differential lockers are highly recommended.

      Route-finding is relatively easy on the first half of Poison Spider Mesa but after the turn for Golden Spike, it becomes difficult. White painted Jeep symbols mark the trail all the way but they are sometimes hard to see. If you go very long without seeing one, you're probably off the trail. Retrace your steps and reexamine your options.

Features: This is one of the most popular trails in Moab and is often combined with Golden Spike (Trail #21) and Gold Bar Rim (Trail #19). Poison Spider Mesa is a fun-filled combination of challenging obstacles and incredible scenery. The second half of the trail passes by impressive Little Arch on the way to an outstanding overlook of the entire Moab area. Mountain biking is extremely popular on this trail. Drive with caution and be courteous to bikers at all times.

Time & Distance: It's 5.3 miles to the start of Golden Spike. The second half loop adds 3.7 miles. The overlook is 0.6 miles each way. It takes more than an hour to reach Golden Spike. The entire round trip back to the start including the overlook takes 5 to 6 hours, not counting stops and extra route-finding time. If you're traveling with a group, add more time. Many people underestimate the amount of time required to drive this trail.

To Get There: Head north from Moab on Highway 191. About 1.5 miles past the river turn left on Potash Road Highway 279. Drive 5.9 miles south and turn right uphill at a parking area.

Trail Description:
      Part I (to Golden Spike): Reset your odometer as you turn off 279 [01]. The trail climbs uphill and swings right up a series of difficult switchbacks. At 1.1 drop down a narrow, rocky chute [02]. The road smooths out at 1.6 at an area called Tie-Rod Flats [03]. It gets rocky again at 2.3 as you enter a canyon. The first major obstacle, called the Waterfall, is reached at 2.5 miles [04]. Stay as far right as possible as you start up. It curves left over

Look closely for arrow and word "BIKE"

Look down to see Little Arch.

Stay far right when starting up the first part of the Waterfall.

Pig Rock is a great landmark. It takes a little imagination to see the piglets.

another ledge then swings right uphill. Several tough spots follow before a wide switchback swings left. Around the corner is another big ledge. Take a few minutes at 2.8 miles [05] to enjoy the view of Behind the Rocks and the La Sal Mountains (see photo page 106). At 2.9 you reach another popular obstacle called the Wedgy [06]. It's a V-shaped groove that can be driven in different ways. It's easy if you straddle it and more difficult if you lean.

Immediately after the Wedgy, there's a confusing sandy stretch. Bikers take a fork to the left. You want to bear right uphill in the sand then make a hard right between the rocks. After swinging left and climbing a big ledge, you reach a high, flat area of slickrock called the Mesa at 3.2 [07]. Head north over a series of rocky whoop-ti-dos [08]. At 4.0 miles there's an easy stretch called the High Speed Mesa [09]. You can make up lost time here but watch for bikers. Along this stretch there's a grave marker on the right at 4.2. Legend has it that a little girl named Mary Jane Francis was buried here in 1896. She allegedly died from—you guessed it—a bite from a poison spider.

The High Speed Mesa ends at about 4.9 miles. At 5.0 [10] the trail swings left downhill a short distance, then swings right (almost reversing direction) through a brief stretch of sand. Watch for Jeep symbols on intermittent slickrock. The trail then swings left onto a higher ridge of slickrock at 5.2 [11]. Black tire marks and Jeep symbols point the way. Once you get on top of the slickrock, bear left following the natural ridge. Stop at 5.3 miles [12] and get out of your vehicle. Look for cairns and a white arrow with the word "BIKE" pointing to the right. When you find the arrow, you have found the official starting point for Golden Spike (Trail #21), which continues on the slickrock straight ahead (northwest). Poison Spider Mesa turns right and follows the arrow off the slickrock. Jeep symbols also continue in this direction.

Part II (the loop): *Reset your odometer as you bear right off the slickrock* [12]. Before you proceed, look northeast to see Pig Rock (see photo). It looks like a pig lying on her side with little piglets suckling. Use this as a reference point as you continue around the loop. At 0.2 miles [13] Jeep symbols go in two directions. This is where the loop ends. You'll come back here later. Bear right now. Climb to the top of a slickrock hill at 0.3 [14]. Descend down the right side. At the bottom swing left and climb gradually. When you reach the top of this hill, you'll drop down a very steep descent between some trees. Continue straight at the bottom on a sandy road. At 0.5 [15] go straight as a lesser road goes left. After passing through a tight spot in the trees, bear left up a very steep section of slickrock. Watch for Jeep symbols. As you start up, there's a dangerous turn to the right that is extremely tippy. Use a spotter. If you get a tire in the wrong spot, you could roll off the slickrock. When you come around the corner at 0.6 [16], you should drive over the word ARCH painted on the rock. An arrow points to the right. Walk this direction to see the arch.

After viewing the arch, continue following symbols. Circle around a giant pothole at 0.9 [17]. At 1.1 after coming down off some rock, bear right where a sandy road goes left [18]. At 1.3 bear left uphill staying on rock [19]. Many people incorrectly turn right here into a sandy gully. At 1.6 bear left at an important fork [20]. Within a hundred feet of this turn you should see a steep section of slickrock covered with black tire marks. Turn right here. Continue around the corner and turn left into a ravine. Watch for symbols; your choices are limited. Meander up and down across a long expanse of slickrock before reaching a major intersection at 2.1 miles [21]. A sign post indicates Jeeps can go left or right. Right takes you to the overlook in 0.6 miles [24]. If you have an extra hour, it's worth the time. Come back to this point when you're finished.

Reset your odometer [21]. Head west continuing around the loop. Bear right at 0.1 at another sign post. The road gets sandy with fewer Jeep symbols. At 0.3 [22] bear left across a large section of slickrock into more sand. At 0.4 turn left as you come up onto a ledge then bear right. You should see more symbols. The road becomes better defined in the sand. You can go either way at 0.7 [23]. Right takes you to the top of a sand hill; left takes you around the sand hill. From here the trail continues southeast and is well marked with Jeep symbols. At 1.5 miles [13] the loop ends. Turn right.

Return Trip: Retrace your steps back the way you came. If you plan to continue on to Golden Spike, remember to turn right at the white painted arrow and the word BIKE [12]. If it's late in the day, you can't complete Golden Spike without camping overnight. Many have spent an unplanned night on this trail.

Services: Closest full services are back in Moab. There's a modern vault toilet at the parking area at the beginning of the trail.

Maps: USGS 7.5 minute map Moab, Utah 38109-E5. Only the first half of Poison Spider Mesa is shown on this map. I plotted the second half using my own GPS equipment.

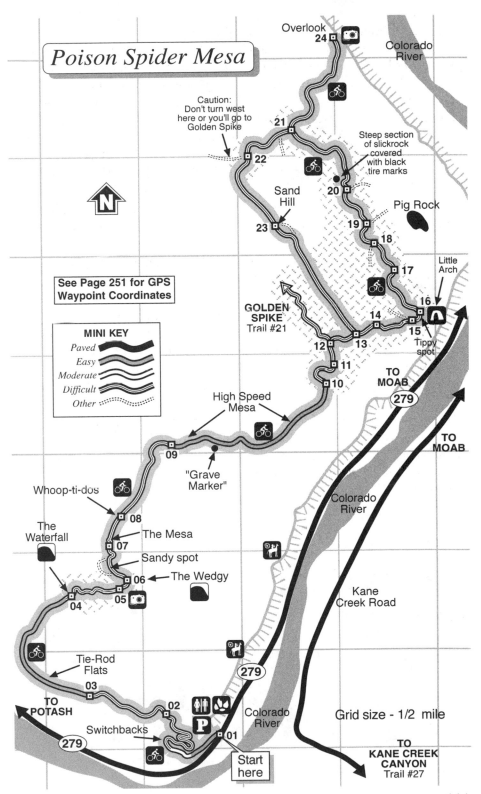

Poison Spider Mesa

Overlook
24

Colorado River

Caution: Don't turn west here or you'll go to Golden Spike

21

22

Steep section of slickrock covered with black tire marks

20

Pig Rock

Sand Hill

23

19

18

17

Little Arch

16

15

N

See Page 251 for GPS Waypoint Coordinates

GOLDEN SPIKE Trail #21

14

Tippy spot

MINI KEY

Paved
Easy
Moderate
Difficult
Other

12

13

11

10

TO MOAB

279

TO MOAB

High Speed Mesa

09

"Grave Marker"

Colorado River

Whoop-ti-dos

08

07

The Mesa

The Waterfall

Sandy spot

06

The Wedgy

05

04

Kane Creek Road

Tie-Rod Flats

03

279

TO POTASH

02

P

Switchbacks

Colorado River

Grid size - 1/2 mile

279

01

Start here

TO KANE CREEK CANYON Trail #27

Obscure start of Golden Spike. Bear left at the bottom of this first ridge of slickrock.

The Launch Pad. What a blast!

Skyline Drive is extremely steep.

Golden Spike symbol.

Countless challenging ledges.

112

Location: West of Moab and Highway 279.

Difficulty: Difficult. One of the toughest hard-core trails in the Moab area. Climb and descend numerous high rock ledges. Daunting slickrock maneuvers. Few bypasses. Differential lockers, high ground clearance, and body protection highly recommended. Vehicle suspension is severely tested.

Route-finding is extremely difficult with few landmarks to guide you. The trail has been painted with gold spike symbols (see photo), but most are worn away. Plans to remark the trail have not materialized at the time of this writing. Without better markings, don't expect this book alone to get you through. The book will help if you've driven the trail before or if you are using GPS. Carry a compass and a detailed topographic map or travel with a group that knows the trail; otherwise, consider hiring a professional guide. (You can't go wrong with Dan Mick, founder of this trail. See appendix under Dan Mick's Guided Tours.) Always travel with at least one other vehicle. Carry at least a gallon of water per person per day. If you get lost, stay with your vehicle until someone comes by. Don't try to walk out.

Features: A dream trail of challenging obstacles which include such well-known names as the Launch Pad, Skyline Drive, Golden Crack, Golden Stairs, and Double Whammy. Much of the trail skirts the edge of high cliffs overlooking Moab. The trail cannot be accessed directly from any paved highway. To reach Golden Spike you must first drive Poison Spider Mesa (Trail #20) from the south or Gold Bar Rim (Trail #19) from the north. Most people drive the trail from south to north.

Time & Distance: The trail, as described here, is about 7 miles. To that, add half of Poison Spider Mesa, all of Gold Bar Rim, and the Gemini Bridges approach road. Counting paved roads, you will have driven over 35 miles by the time you return to Moab—almost half is brutal, hard-core driving. Leave early and plan to get home late. With mechanical problems, it is not uncommon to get stuck overnight, so plan accordingly.

To Get There: Follow directions for Poison Spider Mesa (Trail # 20). At 5.3 miles Poison Spider Mesa turns right off a large slab of slickrock where a large white arrow and the word BIKE are painted on the rock floor. You go straight. Don't follow the arrow. It's possible the arrow may be worn away by the time you read this. If so, continue heading northwest along the ridge of slickrock (see top photo opposite page).

This group has inadvertently wandered back to Poison Spider Mesa. (Pig Rock, top right.)

The Golden Crack.   Photo by Matt Peterson

Double Whammy is for long wheel bases.

Moab from one of the overlooks.

Jeep Arch from the Golden Crack.

Trail Description:
From the start of Golden Spike to the Launch Pad:

> Note: Most people get lost immediately on this first leg. They tend to wander east and completely miss the Launch Pad. They inadvertently end up on the loop portion of Poison Spider Mesa. The correct route to the Launch Pad is almost entirely on slickrock. If you find yourself driving primarily in sand, you're off course. The top photo opposite page shows a group of vehicles that has wandered back over to Poison Spider Mesa. (Note Pig Rock in the background, top right.)

Reset your odometer at the start [01]. Head northwest following the slickrock. It soon ends and becomes sandy. Bear left at 0.4 miles [02]. At 0.5 there's a steep downhill section. After that, bear slightly right. You should see a few spike symbols or plain white dots painted on the rocks. Continue to follow a poorly defined ridge at 0.6 miles [03]. Arrive at the Launch Pad at 0.9 [04]. This obstacle is steep but not that difficult. There's a bypass to the right although it is difficult to find.

From the Launch Pad to the first overlook: *Reset your odometer at the bottom of the Launch Pad.* [04]. Once up the Launch Pad, continue straight to the top of the dome (don't turn to the left). As you start back down the other side of the dome, there's a steep descent to the right [05]. Use a spotter here to get properly lined up before you start down. The trail continues northwest and is defined for a while. It swings left just before approaching the bottom of Skyline Drive at 0.5 miles [06]. Skyline Drive is simply a giant dome that's fun to go up and down. Although optional, I've included the mileage because most people try it. Go up the right side and down the left. There's a fence post at the top [07] that looks like an antenna. Sometimes you can see this from a distance.

After Skyline Drive, continue northwest into a ravine at 1.1 [08]. Once at the bottom of the narrow ravine, turn right. The ravine widens and goes left over a big, round ledge. As you exit the canyon above the ledge, follow cairns as the trail twists back and forth. After dropping into another small ravine, climb up a stretch of tippy, rippled red rock. This ridge turns left and heads downhill into yet another ravine. Before you start to climb out of this ravine, watch for a cairn and a small gnarly tree at 1.8 miles [09]. Turn right here and climb a road parallel to the one you would have been on if you hadn't turned. The other road narrows to a bike path. At 1.9 bear right uphill as a trail comes in on the left [10]. Watch for a painted Golden Spike inside a white circle (see photo). The road becomes better defined as you gradually climb out of a valley. At 2.3 miles bear left as a lesser road goes right [11]. Drop down a tough ledge before coming to a T intersection at 2.8 miles. Stop here and walk uphill a short distance to the right to the first overlook [12].

From the first overlook to the Golden Crack: *Reset your odometer at the T intersection below the overlook* [12]. Turn left at the T and head downhill. You'll zig-zag through some very tight and difficult obstacles. At 0.3 miles go right at another T [13] and cross more slickrock following cairns as best as you can. Bear right at 0.7 miles where a tree splits the trail at a ledge [14]. Left of the tree is easier. At 0.9 you approach the cliff edge again then begin to swing left [15]. At one point, you have to drop down two very high ledges. Inspect them carefully for the right line. At 1.1 miles turn left and head downhill [16]. You're faced with another huge slab of rock after coming over a ridge at 1.4 miles [17]. Head downhill in a southwest direction looking for cairns. Turn right and head uphill where a road appears to come in on the left at 1.5 miles [18]. At 1.7 you're back near the cliff edge again. This is perhaps the best of all the overlooks [19]. After this point, you gradually swing downhill again. At 1.9 miles choose from three places to go up a high ledge [20]. Once on top, bear right uphill back to the cliff edge. Follow the edge and cross over a ridge at 2.2 miles [21]. Now head earnestly downhill across a wide area of slickrock. Gradually swing right in a wide arc, crossing the slickrock in a southwest direction. The Golden Crack lies in front of a rock outcropping at 2.4 miles [22]. From this point, if the light is right, you can see Jeep Arch to the south.

From the Golden Crack to the top of Gold Bar Rim: *Reset your odometer at the Golden Crack* [22]. Once over the Golden Crack, pass through a narrow section and turn hard left up over some ledges. Turn right around the corner and make a large S curve downhill. Traveling west, you encounter a long ledge at 0.3 miles [23]. Pick a good spot to go down. After the ledge turn right and head uphill. You'll weave around another point and swing right to reach the Golden Stairs at 0.5 miles [24]. Bear left after the stairs and climb down through a rough area. Bear left at the bottom. You'll curve uphill and run into some giant ledges at 0.9 miles. Double Whammy is around the next corner on the right [25]. Unless you have a long wheel base and very big tires, forget Double Whammy. Take the bypass left. As the trails merge directly above Double Whammy, continue uphill and climb through a narrow, steep chute on the left called "The Body Snatcher". Continue uphill and bear left. You'll drop down another ledge next to a hard-to-see turnaround loop on the right. This is the upper end of Gold Bar Rim at 1.2 miles [26].

Return Trip: Follow downhill directions for Gold Bar Rim (page 104).

Services: There is a service station near the intersection of Highways 191 and 313 and a modern vault toilet at the parking area at the start of Poison Spider Mesa.

Maps: I plotted all of this trail using my own GPS equipment on USGS 7.5 minute maps Moab 38109-E5 and Gold Bar Canyon 38109-E6.

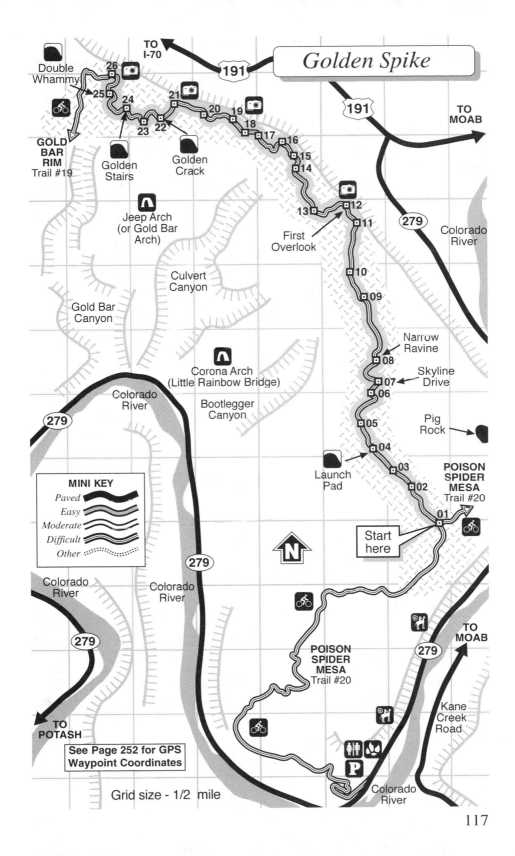

TO
I-70

191

Golden Spike

191

TO
MOAB

26

25
Double
Whammy

24

GOLD
BAR
RIM
Trail #19

23

21

22

20

19

18

17

16

15

14

Golden
Stairs

Golden
Crack

Jeep Arch
(or Gold Bar
Arch)

13

12

11

First
Overlook

279

Colorado
River

Culvert
Canyon

10

09

Gold Bar
Canyon

Narrow
Ravine

08

Corona Arch
(Little Rainbow Bridge)

07

Skyline
Drive

06

Colorado
River

Bootlegger
Canyon

05

Pig
Rock

279

04

03

02

Launch
Pad

POISON
SPIDER
MESA
Trail #20

MINI KEY
Paved
Easy
Moderate
Difficult
Other

01

Start
here

Colorado
River

Colorado
River

279

N

POISON
SPIDER
MESA
Trail #20

279

TO
MOAB

279

Kane
Creek
Road

TO
POTASH

P

**See Page 252 for GPS
Waypoint Coordinates**

Colorado
River

Grid size - 1/2 mile

Typical trail conditions on the east side.

This difficult ledge is in the middle of a narrow shelf road.

Heavy rainstorm swells Kane Creek.   Photo by Matt Peterson

View from the final overlook.

Cliff Hanger ◆22◆

Location: Southwest of Moab and west of Kane Creek Road. When looking for this trail on any map, look for its official name—Amasa Back.

Difficulty: Difficult. The trail starts downhill, crosses Kane Creek, then climbs rapidly up a very rocky, steep grade. Kane Creek can rise quickly after a heavy rain. Obstacles are tall, challenging, and frequent. The second half of the trail smooths out but not before crossing a challenging narrow road on a shelf about 400 feet high. This trail is not suitable for stock vehicles. Extra-high ground clearance and lockers are recommended.

    The trail is fairly obvious most of the way with the exception of a couple of short stretches of slickrock. Spur roads are limited making route-finding fairly easy.

Features: The thing you'll remember most about this trail is not the incredible scenery, but a 4-foot high ledge across a narrow shelf road perched high on sheer canyon walls. Although just one obstacle of many, this one will get your undivided attention. I've added one short side trip that offers a near aerial view of the beginning of Poison Spider Mesa (Trail # 20). Remember to pack your binoculars.

    This is a popular biking trail so use appropriate caution and courtesy. Pull over and let bikers pass if they approach you from behind. On a trail like this, they will often make better time than you.

Time & Distance: As described here, this trail is 4.3 miles from the start to the final overlook. With a properly equipped vehicle, you can complete the round trip in 2 to 3 hours. Add a little more time for the side trip to the overlook of Poison Spider Mesa.

To Get There: From the south side of Moab at the McDonald's Restaurant on Main Street, take Kane Creek Road west. Bear left at the first fork and head south along the Colorado River. The pavement ends before reaching the trailhead on the right at 5.8 miles. A sign here says Amasa Back Trail.

Trail Description: Reset your odometer as you turn off Kane Creek Road. Air down immediately—the trail is difficult from the start [01]. Drop down a short hill and cross Kane Creek. Normally it is shallow but it swells quickly after a heavy rain (see photo at left). Quicksand is possible at this location (see page 33). After the creek, follow the trail to the left over a difficult rock ledge. The trail is well defined as you climb continually over frequent

119

obstacles. At 1.5 miles bear to the right side of a large slab of rock. There's a major obstacle at 1.8 miles (see bottom photo on front cover). You reach the top of the ridge at 2.2 miles and get your first look at the other side. This area is called Jackson Hole and is marked by a tall picturesque butte. The trail swings north and another road goes right uphill [02]. This spur road goes to an overlook of Poison Spider Mesa. You will come back here later so bear left now. Soon the shelf road begins. At 2.6 miles you'll drive down the big ledge described earlier [03] (See center photo on page 118.) Its position along the cliff makes it very intimidating. Take your time and use a spotter.

As you move along this shelf road, you can see the Potash Plant to the west and the evaporation ponds farther south. Shafer Trail (Trail #42) passes through this area. You'll get a much better view of this area at the end of the trail.

After the shelf road, the trail gradually swings to the west and crosses a gentle plateau where you can make better time. At 3.6 miles [04] make a hard right uphill over a big ledge. It may be a little easier to the left. After coming back down this ledge you'll encounter a slickrock section where the trail disappears. Aim for the notch at the top. More slickrock follows as you continue to climb. The trail is not obvious but if you head generally in a southwest direction, you will reach the overlook at 4.3 miles [05]. I try to time the trip so that I reach this point about lunch time. It's a great place to relax.

Return Trip: You can explore the Amasa Back area north of the overlook but you eventually must return the way you came. On the way down, drive out to the overlook of Poison Spider Mesa. Turn left at the fork that I mentioned as you were coming up [02]. Going down, it will be just after the shelf road. The overlook spur heads uphill over a few small ledges. Continue straight at the top as a lesser road goes to the right. Cruise downhill over a stretch of soft sand before reaching the overlook. This side road measures 0.7 miles one way.

Services: Return to Moab.

Maps: The Latitude 40°, Inc. *Moab West* Biking Map is adequate for this road. For more detail, use USGS 7.5 minute maps Moab 38109-E5 and Gold Bar Canyon 38109-E6.

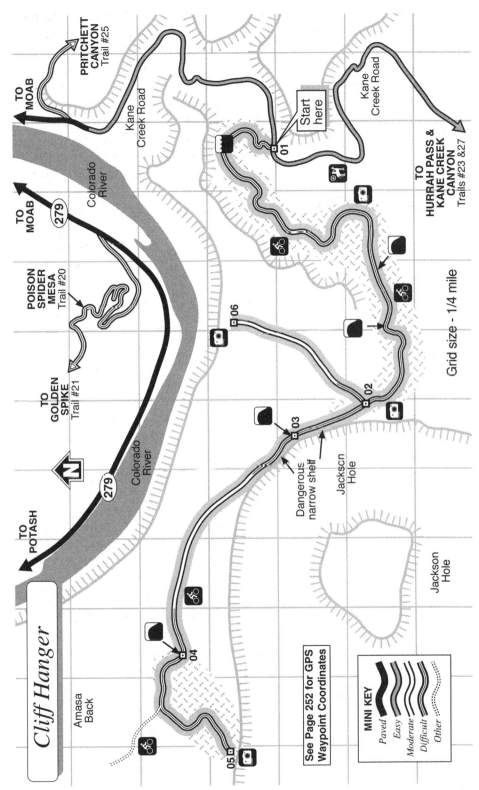

Cliff Hanger

MINI KEY
Paved
Easy
Moderate
Difficult
Other

See Page 252 for GPS
Waypoint Coordinates

Grid size - 1/4 mile

Start here

Kane Creek Road

PRITCHETT CANYON Trail #25

TO MOAB

TO HURRAH PASS & KANE CREEK CANYON Trails #23 &27

Colorado River

TO MOAB

279

POISON SPIDER MESA Trail #20

TO GOLDEN SPIKE Trail #21

N

279

Colorado River

TO POTASH

Amasa Back

Dangerous narrow shelf

Jackson Hole

Jackson Hole

01

06

02

03

04

05

The Birthing Stone with Indian petroglyphs. On right 1.3 miles from start.

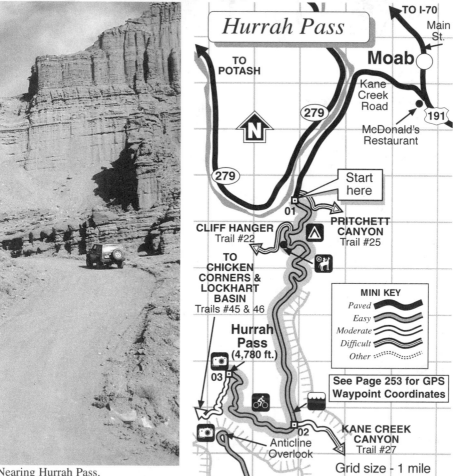

Nearing Hurrah Pass.

Hurrah Pass

TO I-70

Main St.

Moab

TO POTASH

Kane Creek Road

279

191

McDonald's Restaurant

Start here

01

PRITCHETT CANYON
Trail #25

CLIFF HANGER
Trail #22

TO CHICKEN CORNERS & LOCKHART BASIN
Trails #45 & 46

Hurrah Pass
(4,780 ft.)

03

MINI KEY
Paved
Easy
Moderate
Difficult
Other

See Page 253 for GPS Waypoint Coordinates

02

Anticline Overlook

KANE CREEK CANYON
Trail #27

Grid size - 1 mile

122

Hurrah Pass ㉓

Location: Southwest of Moab, west of Kane (Cane) Creek Road.

Difficulty: Easy. A wide gravel road most of the way. Closer to the pass, it narrows somewhat and becomes rockier with mild, tippy spots. Suitable for two-wheel drive vehicles with high ground clearance under ideal conditions. Several water crossings on Kane Creek Road are usually shallow, but they can be very deep and unsafe to cross in the spring or after a heavy rain. Route-finding is extremely easy.

Features: This short drive takes you through the easy parts of Kane Springs Canyon to pleasant views from relatively low Hurrah Pass. Stop along the way to see extraordinary Indian petroglyphs on a large boulder next to the road. Camping is permitted along the route but only in designated sites while in the Colorado Riverway. Fees arc required and vault toilets are provided. Beyond the Riverway boundary, please bring a portable toilet if you plan to camp.

Time & Distance: Hurrah Pass is 9.7 miles from the end of the pavement of Kane Creek Road. Allow 2 to 3 hours for the round trip.

To Get There: From the south side of Moab at the McDonald's Restaurant on Main Street, take Kane Creek Road west. Bear left at the first fork and head south along the Colorado River. The pavement ends at 4.7 miles where the road swings left away from the river.

Trail Description: *Reset your odometer where the pavement ends* [01]. Continue on a wide gravel road cut across high canyon walls. At 1.3 miles look right for Indian writings on a large boulder. (See photo at left.) Walk up close, but please don't touch. Bear right after crossing of Kane Creek at 6.3 miles. At mile 6.6 Kane Creek Canyon Trail (#27) goes left [02]. Swing right and begin a gradual climb. At 8.9 miles a lesser road on the right goes to a small overlook. The pass is reached at 9.7 miles [03]. Beyond the pass starts a more difficult descent to Chicken Corners (Trail #45) and Lockhart Basin (Trail #46).

Return Trip: Return the way you came. All services in Moab.

Maps: Latitude 40°, Inc. *Moab West* Biking Map, USGS 7.5 minute maps Moab 38109-E5 and Troughs Springs Canyon 38109-D5.

The ledge road at the start is very tippy and close to the cliff edge.

Many tough ledges within the first mile.

Approximately 2 miles from the start.

Incredible scenery on the east side.

Spanish Valley below the final overlook.

Moab Rim ◆24◆

Location: On the high plateau immediately southwest of Moab.

Difficulty: Difficult. This trail wastes little time getting down to business. The first mile scares the wits out of most people. I've driven it many times and still get nervous. A long climb of tight, tippy, and extremely difficult ledges requires excellent driving skills and a very capable vehicle. Roll-overs are not unusual. You must come down the same way you go up. Stock vehicles and inexperienced drivers should stay off this trail. Lockers are highly recommended. Do not drive this trail alone.

Route-finding is aided by frequent sign posts and painted white dashed lines in places. Gaps in these markings, however, still require that you pay close attention to directions. **Do not, under any circumstances, wander into the Behind the Rocks Wilderness Study Area. Stay on the route at all times.**

Features: Conveniently located at Moab's back door, this trail offers a four-wheeling experience that you will talk about for a long time. It has always been busy with plenty of hikers and bikers. A new chair lift, now in operation, will increase traffic significantly. Keep your eyes open for wandering children and hiker wannabes. Use extreme caution and be courteous at all times.

Time & Distance: The round trip described here measures 8.2 miles. With capable vehicles, it can be driven in 3 to 4 hours. Allow more time for larger groups.

To Get There: From the south side of Moab at the McDonald's Restaurant on Main Street, take Kane Creek Road west. Bear left at the first fork and head south along the Colorado River. As soon as you round the bend, begin watching for a trail sign on the left at 2.7 miles.

Trail Description: Reset your odometer when you turn off the pavement [01]. Bear left and follow a narrow shelf that tilts precariously outward with a sheer drop-off to the left. Perhaps the toughest and most dangerous spot is just a short walk up the hill. If you have any doubts about your driving skills or vehicle capability, walk up first and take a look. Once you begin, there's no easy place to turn around on this lower section. The first obstacle, called the Devils Crack, is a high, irregular ledge that must be traversed while making an awkward right turn. Exact tire placement is important so use a spotter. A rollover here could send you tumbling off the cliff. The next two ledges look less harrowing, but actually tilt you sideways more than the first obstacle. Choose your line very carefully. Another half mile of very difficult obstacles follows on a zig-zag course to the top. Follow the white dashed lines which show the correct four-wheel-drive route.

You reach the top at 1.1 miles [02]. Here you cross private property. Please respect the owner's openness. Park and walk north to see a fantastic view of Moab below and the La Sal Mountains to the east. Watch for sightseers who have come up the chairlift. Once at the top, the trail swings around to the south. Bear right at 1.4 miles before encountering more challenging terrain. Stay clear of two vehicle-size potholes below a sandstone ridge. Left undisturbed, these potholes contain small organisms that come to life after a rain. These organisms are an important part of nature's food chain. Whether wet or dry, never drive through a pothole in the slickrock.

Important: Most of this trail follows the boundary of the Behind the Rocks Wilderness Study Area. It is extremely important that you stay on the route at all times. This part of the trail is confusing. Do not wander too far west or south into the W.S.A.

Bear right at a fork at 1.8 miles [03]. You will return to this spot later from a different direction. The trail swings west for a short distance before turning south again. (Don't continue west into the W.S.A.) At 2.4 miles it swings east and climbs an extremely steep slickrock dome [04]. There are no signs of the trail here but they resume on the other side just after an extremely steep downhill section at 2.6 miles. Spur roads begin to branch off in various directions but most are marked with sign posts. Stay on the trail. Go straight at 2.7 miles, right at 3.0 miles, and right again at 3.1 miles. At 3.5 a sign indicates Hidden Valley Hiking Trail to the right; you go left [05]. Bear right at 4.1 before reaching the overlook at 4.3 miles [06]. From here you can see Spanish Valley and the La Sal Mountains.

Return Trip: Turn around and retrace your steps for about a mile then bear right [07] as the trail drops rapidly into a sandy ravine. At 5.6 miles there's a steep, sandy hill on the left [08] that many people attempt to drive. Continue down the ravine until mile 5.9 [09]. Bear left and begin a rocky, twisting climb out of the ravine. At 6.4 you return to the fork mentioned earlier [03]. From here, turn right and go out the way you came in.

Services: No services on the trail. Return to Moab.

Maps: Latitude 40°, Inc. *Moab West* Biking Map, USGS 7.5 minute map Moab 38109-E5.

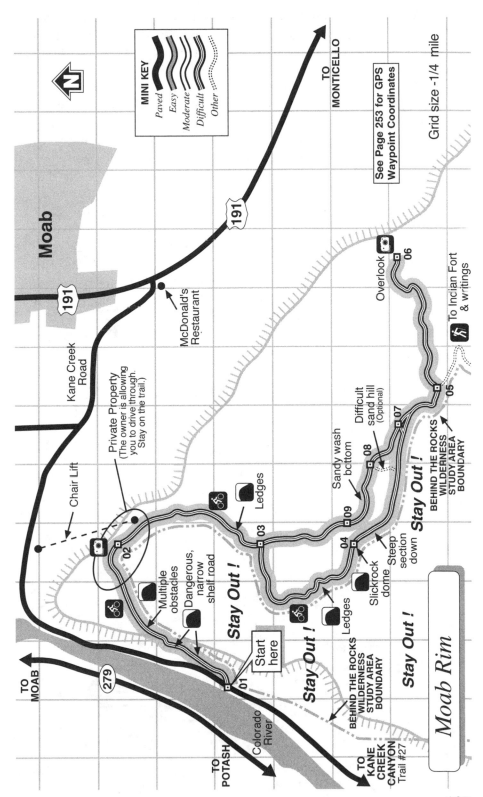

MINI KEY
Paved
Easy
Moderate
Difficult
Other

N

Moab

191

191

Kane Creek Road

McDonald's Restaurant

TO MONTICELLO

See Page 253 for GPS Waypoint Coordinates

Grid size -1/4 mile

Overlook

06

To Incian Fort & writings

Chair Lift

Private Property
(The owner is allowing you to drive through. Stay on the trail.)

Difficult sand hill (Optional)

Sandy wash bottom

BEHIND THE ROCKS WILDERNESS STUDY AREA BOUNDARY

05

07

08

Stay Out !

Ledges

02

03

09

Multiple obstacles

Dangerous, narrow shelf road

Stay Out !

04

Ledges

Slickrock dome

Steep section down

Stay Out !

TO MOAB

279

Start here

01

Stay Out !

BEHIND THE ROCKS WILDERNESS STUDY AREA BOUNDARY

TO POTASH

Colorado River

TO KANE CREEK CANYON Trail #27

Moab Rim

The rugged canyon is almost always driven from bottom to top.

Rocker Knocker, the second toughest obstacle, seems to have worsened in recent years.

Most vehicles require a winch or tow strap to get over The Rock Pile. There's no bypass.

Pritchett Canyon

Location: Southwest of Moab. The trail begins from Kane Creek Road and exits southeast at Highway 191.

Difficulty: Difficult. Considered by many to be the toughest four miles in all of Moab. (Other trails have more difficult individual obstacles—Behind the Rocks' White Knuckle Hill and High Dive are two that come to mind.) I've driven Pritchett Canyon several times, always with a large group. It's rare not to have at least one or two vehicles with major breakdowns. If you have any weak points in your vehicle, this trail will likely expose them. Differential lockers and/or winches are basic requirements.

Surprisingly, route-finding is not too difficult. The canyon is narrow so you can't stray far. Spur roads dead end quickly. Once out of the canyon, roads are fairly well-defined, although you have to follow directions carefully because there are many spurs.

Features: This trail is best known for its toughest obstacle—The Rock Pile—a gigantic ledge with no bypass. It gets its name from rocks piled at its base to make it easier. Unfortunately, the rocks get thrown out quickly by spinning tires. Vehicles with very large tires and a long wheel base have the best chance of getting up unaided. Most vehicles require a winch. Broken axles are common, usually the result of macho drivers who refuse to give up.

Time & Distance: It's 4.4 miles to the top of the canyon and another 14.5 to reach Highway 191. A trouble-free run through the canyon should take only 2 to 4 hours plus another hour to drive out. It's more likely, however, to take an entire day. Larger groups take longer.

To Get There: From the south side of Moab at the McDonald's Restaurant on Main Street, take Kane Creek Road west. Bear left at the first fork and head south along the Colorado River. At 4.6 miles, before the pavement ends, turn left into a private campground marked by a split-rail fence. Because the start of the trail passes through private property, you are asked to pay a small fee.

Trail Description: *Reset your odometer at the start* [01]*.* Bear left into a sandy ravine that runs along the east side of the campground. The trail heads north briefly then turns right and follows the narrow canyon. Pass through a gate before reaching a tricky step-down ledge at 0.3 miles [02]. The canyon widens at 0.5 miles. Bear right unless you're interested in attempting a giant ledge on the left. The trail is easy until 1.5 miles where you round a corner and pass through a spring-fed muddy section. Stay out of a deep water hole on the right. At 1.7 miles [03], there's a steep descent to the left followed by a major rock obstacle at the bottom. (It can be bypassed on the right.) After the obstacle, turn right and continue up the canyon. Continue straight as a spur road goes left to a side canyon at 2.5 miles [04].

There are some optional obstacles on the right at 3.5 miles before reaching Rocker Knocker at 3.6. This is a very nasty spot [05]. At first you think you can drive right up, but after a few tries it becomes apparent that this is no ordinary obstacle. The harder you try, the more you get wedged against the rock wall on the left. Winching is difficult because it has to be done from the side at an awkward angle. After this spot the trail switchbacks up a steep hill.

At 3.9 miles bear left as a spur goes right in the direction of Pritchett Arch. This is not the best way to get to the arch (See Trail #26). There's a driver's choice at 4.0 followed by a fairly tough spot before reaching the Rock Pile at 4.2 miles [06]. This is a frequent spot of congestion as drivers take time to find the best way up. Often, repairs are being made. Relax, watch the action, and learn as much as you can. Your turn is next.

After the Rock Pile, several tough obstacles on a steep hill remain. If you have a serious breakdown at the Rock Pile, it can take hours to winch a vehicle the remaining short distance to the top.

Once you reach the crest of the hill at 4.4 miles [07], the road swings right and winds downhill. At 5.7 miles another spur road goes right to Pritchett Arch [08]. (Refer to Trail #26 for directions to the arch. A short, steep hike is required.) The road splits briefly and comes back together before reaching an intersection with Behind the Rocks (Trail #28) at 6.1 miles [09]. Continue straight from here. It's 14.5 miles to Highway 191. See directions below.

Return Trip: Follow west to east directions for Pritchett Arch (page 134).

Services: Return to Moab.

Maps: Latitude 40°, Inc. *Moab West* Biking Map, USGS 7.5 minute maps Moab 38109-E5, Troughs Springs Canyon 38109-D5, and Kane Springs 38109-D4.

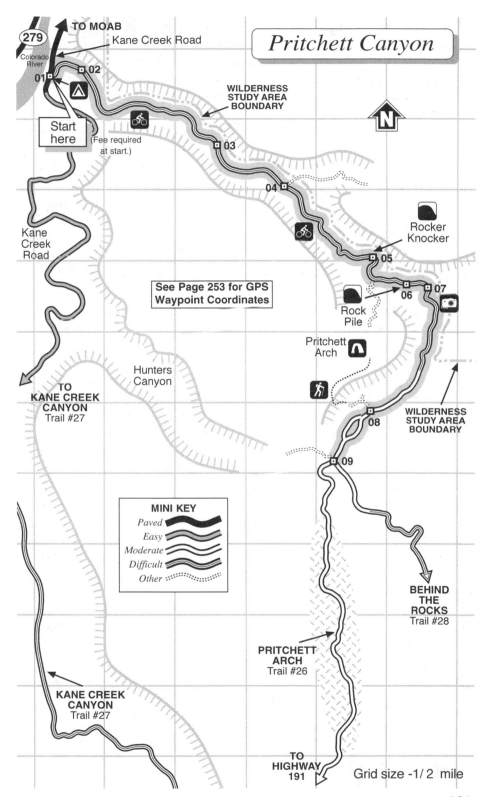

279

Colorado River

TO MOAB

Kane Creek Road

01 — 02

Start here

(Fee required at start.)

Kane Creek Road

Pritchett Canyon

WILDERNESS STUDY AREA BOUNDARY

N

03

04

Rocker Knocker

05

See Page 253 for GPS Waypoint Coordinates

06 — 07

Rock Pile

Pritchett Arch

Hunters Canyon

TO KANE CREEK CANYON Trail #27

08

WILDERNESS STUDY AREA BOUNDARY

09

MINI KEY

Paved
Easy
Moderate
Difficult
Other

BEHIND THE ROCKS Trail #28

PRITCHETT ARCH Trail #26

KANE CREEK CANYON Trail #27

TO HIGHWAY 191

Grid size -1/2 mile

131

Pritchett Arch cannot be seen very well from the trail. A short, steep hike is required.

Road is close to rim of Kane Creek Canyon.

This steep spot is the toughest you'll cross.

Most of the road is wide and easy with intermittent rocky sections.

Pritchett Arch 26

Location: Southeast of Moab, west of Highway 191.

Difficulty: Moderate. This trail is mostly easy except for the last several miles where it becomes increasingly rocky with one challenging spot. (See photo at left.). With careful maneuvering, some driving skill, and a good spotter, stock vehicles can get through without mishap. Skidplates are recommended.

Although there are many spur roads, route-finding is fairly easy, provided instructions are carefully followed. Loose gravel and cairns help define the trail across two short sections of slickrock.

Features: Much of this trail follows the eastern rim of Kane Creek Canyon. Several side roads lead to overlooks along the rim where Hurrah Pass can be seen in the distance and Kane Creek Canyon Trail can be seen below. The trail takes you close to magnificent Pritchett Arch but you must hike about 15 minutes to see the arch up close. Although short, the hike is very steep and requires some climbing at the start. Make sure you carry plenty of drinking water.

Time & Distance: From Highway 191 to the parking area below the hiking trail is 15.2 miles. Travel is fast on the easy parts of the trail but you'll have to slow down through the rocky sections. Allow about 2 hours driving time in each direction plus another hour for the round trip hike to the arch. The start of the trail is about 30 minutes from Moab.

To Get There: From the McDonald's Restaurant on the south side of Moab, drive 12.3 miles south on Highway 191. After a long hill, turn right and cross a cattle guard. There's a sign here for Pritchett Arch and other trails.

Trail Description (East to West): Reset your odometer as you turn off 191 [01]. There are many spur roads at the start of the trail. The road briefly swings north then curves back to the east. Stay on the widest part of the road. Bear left at 0.3 and 0.4 miles. Go straight at 2.3 as a lesser road goes left. At 2.6 bear left. Continue straight across a normally dry creek bed at 2.7. Bear right at 3.0 miles following a sign to Pritchett Arch [02]. The road alternates between smooth sand and patches of rock. At 4.0 miles bear left. Go around the south end of Lone Rock at 5.0 miles. You'll begin a gradual descent to a sandy stretch of road that swings left at 6.7 miles [03]. The two roads on the right are part of Behind the Rocks (Trail #28). As you continue, the road climbs, swings north, and crosses a shelf. (A short spur road goes left at 10.0 miles to an overlook of Kane Creek Canyon.) Go straight at 10.5 as a good-size road goes right [04]. Continue on the widest part of the road past more spur roads. Another wide road goes right at 12.3 miles [05]. You continue straight.

Continue straight across slickrock at 13.0 miles. Cairns and loose gravel help mark the route. Soon you'll encounter a fairly tough spot. Get out of your vehicle and study the contour of the rocks to determine the best line. Remember to place you tires on the high points. Shift into low range if you haven't already done so. Use a spotter if necessary.

At 14.5 miles [06], you intersect with Behind the Rocks Trail on the right. A lesser road goes left. You continue straight as the road gets easier. It splits briefly and comes back together before reaching the turn to Pritchett Arch at 15.0 miles [07]. Turn left. When it forks, turn left again. Stop at 15.2 miles [08] at a small parking area.

The hiking trail switchbacks up a steep embankment for a short distance than swings right across a high ledge. Head north a short distance bearing right of the rock wall before turning left uphill across a rippled slickrock dome. Cairns mark the route but you have to look carefully to find them.

Trail Description (West to East): Return to the main trail and turn right to the intersection with Behind the Rocks [06]. *Reset your odometer at this point.* Continue straight as the road curves uphill to the right. After climbing a rocky stretch, continue straight across slickrock at 1.5 miles. Go straight at 2.2 [05] and again at 4.0 miles [04]. The road curves left downhill and crosses a shelf at 4.5 miles. The road remains wide and is easy to follow. Soon the road curves left and heads northeast. It splits and comes back together. A broad valley can be seen ahead with Lone Rock in the distance. Bear right through a sandy stretch at 7.8 miles [03] and begin a gradual climb.

Pass around the south side of Lone Rock at 9.5 miles. Bear left as a major road goes right at 11.5 miles [02]. Continue straight across a dry creek bed at 11.8. Ignore all spur roads. Bear right at 14.1 and 14.2 before reaching Highway 191 at 14.5 miles [01].

Return Trip: Turn left (north) on 191 and head back to Moab. It's 12.3 miles to the McDonald's Restaurant on the south side of town.

Services: There's a nice rest stop about 2 miles south on Highway 191 but nothing north until you get close to Moab.

Maps: Latitude 40°, Inc. *Moab West* Biking Map, USGS 7.5 minute maps Moab 38109-E5, Troughs Springs Canyon 38109-D5, and Kane Springs 38109-D4.

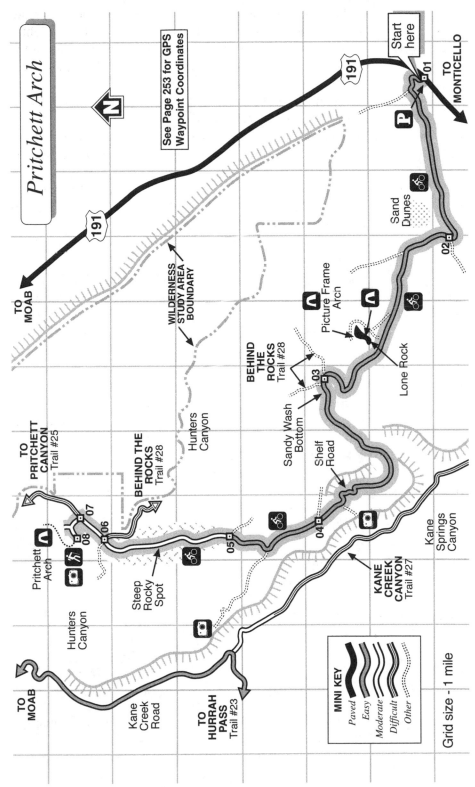

Pritchett Arch

N

See Page 253 for GPS Waypoint Coordinates

191 TO MOAB

191

TO MONTICELLO

Start here

01

P

Sand Dunes

02

WILDERNESS STUDY AREA BOUNDARY

Picture Frame Arch

Lone Rock

BEHIND THE ROCKS Trail #28

03

Sandy Wash Bottom

Shelf Road

Hunters Canyon

TO PRITCHETT CANYON Trail #25

BEHIND THE ROCKS Trail #28

07

06

08

Pritchett Arch

Hunters Canyon

Steep Rocky Spot

05

04

Kane Springs Canyon

KANE CREEK CANYON Trail #27

TO MOAB

Kane Creek Road

TO HURRAH PASS Trail #23

MINI KEY
Paved
Easy
Moderate
Difficult
Other

Grid size - 1 mile

135

Erosion has cut into the trail in a few places.

Water crossings are too numerous to count.

Perhaps the toughest spot on the trail.

Climbing out of the canyon.

Kane Creek Canyon 27

Location: South of Moab. Starts from Kane Creek Road and exits at Highway 191.

Difficulty: Difficult. This trail is on the borderline between moderate and difficult. Stock vehicles with skid plates can get through although some experience is necessary. Tight brush, in a few places, will rub against the sides of your vehicle. Avoid this trail during periods of heavy runoff as stream crossings may be too deep. There is a high shelf road as you near the end of the trail. Backing may be required to pass. Be aware of the possibility of flash floods in the narrow canyon.

Route-finding is easy except for a brief spot at the beginning. Although there are spur roads that depart into side canyons, the main trail is obvious most of the way.

Features: The trail winds back and forth across the floor of Kane Creek Canyon and crosses Kane Creek many times. It then climbs rapidly up the narrow end of the canyon, providing some terrific photo opportunities and a few small challenges. Officially this canyon is called Kane Springs Canyon, but most people refer to it as Kane Creek. I don't recommend you drive this trail during the hot summer months when biting flies become a problem.

Time & Distance: From Kane Creek Road to Highway 191 is 13.6 miles. Allow 3 to 4 hours driving time once on the trail.

To Get There: From the south side of Moab at the McDonald's Restaurant on Main Street, take Kane Creek Road west. Bear left at the first fork and head south along the Colorado River. After the pavement ends, the road swings east away from the river. The road continues south, crossing Kane Creek several times. Just before the wide dirt road swings right in the direction of Hurrah Pass, turn left on a single lane road 11.3 miles from McDonald's.

Trail Description: Reset your odometer at the start [01]. As you head east, you immediately encounter a jumble of spur roads. Make a left, a right, and a left. The last turn should send you across Kane Creek at a rocky spot. Continue straight at 0.4 miles and the road should soon head south. From this point, ignore all spur roads that head east and west.

You'll cross a variety of interesting obstacles as the trail twists in every direction. At several points, erosion has eaten away the right side of the trail, forcing you left over some challenging terrain. At 3.7 miles pass a steep hill on the right [02] where a spur goes up and down the hill in the shape of a horseshoe. At 4.5 miles [03] the stream becomes overgrown with tamarisk, an aggressive brush used for erosion control. The trail narrows as it passes through the brush and weaves in and out of the shallow creek many times. At 6.6 miles [04] pass through an opening in a barbed wire fence. At 10.0 miles the trail follows the rocky creek bed for a distance before beginning an earnest climb out of the canyon.

Perhaps the toughest spot on the trail is encountered at 10.7 miles [05]. It's steep and rocky (see photo). Several attempts may be necessary for stock vehicles. The road continues up the canyon wall across a narrow shelf. Use caution around blind curves. There's another challenging spot at 11.4 miles as you cross a small stream that feeds into Kane Creek. This is a nice place to stop for lunch.

At 12.8 miles [06] cross Kane Creek and head uphill on a better road. Bear right at 12.9. Pass through an area identified as having an underground pipeline. Turn left at a T intersection at 13.2 miles to connect with Highway 191 at 13.3 miles [07].

Return Trip: Turn left and head back to Moab. It's about 15 miles.

Services: There's a well-maintained roadside park with modern restrooms north on Highway 191. The Hole-in-the-Rock Home and Gift Shop has snacks and drinks when they're open. Return to Moab for all other services.

Maps: Although this trail is not a recommended biking route, it is shown on the Latitude 40°, Inc. *Moab West* Biking Map. USGS 7.5 minute maps include Moab 38109-E5, Trough Springs Canyon 38109-D5, and Kane Springs 38109-D4.

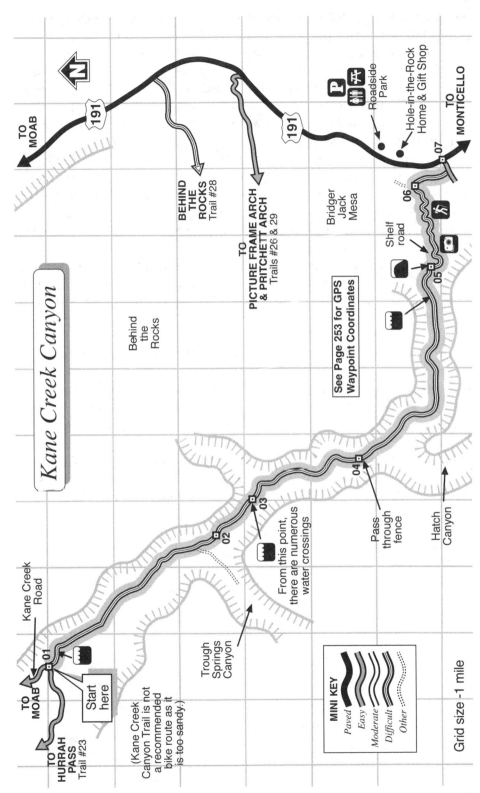

Kane Creek Canyon

N

TO MOAB

191

191

TO MOAB

TO MONTICELLO

P

Roadside Park

Hole-in-the-Rock Home & Gift Shop

07

06

Shelf road

05

Bridger Jack Mesa

BEHIND THE ROCKS
Trail #28

TO **PICTURE FRAME ARCH & PRITCHETT ARCH**
Trails #26 & 29

Behind the Rocks

See Page 253 for GPS Waypoint Coordinates

04

Pass through fence

Hatch Canyon

03

02

From this point, there are numerous water crossings

Trough Springs Canyon

Kane Creek Road

01

TO MOAB

Start here

(Kane Creek Canyon Trail is not a recommended bike route as it is too sandy.)

TO **HURRAH PASS**
Trail #23

MINI KEY
Paved
Easy
Moderate
Difficult
Other

Grid size - 1 mile

High Dive is extremely dangerous.

Roller Coaster—what a ride!

Don't get sideways on Hummer Hill.

Going up White Knuckle Hill. Photo by Matt Peterson

Coming down White Knuckle Hill requires complete confidence in your spotter.

Behind the Rocks 28

Location: South of Moab, west of Highway 191.

Difficulty: Difficult. Behind the Rocks' most difficult obstacle—White Knuckle Hill—may be the most dangerous and terrifying obstacle in Moab. It's akin to driving off a series of small cliffs. Many drivers attach a safety strap to the rear of their vehicle to avoid tipping forward and tumbling down the hill. Others do it cold turkey. Incredibly, some people actually turn around and drive back up. To make matters worse, White Knuckle Hill has no bypass. You must avoid this entire portion of the trail or turn around. Remaining obstacles are not much easier. High Dive and Upchuck are appropriately named. I've seen stock vehicles get through this trail, but not without a great deal of assistance and body damage. Lockers and extra high ground clearance are highly recommended. Even then, damage is possible.

    While landmarks and defined roads make route-finding manageable, the route is complex. Instructions must be followed carefully. Fortunately, if you get lost, the exit route is not far away. Many spurs that head south lead to the county road. From there a left turn takes you back to Highway 191. There are several places along the trail that come back to the main road, allowing early departure if this becomes necessary.

Features: This trail starts just south of the Behind the Rocks Wilderness Study Area. This particular WSA is completely closed to motorized travel to preserve its incredible beauty. This fantasy land of Navajo sandstone fins and domes is perhaps the most photographed area in Moab. Between difficult obstacles are stretches of easy terrain and unique arches. The trail concludes with a wild descent through remote Hunters Canyon.

Time & Distance: The trail itself measures 14.1 miles. Add to that another 15 miles for the return on Pritchett Arch Trail (#26) to Highway 191. An entire day should be allowed for this run. Don't be surprised if you arrive home late for dinner.

To Get There: From the McDonald's Restaurant south of Moab, drive 10.8 miles south on Highway 191. About 0.6 miles south of mile post 115, turn right on an unmarked dirt road. If you begin climbing a long hill on 191, you've gone too far.

Trail Description:
    From the start to High Dive: *Reset your odometer as you turn off*

An easy stretch of road alongside Behind the Rocks Wilderness Study Area.

Upchuck is short but steep. To get over it takes the right blend of power and finesse.

Dodging a brief rainstorm under an overhang in Hunters Canyon.

142

191 [01]. Air down and shift into low range immediately. Challenges are just ahead. At 0.6 miles there's a steep rocky hill that's easier with lockers. Turn right when you intersect with a wider road at 0.9 miles [02]. A left turn here would take you to the start of Pritchett Arch Trail (#26). Go straight at 1.0 miles as a lesser road comes in from the right. At 1.3 miles [03] spur roads depart in several directions. Take the left-most spur, followed by another left immediately. Stay on the most traveled part of the trail as you pass frequent spurs. The trail widens at 2.3 miles [04] and descends rapidly over some tough ledges. Left here is the easier route. Numerous other smaller challenges follow. Go straight at mile 3.0 as an equal size road crosses perpendicularly [05].

At 3.6 miles you reach High Dive and Upchuck [06]. Get out of your vehicle and take a close look at High Dive. I recommend first-timers connect a tow strap to the heaviest vehicle available. This vehicle follows at a speed that leaves just a few feet of slack in the tow line, preventing a serious tumble. If you don't feel comfortable going down this obstacle, turn around; the trail only gets worse. The tall ledge immediately after High Dive is Upchuck. Use caution here as well. It's tougher than it looks.

From High Dive to White Knuckle Hill: *Reset your odometer at the bottom of High Dive.* At the top of the canyon at multiple spurs, take a hard left and head southwest. The road becomes sandy with a fun stretch of whoop-ti-dos. Continue straight at 1.1 miles [07] as a road crosses diagonally. At 2.0 miles [08] turn right and head directly towards Lone Rock (called Prostitute Butte on biking map). Turn right again when you reach the Lone Rock. Balcony Arch is directly above you. Head northeast then curve left around the back side of the butte where you encounter Picture Frame Arch on the left at 2.5 miles [09]. This is usually a good place to stop for lunch. I like to climb up inside the arch and take pictures looking down. Climbing up on the left side is easier.

After Picture Frame Arch, make a hard right and head downhill. Don't continue around the butte. Follow a smooth sandy road that heads northeast. It curves north and crosses straight over a short section of slickrock. Turn left at a 4-way intersection at 3.7 miles [10]. The road is easy for a short distance before it drops over a steep ledge. Continue straight until you run into the main road at 5.0 miles [11]. Bear right, then right again immediately off the main road heading northwest. Go straight at 5.4 miles as a road joins on the right [12].

Bear left as you encounter several spur roads at about 5.7 miles. Look right for a steep hill blackened by tire marks. This is called Hummer Hill [13]. It got its name from the fact that some Hummers have parked sideways on the hill without rolling over. My advice is to drive straight up and down regardless of vehicle type. Bear left after Hummer Hill. There's yet more challenge before reaching a major intersection at 6.1 miles [14]. A hard left here, marked by a sign to Pritchett Arch, would take you back to the main road. Continue partially left uphill on a sandy road. After some more whoop-ti-dos, it gets rocky again. The trail becomes somewhat obscure but you can find your way through without too much trouble. At mile 6.7 there's a rounded-off series of ledges that I found really fun to go down [15]. No one in our group knew an official name for this obstacle, so I've dubbed it Roller Coaster. Continue straight at 6.8 as a lesser road joins on the left. I think this is the last chance to avoid White Knuckle Hill. I didn't drive this road myself, so I'm only guessing after studying a detailed USGS map.

At 6.9 miles turn left down a steep, rocky, tippy spot. Once past here, you're committed to White Knuckle Hill, which follows immediately [16]. Walk down and survey the area before you go any farther. White Knuckle Hill is the ultimate four-wheel commitment. If you decide to continue, you'll need an excellent spotter—an experienced four-wheeler in whom you have complete trust. Consider using a safety strap as described earlier. It feels like you're driving off the edge of a cliff. You can see nothing ahead except blue sky. Make sure your spotter stands within your view.

From White Knuckle Hill through Hunters Canyon: *Reset your odometer after completing White Knuckle Hill* [16]. Turn right and head north toward Hunters Canyon. Turn left at 1.0 miles [17]. As you begin to descend, you'll encounter an obscure section of slickrock. Gradually curve right in a northwest direction. You'll drop down some challenging ledges as the canyon narrows. At 1.3 miles you can see the bottom of the canyon as the trail bends around in a sweeping S curve—first right, then left. The trail is well-defined as it zig-zags through the canyon. In places, the canyon is too narrow to receive a GPS signal. At mile 2.7 bear right as the trail passes under an overhang. You cross back and forth across the creek bed before reaching the end of the trail at 3.6 miles [18].

Return Trip: To return to Moab, turn left and follow the "west to east" trail description for Pritchett Arch (page 134). If you have time to visit Pritchett Arch, turn right on an easy road, go 0.5 miles and turn left at the sign to Pritchett Arch. At the next fork, turn left. A short but steep hike is required.

Services: Return to Moab.

Maps: Parts of this trail are shown on the Latitude 40°, Inc. *Moab East* Biking Map and USGS 7.5 minute maps Moab 38109-E5, Troughs Springs Canyon 38109-D5, and Kane Springs 38109-D4. Some of this trail I plotted using my own GPS equipment.

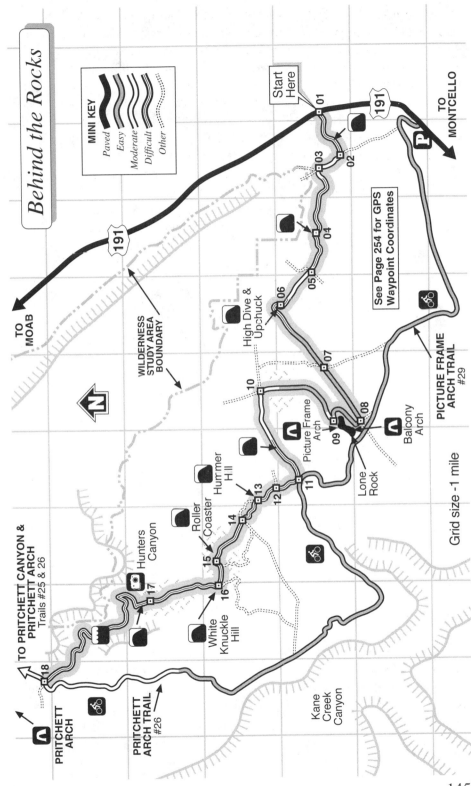

Behind the Rocks

MINI KEY
Paved
Easy
Moderate
Difficult
Other

Start Here

TO MOAB

191

TO MONTCELLO

191

P

WILDERNESS STUDY AREA BOUNDARY

See Page 254 for GPS Waypoint Coordinates

PICTURE FRAME ARCH TRAIL #29

N

High Dive & Upchuck

Picture Frame Arch

Balcony Arch

Lone Rock

Hummer Hill

Roller Coaster

Hunters Canyon

White Knuckle Hill

Grid size -1 mile

TO PRITCHETT CANYON & PRITCHETT ARCH
Trails #25 & 26

PRITCHETT ARCH

PRITCHETT ARCH TRAIL #26

Kane Creek Canyon

01
02
03
04
05
06
07
08
09
10
11
12
13
14
15
16
17
18

Most of the road is easy cruising.

Photo taken from inside Picture Frame Arch.

Balcony Arch is on southeast side of Lone Rock. Picture Frame Arch is on the northwest side.

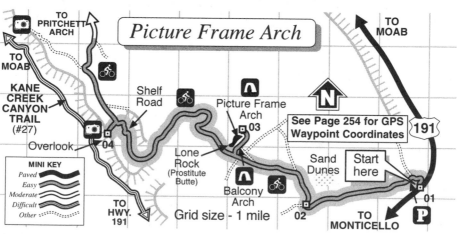

Picture Frame Arch

TO PRITCHETT ARCH

TO MOAB

TO MOAB

KANE CREEK CANYON TRAIL (#27)

Shelf Road

Picture Frame Arch
03

Overlook
04

Lone Rock
(Prostitute Butte)

See Page 254 for GPS Waypoint Coordinates

191

Sand Dunes

Start here

01

Balcony Arch
02

MINI KEY
Paved
Easy
Moderate
Difficult
Other

TO HWY. 191

Grid size - 1 mile

TO MONTICELLO

P

Picture Frame Arch

Location: Southeast of Moab, west of Highway 191.

Difficulty: Easy. The road alternates between smooth, well-packed sand and mild rocky sections. You probably won't have to shift into four-wheel drive unless it's wet. Route-finding is fairly easy, although numerous spur roads require that you pay attention to directions.

Features: Drive up close and climb inside Picture Frame Arch if you can. Be careful; you have to climb up a steep wall left of the arch. Picnic at a secluded overlook along Kane Creek Canyon Rim (same as Kane Springs Canyon). Enjoy a short, relaxing day away from the crowds.

Time & Distance: From Highway 191, it's about 5 miles to Picture Frame Arch and another 5 miles to the overlook of Kane Creek Canyon. Allow about 3 hours for the complete round trip.

To Get There: From the McDonald's Restaurant on the south side of Moab, drive 12.3 miles south on Highway 191. After a long hill, turn right and cross a cattle guard. There's a sign here for Picture Frame Arch and other trails.

Trail Description: Reset your odometer as you turn off 191 [01]. There are many spur roads at the start of the trail. The road briefly swings north then curves back to the east. Stay on the widest part of the road. Bear left at 0.3 and 0.4 miles. Go straight at 2.3 as a lesser road goes left. At 2.6 bear left. Continue straight across a normally dry creek bed at 2.7. Bear right at 3.0 miles following a sign to Pritchett Arch [02]. At 4.0 miles bear left. At 5.0 miles turn right into Lone Rock. You can turn when you're alongside Lone Rock or at a Y just before Lone Rock. Go past Balcony Arch heading in a northeast direction. Follow the trail around to the northwest side of the arch. Picture Frame Arch is on the left at 5.4 miles [03]. Go back out the way you came in.

To visit the overlook on Kane Creek Canyon Rim, get back on the main road and continue another 5 miles. At the top of a hill after a shelf road the main road swings northwest. Watch for a single lane road on the left. The overlook is just another 0.2 miles down this road [04].

Return Trip: Return the way you came.

Maps: Latitude 40°, Inc. *Moab East* Biking Map.

This stretch of slickrock is very tippy and route-finding requires patience.

Follow nature's red brick road.

Tilt-a-Whirl is steep and tippy.

Flat Iron Mesa ◆30◆

Location: Southeast of Moab, west of Highway 191.

Difficulty: Difficult. Two obstacles on this trail need special mention. Tilt-a-Whirl turns you sideways on a steep hill, forcing you into an uncomfortable lean. Good spotting is necessary to get through safely. Easter Egg Hill squeezes you through a narrow opening between two jagged rocks while negotiating a steep, challenging, rocky descent. Body damage is a real possibility. Both Tilt-a-Whirl and Easter Egg Hill can be bypassed. Many other challenging obstacles remain, including a tight corner hundreds of feet above Coyote Canyon, a tributary of Hatch Wash. This trail is not recommended for stock vehicles. Lockers and/or excellent articulation are required. Do not drive this trail alone.

Route-finding is fairly complicated as the trail departs from and rejoins a maze of easy county roads. There is little confusing slickrock, but a spaghetti-works of roads near the overlook of Hatch Wash will have you scratching your head. The map in this book, as far as I know, is the only one that shows the difficult portions of this trail. I plotted these areas using my own GPS equipment. Make sure you carry another map with topographic information in case you get off-course. Also, carry a compass. You'll need to know your direction of travel to verify that you're on the right road. A GPS receiver is a real benefit on this trail. It's best to go with someone who has driven the trail before.

Features: A lesser-known but great hard-core trail. It's popular during the Easter Jeep Safari because a guide is provided. The rest of the year people seem to have trouble finding it. Consequently, it sees light travel. Besides a variety of very difficult obstacles, the trail offers some outstanding scenery across Flat Iron Mesa and along the rim of 800-ft.-deep Hatch Wash.

Time & Distance: The trail, as described here, measures 15.0 miles. Allow 4 to 5 hours driving time. (Note: This trail is 1.3 miles shorter than the full-blown Safari version. I eliminated one confusing and, in my opinion, tedious side trip between waypoints 11 and 12.)

To Get There: From the McDonald's Restaurant on the south side of Moab, drive 17.5 miles south on Highway 191. Watch for the trail on the right 2.4 miles past Hole-in-the-Rock Home & Gift shop.

Hatch Wash at overlook. Upper left, the flat-iron-shaped butte that gives the mesa its name.

The top of Easter Egg Hill is extremely tight and tippy. You need a good spotter.

This narrow corner is just after Easter Egg Hill above Coyote Canyon.

Trail Description: .

From the start to Tilt-a-Whirl: *Reset your odometer as you turn off Highway 191* [01]. As you get off the highway, turn around and head north on a dirt road that parallels 191. Pass through a gate and cross a small ravine heading west. Turn right at 0.3 miles [02]. At 0.6 the road swings uphill and crosses the first obstacle [03]. The trail seems to end at a small turnaround area. It actually continues to the right between a large rock and a tree. After passing through a narrow section with a few challenges, you'll reach the base of Rubble Hill at 1.5 miles [04]. Bear right up the hill. Left is a bypass. Rubble Hill doesn't look like much, but the loose rock is a challenge for open differentials. When you reach the top of the hill, swing left and follow the trail down a steep, twisting descent.

At 1.8 turn left at the bottom of the hill [05] and follow an easy road that parallels a buried pipeline. Turn right at 2.2 miles [06]. Cross an area that looks like red bricks [07] then climb a series of ledges. At 3.1 you reach the base of a steep section of slickrock [08]. Climb the rock following black tire marks as best as possible. The trail swings to the right, then drops down a steep tippy spot, then turns left back uphill. You level off briefly before turning left uphill off the slickrock over a couple of tough ledges at 3.2 miles. You should end up heading in a southeast direction [09]. Be careful to stay on the established route. It's easy to get lost in this area.

Bear left as a lesser road goes right at 3.3. Go straight at 3.5 as a road joins on the left [10]. The road becomes wider and easier. Bear right at 4.2 miles [11] then right again heading northwest. Go straight at 4.8 as a lesser road goes right [12]. Continue on this easy road for a while. A good size road goes left. Pass this road and continue to 6.5 miles and turn left uphill on a much lesser road [13]. The road crosses several ledges before reaching a fork at 7.3 miles [14]. Right takes you down Tilt-a-Whirl; left is a bypass. Get out of your vehicle and examine the obstacle before starting down. You'll need the help of a good spotter to do it safely.

From Tilt-a-Whirl to the overlook: *Reset your odometer.* At the bottom of Tilt-a-Whirl make a hard right then an immediate left down a steep, rocky trench. There are some challenging spots through this section. Go straight at 0.4 as a lesser road goes right to an overlook of Hatch Wash [15]. Go straight again at 0.5 as the bypass road road joins on the left. Go right at 0.9 as you pass through a shallow canyon. At some point, you should see Hatch Wash on the right. Bear left at 1.3 as a lesser road goes right to another overlook [16]. At 1.7 the main road appears to go straight [17]; you go right.

A confusing area begins at 2.4 miles [18]. Drop down a big ledge (there's a bypass) and bear left, then make an immediate right turn. The road swings west towards the overlook. Try not to be confused by criss-crossing spurs. You reach the overlook at 2.7 miles [19]. Hatch Wash is about 500 ft. deep at this point and the views are spectacular.

From overlook to end of trail: *Reset your odometer at the overlook.*
Reverse direction and head east. Bear right as two spurs go left at 0.2 miles
[20] continuing east. The road swings right at 0.6 miles and joins a better
road [21]. You should be able to see distinctive Hammerhead Rock ahead.
You'll know it when you see it.

Turn right at 0.9 miles [22] for Easter Egg Hill or take the bypass
left. You reach Easter Egg hill at 1.2 miles [23]. If you attempt this obstacle,
be prepared for body damage. It is a complex driving maneuver and requires
an excellent spotter. Just after Easter Egg Hill, there's a narrow point only
a few feet from the edge of the canyon. Once again, you'll want a reliable
spotter to guide you through. At 1.5 miles [24] there's a parking and turnaround area for those who took the bypass. From there you can walk back
and watch the action on Easter Egg Hill.

From the turnaround area, head north uphill. Bear left at the first
fork then right at 1.7 miles [25] heading east. You'll climb out of one valley
then dip into another. The road changes back and forth from sandy to rocky.
Bear right as a lesser road goes left at 2.4 miles [26]. You reach the county
road at 3.2 miles [27]. Turn right and stay on the main road until you reach
Highway 191 at 5.0 miles [28].

Return Trip: Turn left on Highway 191 to return to Moab. It's about 20
miles north.

Services: The Hole-in-the-Rock Home & Gift Shop has snacks when they're
open. For restrooms, continue north on 191 to a modern roadside park just
past the gift shop. Return to Moab for all other services.

Maps: USGS 7.5 minute map La Sal Junction 38109-C4.

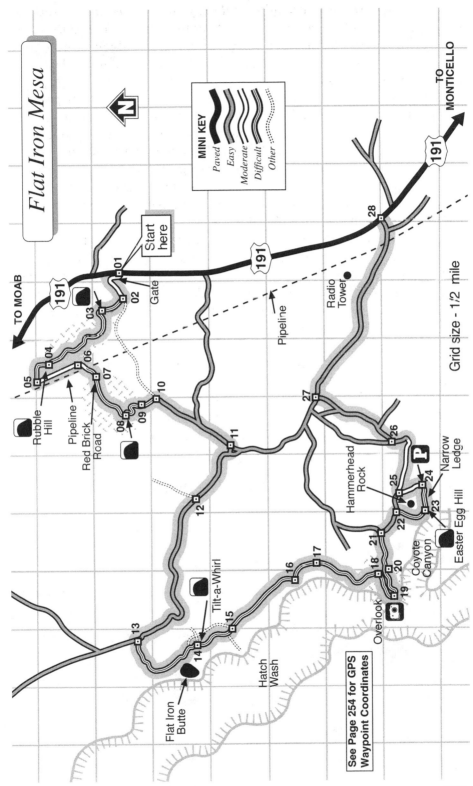

Flat Iron Mesa

N

MINI KEY
Paved
Easy
Moderate
Difficult
Other

TO MOAB

191

191

TO
MONTICELLO

Start here

Gate

01
02
03
04
05
06
07
08
09
10
11
12
13
14
15
16
17
18
19
20
21
22
23
24
25
26
27
28

Rubble Hill

Pipeline

Red Brick Road

Pipeline

Radio Tower

Tilt-a-Whirl

Flat Iron Butte

Hatch Wash

Overlook

Coyote Canyon

Hammerhead Rock

Narrow Ledge

Easter Egg Hill

P

Grid size - 1/2 mile

See Page 254 for GPS Waypoint Coordinates

153

#1) Follow yellow flame symbols.

#2) Start of trail.

#3) The first big slickrock dome.

#4) Don't go up this knoll. Turn right here.

#5) Continue straight up next dome.

#6) The first crossing of the Slickrock Bike Trail. Don't follow dashed lines.

Location: Northeast of Moab just outside of town.

Difficulty: Difficult. Numerous steep climbs and descents over sandstone domes and ledges. Excellent traction enables vehicles to surmount inclines of incredible steepness but plenty of power is necessary. Make sure your vehicle is properly geared. Several tippy spots will test the leaning ability of most vehicles. It's important to have excellent front and rear approach angles on your vehicle and good articulation. Not recommended for stock vehicles.

       This trail is now marked with painted yellow flame symbols (photo #1). With these symbols, you have a fighting chance of finding the trail, although it's always best to travel with someone familiar with the trail. As the symbols wear away, route-finding will get progressively more difficult. Without symbols, the trail is almost impossible to find unless you've been on the trail before or are using GPS. These directions are helpful but should not be solely relied upon, especially when the trail markings fade. Carry a detailed topographic map and a compass. If you get disoriented, it's likely that someone will come along soon. Please be sure to stay on the trail. If you get confused, get out and find the trail on foot. Do not drive around aimlessly looking for the trail. Carry at least one gallon of water per person per day.

Features: The trail is as beautiful as it is confusing. It has a high vantage point with beautiful views of the La Sal Mountains and Negro Bill Canyon to the east and, from the overlook, the Colorado River. The area is also known for the Slickrock Bike Trail which draws avid bikers from all over the world. The four-wheel-drive and biking trails crisscross several times but never share the same route. Never drive on the biking trail, which is marked with painted white dashed lines. Be very careful at the crossing points. Always be courteous and friendly—it's contagious.

Time & Distance: The trail is 8.5 miles long and can be driven in 3 to 4 hours under ideal circumstances. However, it's likely to take much longer, especially if you're traveling with a group. Allow 5 to 7 hours to be safe.

To Get There: (See town map on page 242) From Main Street and Center Street in the middle of Moab, go four blocks east to 400 East Street. Head south to Millcreek Drive and turn left. Go straight at the stop sign near the cemetery and follow Sand Flats Road 1.7 miles to the entrance booth of the

#7) Proceed right of Black Hole seen in distance.

#8) Jeep follows trail south above Black Hole.

#10) Weave northeast through here.

#9) A spotter is helpful descending this steep slope.

#11) Tip-Over Challenge.

#12) Hardtops use caution here.

Sand Flats Recreation Area (fee required). Turn left after the entrance booth within a few hundred feet. You'll see a slickrock fin with yellow flame markings that goes to the left.

Trail Description:

From the start to the overlook: Reset your odometer as you turn left off Sand Flats Road [01]. Climb a big hump onto a slickrock fin and follow it left (photo #2). After the fin, pass through a sandy area. At 0.2 miles there's a low spot between the rocks. When dry, it's barely noticeable. In the spring or after heavy rains, however, this spot fills with water and can be a quagmire. During those times, it's dubbed Lake Michigan. Pass through a fence at 0.4 [02] and turn left following the fence line. The road appears to go straight here so don't miss this turn. Along the fence you can see Lion's Back on the left. Turn right at a 4-way intersection at 0.6. Bear left up a steep fin at 0.7 [03]. You should see flame symbols on the side of the fin. You'll swing to the right somewhat above the fin then descend to the left down a steep section of slickrock. Climb and descend a massive dome of slickrock (photo #3). At 1.0 [04] a sandy road goes right. You continue straight up another large dome (photo #5).

The trail seems to end at 1.2 [05]. Make a hard right down a steep rock slope. Pass precisely between two painted lines or risk a rollover. After this short drop, hug a rock wall on the right and round a corner. At 1.3 bear left downhill at a spot with a great deal of sideways tilt. Choose your line carefully; this is a tricky spot. At the bottom of this hill, bear left into the sand then start across slickrock. The trail swings right off the slickrock at 1.4 [06]. This is another turn easily missed. At 1.5 [07] the trail appears to follow black tire marks up a small, steep knoll (photo #4). Don't go up; turn right. You'll weave through the sand and climb over some rocks before reaching an intersection with the Slickrock Bike Trail at 1.6 miles [08] (photo #6). Watch for bikers speeding down the hills on each side of the 4-wheel trail. Go straight here between the rocks on a sandy road. Bear right through a small turnaround area at 1.8. Go straight at 1.9 [09] as a lesser road goes left. Bear left over some steep rocks at 2.1 [10]. A bypass goes right.

At 2.5 miles [11] turn right for the overlook. Follow a very rocky road, ignoring several spur roads left. The trail ends at 3.1 where it climbs up slickrock, swings around and comes back down [12]. Park on top and enjoy the views of the Colorado River and Negro Bill Canyon.

From the overlook to Tip-Over Challenge: Reset your odometer at the overlook [12]. Return to the start of the overlook spur [11] and turn right. You'll climb to the top of another large dome. There are various choices, one of which is quite steep and is quickly identified by black tire marks. At the top of this dome, swing left around a natural rock wall to a gravelly spot at 0.8 miles [13]. Turn right and head downhill following flame symbols. The trail swings right and then left down a switchback on the barren rock.

As you come down off this hill, swing right towards a large dead tree lying on the ground and drop into the sand at 0.9 [14]. Follow a sandy trail until it intersects with the bike trail again at 1.2 [15]. Look southwest for a large indentation in a massive slickrock mountain. This is called the Black Hole but only appears that way when the sun is low (photo #7). Use this as a reference point. The trail goes around the top of the Black Hole starting on the right side. Here's where the flame symbols become essential. Without them, the trail is almost impossible to follow. After several steep spots, swing left and pass between a small tree and the edge of the Black Hole at 1.7 [16] (photo #8). There's plenty of room even though it looks intimidating. From here the trail goes up to the right, then swings to the left around a series of large depressions filled with trees at approximately 1.8 [17] (photo #10). You'll pass a deep vehicle-size depression before starting down a steep ridge line off the slickrock at 2.2 miles [18]. Use a spotter. A miscue here could send you tumbling down the slope (photo #9). Once down off the slickrock, turn right and follow a sandy trail. Bear right at a fork at 2.6 [19]. At 2.7 [20] you begin climbing up a canyon. Stay to the left as you go up. A road goes left at 2.9. Go right and almost immediately you'll see Tip-Over Challenge on the left [21] (photo #11). It can be bypassed to the right. If you try this obstacle, turn right after it and merge with the bypass.

From Tip-Over Challenge to end of trail: *Reset your odometer at Tip-Over Challenge* [21]. Head northwest as slickrock becomes a rough gravel road for a short distance. Bear left at a fork at 0.2 [22] and left again at 0.3. At 0.4 [23] climb a steep wall onto a fin and turn right. At 0.6 [24] bear left and reverse direction. You should be on a rough but defined road. At 0.8 [25] climb Rubble Trouble—a steep, loose-rock hill. Go straight at 1.0 as a good size road goes right [26]. You'll descend along the base of Lion's Back before passing through a narrow, tippy spot at 1.5 miles [27]. Hard-top vehicles have a tough time here trying to avoid nipping a roof edge (photo #12). Bear right at a vandalized gate at 1.6 [28] and drop through some tough rocks turning left. Pass through a beach-like area with roads going in every direction. Continue to head southeast. You'll soon intersect with Sand Flats Road at approximately 2.5 miles [29].

Return Trip: Turn right and head back to Moab.

Services: Return to Moab. There is fee camping inside the Sand Flats Recreation Area and at the base of Lion's Back.

Maps: The most detailed map for this area is the USGS 7.5 minute map Moab 38109-E5. The trail itself is not shown but the map provides helpful topographic information. I plotted this trail using my own GPS equipment.

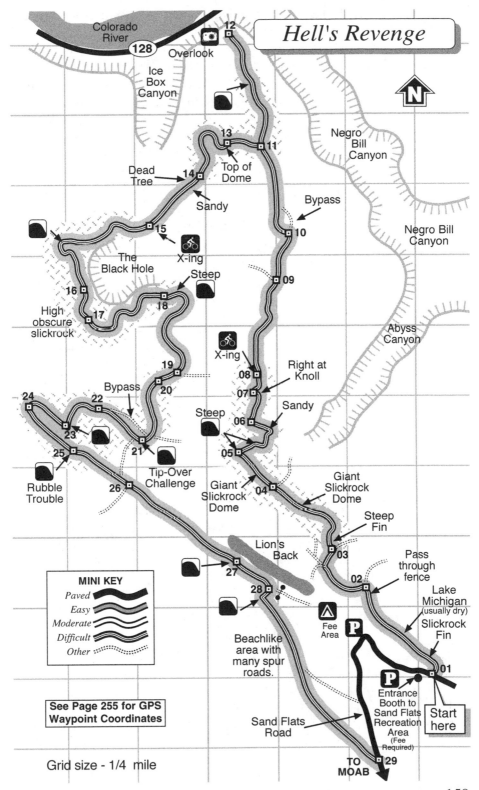

Hell's Revenge

N

Colorado River
128
Overlook
Ice Box Canyon

12
11
Negro Bill Canyon

13
Top of Dome

14
Dead Tree
Sandy

Bypass
10
Negro Bill Canyon

15
X-ing
The Black Hole
09

Steep
16
18
17
High obscure slickrock

19
20
X-ing

08
Right at Knoll
07
Sandy

Abyss Canyon

Bypass
24
22
23
21
Steep
06
05
Giant Slickrock Dome

25
26
Tip-Over Challenge
Giant Slickrock Dome
04

Rubble Trouble

Giant Slickrock Dome
Steep Fin

03
Lion's Back

MINI KEY
Paved
Easy
Moderate
Difficult
Other

27
28
Pass through fence
02
Lake Michigan (usually dry)
Slickrock Fin

Fee Area

P
P

01

Beachlike area with many spur roads.

Entrance Booth to Sand Flats Recreation Area (Fee Required)

Start here

See Page 255 for GPS Waypoint Coordinates

Sand Flats Road

Grid size - 1/4 mile

TO MOAB
29

159

Heading down Frenchy's Fin—short but extremely steep.

Trail is marked well with stegosaur symbols.

Amazing natural rock formation.

One of many giant fins.

La Sal Mountains are a backdrop to the area.

Location: East of Moab inside the Sand Flats Recreation Area.

Difficulty: Difficult. Dominated by undulating slickrock with intervals of soft sand and a few rocky sections. Excellent traction on dry slickrock permits vehicles in low gear to ascend and descend extremely steep sections of dry slickrock. Be more careful under wet conditions. Approach steep sections head-on rather than sideways across the hill. Stock vehicles should have good articulation, high ground clearance, and adequate front and rear approach angles.

> The trail is well marked with stenciled stegosaur symbols (see photo at left). A few confusing spots remain, however, so pay close attention to directions. Use the radio tower for a landmark. Please be sure to stay on the trail. If you get confused, get out and find the trail on foot. Don't drive around aimlessly looking for the route.

Features: A thrilling drive of steep climbs and heart-pounding descents with the La Sal Mountains providing a beautiful backdrop. Part one, on the south side of Sand Flats Road, is very scenic and steep but the fins are less dramatic. Part two, on the north side, starts gradually but ends with a roller-coaster ride you'll never forget. This route duplicates that driven during the Easter Jeep Safari with the exception of one short out-and-back side trip at waypoint 12.

Time & Distance: The trail measures 9.4 miles as described here and takes 3 to 4 hours.

To Get There: (See town map on page 242) From Main Street and Center Street in the middle of Moab, go four blocks east to 400 East Street. Head south to Millcreek Drive and turn left. Go straight at the stop sign near the cemetery and follow Sand Flats Road 1.7 miles to the entrance booth of the Sand Flats Recreation Area (fee required). Stay on Sand Flats Road another 2.0 miles and turn right into Campsite Cluster E. Drive in a short distance. The trail starts on a patch of slickrock to the right of camping spot #5.

Trail Description:
> *South side: Reset your odometer where the trail starts next to camping spot #5* [01]. The trail swings around the back of the campsite to the left where you'll see stegosaur symbols immediately. Pass over a sand hill at 0.3 miles. In places, rocks are lined up on each side of the road to

161

One of many great views on the south side. A totally enjoyable drive.

Steep descent on the south side.   Kenny's Climb.

Pass through this point two times in opposite directions. Vehicles shown are heading out.

help define the trail. At 0.5 [02] bear right at a fork. The trail turns north for a while then swings south again along the top of a fin. A diversion at 0.8 [03] drops off the fin to the right then immediately climbs back up. At 0.9 it drops off the fin again to the right and then swings left. After the trail reverses direction again, descend through a steep, narrow ravine at 1.4 miles. Bear right at a fork at 1.5 [04]. Make a hard right at 1.6. You meet a larger road at 1.8 [05] at Campsite 4F. Turn right and climb a steep, rocky hill following signposts. Bear left at 1.9 as you go around in a circle. At 2.1 miles [06] bear right on a lesser road uphill before you return to campsite 4F. (Are you dizzy yet?) When you run into a larger road at 2.2 bear right. At 2.4 bear right again at a T intersection. You're now in Campsite Cluster H. Continue east across a small plank bridge before reaching Sand Flats Road at 2.5 miles [07]. Turn right and drive 0.5 miles [08] to campsite K5 on the left.

North side: Reset your odometer as you you turn left off Sand Flats Road [08]. Pass straight through Campsite K5 following Fins & Things signposts. Look hard for the stegosaur symbols—they're there. Climb over a small rock outcropping and drop down a steep incline. At 0.1 [09] bear right at a T intersection following a sandy groove. Go straight at 0.3 and left at 0.5 [10]. Bear right uphill at campsite L1. Bear right at 0.6 [11]. Watch for signposts. Go straight past campsite L3 at 0.7. Cross a cattle guard heading north before reaching a T intersection at 1.1 miles [12]. Turn left on a sandy road. At 1.6 miles [13] bear left as a lesser road goes right. Bear right at a fork at 1.7. Descend an area between tall rocks and pass through a fence. Go straight at 2.4 as a lesser road goes right. At 2.5 stay right on the rocks.

Bear right at 2.6 miles [14] where stegosaur symbols point both ways. Left exits past the radio tower. You'll climb on top of a fin heading west. At 2.8 bear right following symbols up a steep section of slickrock. Bear right at a T at 3.0 miles [15]. Left goes to the radio tower again. Bear left at 3.1 at a sign indicating limited use area ahead. That would be the Negro Bill Wilderness Study Area. Make left turns at 3.1 and 3.2.

At 3.7 [16] you'll pass a canyon on the right that goes to Morning Glory Arch (hiking required). Look for the natural dinosaur rock formation directly south (see photo on page 160). The main trail appears to go straight at 4.0 [17] so watch carefully. Turn right, drop down into a sandy spot and climb back up a steep section of slickrock. You'll see stegosaur symbols again after you make the turn. Bear right at 4.1 [18] as yet another road returns to the radio tower. Cross more sand before climbing onto another fin at 4.3. Make a hard right off the fin at 4.4 [19]. At 4.7 [20] turn right onto a fin as a sandy road goes left to the exit. But don't quit now, the real fun is about to begin.

Continue to follow stegosaur symbols. Straddle a narrow spot at 4.9. Climb to the top of a tall fin and descend the other side. When you reach the bottom, turn right off the slickrock at approximately 5.1 miles [21]. This is a key intersection. You'll loop around and come back to this spot in just a few minutes. At 5.3 miles [22] you can take a shortcut up a steep spot on the left called Kenny's Climb or go around. As you continue, drop down a steep section into the sand as the trail meanders to Frenchy's Fin at 5.5 [23]. Bear left around a tree and climb this short, steep obstacle. At 5.6 you descend to the intersection crossed earlier [21]. Make a hard right off the fin (see bottom photo, page 162) then immediately turn left back up a steep spot. Follow stegosaur symbols up and down more roller coaster size fins before finally leveling off. Go straight at 6.0 [20] where a sandy road joins on the left. Pass through a fence before reaching Sand Flats Road at 6.4 miles [24].

Return Trip: Turn right to return to Moab. Left takes you on easy Sand Flats Road (Trail #34) and eventually connects to La Sal Mountain Loop Road. On the way you pass the start of Porcupine Rim (Trail #33).

Services: All of the campground clusters have vault toilets. Individual campsites are more primitive and a portable toilet is required. Return to Moab for full services.

Maps: I plotted this trail using my own GPS equipment and two USGS 7.5 minute maps as follows: Moab 38109-E5 and Rill Creek 38109-E4.

The Sand Flats Recreation Area: This is a unique area restored and developed for your use through the joint efforts of the BLM, Grand County, and the Moab community. Fees are used to construct and maintain campsites, toilets, fencing, roads, parking areas, signage and trail markings. Regulations are established to protect the land so it can be enjoyed by all for many years. The rules are simple and practical: camp only in designated areas, use only routes marked with an arrow, bring your own firewood, and take out all trash and waste. Many people have worked hard to keep this area open for responsible four-wheelers. Please do your part.

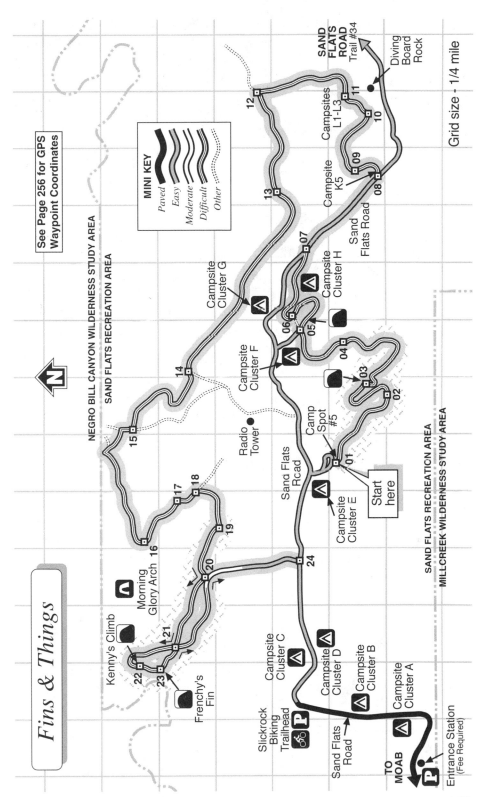

Fins & Things

See Page 256 for GPS Waypoint Coordinates

MINI KEY
Paved
Easy
Moderate
Difficult
Other

NEGRO BILL CANYON WILDERNESS STUDY AREA

SAND FLATS RECREATION AREA

N

SAND FLATS ROAD
Trail #34

Diving Board Rock

12

Campsites L1-L3

11

10

09

Campsite K5

08

13

Sand Flats Road

07

Campsite Cluster H

06

05

Campsite Cluster G

04

Campsite Cluster F

03

02

14

Camp Spot #5

15

Radio Tower

Sand Flats Road

01

Start here

Campsite Cluster E

SAND FLATS RECREATION AREA

MILLCREEK WILDERNESS STUDY AREA

17

18

16 Morning Glory Arch

Kenny's Climb

19

20

21

22

23

Frenchy's Fin

24

Slickrock Biking Trailhead

Campsite Cluster C

Campsite Cluster D

Campsite Cluster B

Sand Flats Road

Campsite Cluster A

Entrance Station (Fee Required)

TO MOAB

Grid size - 1/4 mile

165

Southeastern view from Porcupine Rim. La Sal Mountains in the distance.

Castle Rock, Priest & Nuns.

Looking northeast to Castle Valley.

One of the tougher spots.

Watch for bikers.

Porcupine Rim

MINI KEY
Paved
Easy
Moderate
Difficult
Other

Castle Valley

06

05

04

See Page 256 for GPS Waypoint Coordinates

N

TO FINS & THINGS Trail #32

Negro Bill Canyon

Water tanks

02

01

03

07

TO MOAB

Start here

SAND FLATS ROAD

Alternate Entrance

SAND FLATS ROAD Trail #34

Grid size - 1/2 mile

Porcupine Rim ◆33◆

Location: East of Moab on the western edge of Castle Valley.

Difficulty: Difficult. While there are no major obstacles, the trail is too tough for most stock vehicles. High ground clearance and skid plates recommended. Route-finding is easy.

Features: Incredible views of Castle Valley, featuring the La Sal Mountains, Castle Rock, and Priest and Nuns rock formation. A popular bike route.

Time & Distance: The complete trip back to the starting point is 8.8 miles. Allow 2 to 3 hours. This is a significantly shorter version than that driven during the Easter Jeep Safari.

To Get There: From Main Street and Center Street in the middle of Moab, go four blocks east to 400 East Street. Head south to Millcreek Drive and turn left. Go straight at the stop sign near the cemetery and follow Sand Flats Road 1.7 miles to the entrance booth of the Sand Flats Recreation Area. This is a fee area. Continue 7.1 miles farther and turn left on a lesser road at some water tanks. Please sign in at the registration box.

Trail Description: Reset your odometer as you turn off Sand Flats Road [01]. Follow a narrow road northeast around a ridge. Continue straight at 0.3 as a connecting road to Fins & Things (Trail #32) joins on the left [02]. Bear right uphill at 1.7. Continue straight at 1.9 miles [03]. You'll exit here later. The road splits and remerges. The first overlook is on the right at 3.1 miles [04]. Get out of your vehicle for the best view. The trail continues downhill to the left then returns to the rim several more times at 3.7 [05], 3.9, and 4.2 miles [06]. Bikers call the final overlook High Anxiety. *Reset your odometer at this point* and head back the way you came. (Although you can continue farther, the trail eventually narrows to a bike trail.) At 2.3 miles [03] turn left uphill and drive out the alternate exit. Bear left at 2.5. Pass through a fence before reaching Sand Flats Road at 2.6 miles [07]. Turn right and drive 2.0 miles back to the starting point.

Return Trip: Continue west on Sand Flats Road to reach Moab. Campsites have vault toilets and a fee is required. Full services in Moab.

Maps: Latitude 40°, Inc. *Moab East* Biking Map and USGS 7.5 minute map Rill Creek 38109-E4.

The road curves to the right here, then heads south into the Manti-La Sal National Forest.

Unique campsites.

The view changes dramatically at the eastern end of Sand Flats Rd.

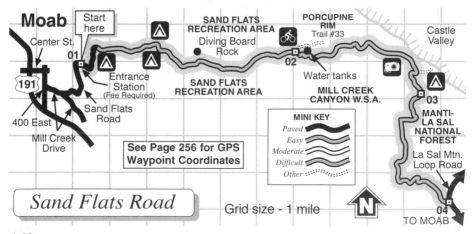

Moab

Start here

Center St.

01

191

400 East

Mill Creek Drive

Sand Flats Road

Entrance Station
(Fee Required)

SAND FLATS RECREATION AREA
Diving Board Rock

SAND FLATS RECREATION AREA

See Page 256 for GPS Waypoint Coordinates

PORCUPINE RIM
Trail #33

02

Water tanks

MILL CREEK CANYON W.S.A.

MINI KEY
Paved
Easy
Moderate
Difficult
Other

Castle Valley

03

MANTI-LA SAL NATIONAL FOREST

La Sal Mtn. Loop Road

04
TO MOAB

Sand Flats Road

Grid size - 1 mile

N

Sand Flats Road 34

Location: East of Moab and along the foothills of the La Sal Mountains.

Difficulty: Easy. A maintained county road subject to occasional deterioration. Possible muddy conditions through the forest during rainy periods. Ask about conditions at the entrance booth. Route-finding is easy.

Features: Many great camping spots (fee required) within the Sand Flats Recreation Area and one along Porcupine Rim in the La Sal National Forest. Sand Flats Road is part of Kokopelli's Bike Trail.

Time & Distance: Just under 20 miles from the entrance station to La Sal Mountain Loop Road. Allow about 1.5 hours one way.

To Get There: From Main Street and Center Street in the middle of Moab, go four blocks east to 400 East Street. Head south to Millcreek Drive and turn left. Go straight at the stop sign by the cemetery and follow Sand Flats Road 1.7 miles to the entrance booth of the Sand Flats Recreation Area. This is a fee area.

Trail Description: Reset your odometer at the entrance station [01]. Continue east past the Slickrock Bike Trailhead where the pavement ends. Pass Diving Board Rock on the left at 3.9 miles. At 7.1 miles [02] Porcupine Rim (Trail #33) goes left. Soon the road crosses a wide shelf as you pass north of the Mill Creek Canyon Wilderness Study Area. Swing right at 9.1 past the alternate entrance to Porcupine Rim Trail before entering the forest at 11.0 miles. Bear right at 11.7 as a lesser road goes left. Kokopelli's Bike Trail departs to the left at 12.4 miles [03]. You continue straight. La Sal Mountain Loop Road is reached at 19.8 miles [04].

Return Trip: Right on scenic La Sal Mountain Loop Road connects to Spanish Valley Drive into Moab (26 miles). Left goes through Castle Valley back to Moab (39 miles). Both ways are pleasant scenic drives on paved roads.

Services: Campsites have vault toilets. Return to Moab for other services.

Maps: Latitude 40°, Inc. *Moab East* Biking Map and USGS 7.5 minute maps Moab 38109-E5, Rill Creek 38109-E4, and Warner Lake 38109-E3.

The start of the trail is well marked. There's also a sign at the other end of the trail.

This shelf road, at the north end of the trail, becomes slippery and dangerous when wet.

This rocky section is encountered after the third stream crossing on the north end.

Steel Bender ◆35◆

Location: Directly southeast of Moab and north of Ken's Lake. When looking for this trail on a map, look under the name of Flat Pass.

Difficulty: Difficult. Many rock challenges and four stream crossings (usually shallow). Differential lockers are highly recommended. Under wet conditions, the shelf road at the north end of the trail becomes extremely slick and dangerous. Under worst-case conditions, it may be impassable.

Although there are many spur roads, the main trail is obvious most of the way. In addition, the trail is well marked for bikers. Watch for signposts indicating Flat Pass.

Features: An extremely popular biking trail most often ridden starting from Ken's Lake. Consequently, I find it easier to drive starting from Moab. This minimizes the leap-frogging effect that often occurs when bikers alternate climbs and descents. When bikers approach, pull over and let them pass.

A very scenic trail through the Mill Creek drainage area. Because of water quality issues, camping is only permitted at designated sites around Ken's Lake. No camping is allowed along the trail.

Time & Distance: From the start of the trail to Ken's Lake is 10.5 miles. Allow 4 to 5 hours driving time. Add time for additional vehicles

To Get There: From the McDonald's Restaurant on the south side of Moab, drive 3.6 miles south on Highway 191 and turn left on Spanish Trail Road. There's a gas station at this corner. After passing through a 3-way stop in about a mile, the road curves to the left. Turn right on Westwater Drive after the curve. The road winds through some condos and homes and heads out of town. In less than a mile, Westwater Drive ends at a gate to a private residential area. The trail is on the right just before the gate.

Trail Description (North to South): Reset your odometer at the start of the trail [01]. The trail begins with some rocky terrain—just a taste of what's to come—then swings right and begins to descend. After a gate it switchbacks to the left. If dry, this portion of the road is easy; however, if wet, it becomes extremely slippery and dangerous. When I drove this trail during the Easter Jeep Safari, we had about 4 inches of melting snow. Only a few vehicles elected to proceed, all of which experienced a near-uncontrollable slide down the hill. At the bottom of hill, make a sharp right.

171

This member of the Red Rock 4-Wheelers leads the way during an Easter Jeep Safari.

Crossing Mill Creek at the southern end. Bikers contemplate how to keep their feet dry.

Looking down from Flat Pass at Spanish Valley and Ken's Lake.

The trail crosses an open area, then enters the trees along Mill Creek. At 0.7 miles bear left at a fork and cross the creek [02]. Cross it again at 0.9. On the other side, bear left and drive parallel to a washed-out ravine. Cross the creek a third time at 1.4 miles [03] and begin a gradual climb out of the valley. The valley ends with a steep rocky climb. Make a hard right as two roads go left at 2.5 miles [04]. Bear right at a fork at 3.1 [05]. There's a wide expanse of slickrock at 3.3, but you can see the trail as it exits the other side. Continue straight as several spurs go uphill to the left.

Pass through a gate at 3.6 [06] and drop down a short, steep hill. There's a nasty ledge about halfway down with a scary drop-off on the right. At 4.7 miles [07] the main road appears to go straight. Turn right and head downhill. Signs point both ways. Straight takes you through an almost impassable section called the Dragon's Tail. At 5.0 [08] you come to a confusing diagonal 4-way intersection. Straight or left comes back together in a short distance. I went left downhill. The Dragon's Tail rejoins the trail on the left at 5.2.

At 6.1 miles [09] there's a driver's choice. The first left is the most difficult route up a very challenging series of ledges. I managed to get up this section during the safari when it was wet and muddy but my Cherokee took some punishment. The bypass goes right then curves up the hill to the left. From this point, the trail is one big ledge after another. A big drop at 6.5 [10] catches my rear bumper every time. After a series of ledges at 6.9 [11], bear left as the trail appears to go straight. Drop down into a ravine and start up the other side. The choice on the right is more difficult.

The highest point on the trail is reached at 7.4 miles. Bikers breathe a sigh of relief at this point. From here you descend quickly through a beautiful, narrow canyon. Pass through a barbed wire gate at 8.5 miles [12] then drop down a steep section. Twist through the canyon before reaching Mill Creek for the last time at 8.7 miles [13]. This crossing is more difficult than the others with a high rock bank on the opposite side. You should turn right after exiting the creek but the turn is too sharp. Circle around to the left at an area provided for this purpose then head northwest along the creek. Turn left uphill on a wide gravel road at 9.1 miles [14]. A cattle guard marks Flat Pass at 9.4. There's a scenic overlook on the right after the cattle guard.

Return Trip: Follow the gravel road downhill past Ken's Lake where the road is paved before reaching Spanish Valley Drive. Turn right and drive north 1.5 miles where a left on County Road 194 takes you to Highway 191. Moab is about 7 miles to the right.

Trail Description (South to North): *(Caution: Do not attempt to drive in this direction under very wet conditions. The clay shelf road at the end of the trail becomes extremely slippery and may be impassable.)*

Cut over from Highway 191 at mile post 118 to Spanish Valley Drive. Go by a gravel operation and turn right. About 1.5 miles south, turn left on the paved access road to Ken's Lake. Continue straight uphill past the lake on a wide gravel road to Flat Pass, marked by an overlook and cattle guard. Continue straight downhill 0.3 miles and turn right on a lesser road marked with a sign for Steel Bender. The trail starts here.

Reset your odometer [14]. Follow a single-lane road along Mill Creek southeast to a turnaround area. The trail drops down a steep bank on the left and crosses Mill Creek at 0.4 [13]. The road twists and climbs through a beautiful canyon before reaching a barbed wire gate at 0.6 miles [12]. Reach the highest point on the trail at 1.7 miles. You'll eventually descend to the bottom of a narrow ravine. Bear right up a series of ledges as you climb out of the ravine at 2.2 miles [11]. There's a big ledge at 2.6 [10] with more to come. At 2.9 miles [09], there's an optional challenge to the right. A bypass goes left then swings right downhill. Continue straight at 3.9 as a road goes left. Bear right at a diagonal 4-way intersection at 4.1 miles [08]. At 4.4 miles [07] turn left at a T intersection.

At 5.4 miles climb a hill with two big ledges and a drop-off to the left. Close the gate [06] at the top of the hill. Continue straight as spurs go right uphill. Continue straight across an expanse of slickrock at 5.7 then bear left at a fork at 6.0 [05]. Make a hard left at 6.6 [04] as two spurs go right. Drop down through a rocky section as you descend into a canyon. Cross Mill Creek three times at 7.7 [03], 8.2, and 8.4 miles [02]. After the last crossing bear right. After crossing an open field, bear left up a shelf road out of the valley. If wet, this shelf road may be impassable. The trail ends at Westwater Drive at 9.1 miles [01].

To reach Moab, turn left on Westwater Drive. Descend 0.9 miles and turn left at Canyonlands Circle onto Spanish Trail Road. The road curves to the right and intersects with Highway 191 in about a mile. Turn right for Moab.

Services: None along the trail. You must return to Moab.

Maps: Latitude 40°, Inc. *Moab East* Biking Map and USGS 7.5 minute maps Rill Creek 39109-E4 and Kane Springs 38109-D4.

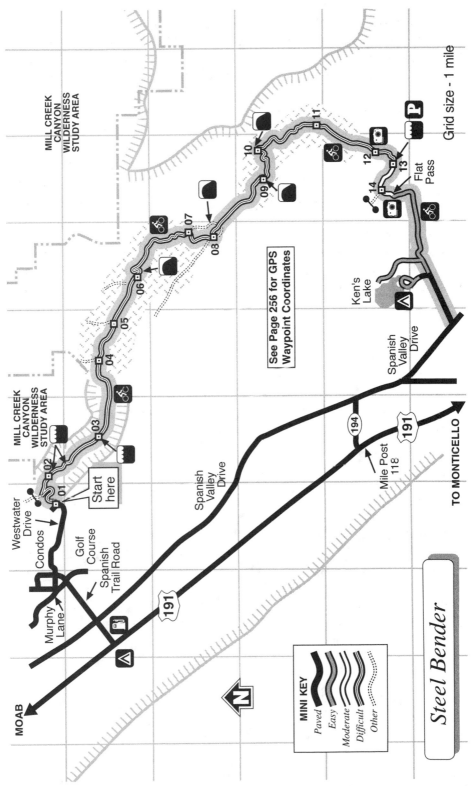

MILL CREEK CANYON WILDERNESS STUDY AREA

Grid size - 1 mile

Flat Pass

See Page 256 for GPS Waypoint Coordinates

Ken's Lake

Spanish Valley Drive

194

191

Mile Post 118

TO MONTICELLO

Spanish Valley Drive

MILL CREEK CANYON WILDERNESS STUDY AREA

Start here

Westwater Drive

Condos

Golf Course

Spanish Trail Road

Murphy Lane

191

MOAB

N

MINI KEY
Paved
Easy
Moderate
Difficult
Other

Steel Bender

175

AREA 3

East Moab &
Manti-La Sal
National Forest

36. Onion Creek,
    Fisher Towers
37. Top of the World
38. Rose Garden Hill
39. Thompson Canyon
40. Geyser Pass
41. La Sal Pass

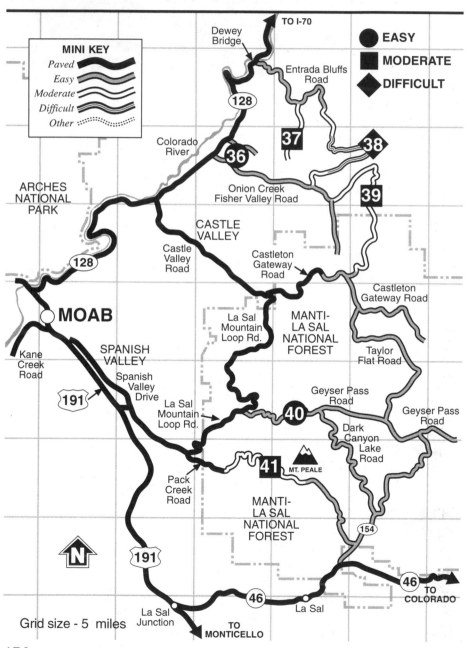

MINI KEY
Paved
Easy
Moderate
Difficult
Other

● EASY
■ MODERATE
◆ DIFFICULT

TO I-70

Dewey
Bridge

Entrada Bluffs
Road

128

Colorado
River

37

38

36

ARCHES
NATIONAL
PARK

Onion Creek
Fisher Valley Road

39

CASTLE
VALLEY

Castle
Valley
Road

Castleton
Gateway
Road

Castleton
Gateway Road

128

MANTI-
LA SAL
NATIONAL
FOREST

MOAB

Kane
Creek
Road

SPANISH
VALLEY

La Sal
Mountain
Loop Rd.

Taylor
Flat Road

Spanish
Valley
Drive

191

La Sal
Mountain
Loop Rd.

Geyser Pass
Road

40

Geyser Pass
Road

Dark
Canyon
Lake
Road

41 MT. PEALE

Pack
Creek
Road

MANTI-
LA SAL
NATIONAL
FOREST

154

N

191

46

TO
COLORADO

Grid size - 5 miles

La Sal
Junction

46

La Sal

TO
MONTICELLO

176

East Moab & Manti-La Sal National Forest

When hot summer months arrive in Moab, beat the heat by heading east to the La Sal Mountains. Within minutes, you'll find yourself looking down on Moab and Spanish Valley from elevations above ten thousand feet. On a clear day, from La Sal Pass (#41) and Top of the World (#37), you can see neighboring Colorado. Select from all levels of difficulty, including easy Onion Creek (#36) and Geyser Pass (#40) to difficult Rose Garden Hill (#38). In between, choose from three moderate adventures, including Thompson Canyon (#39) which doubles as a part of popular Kokopelli's Bike Trail. Just driving to the trails is enough beauty for most people. Enjoy the serenity of the majestic Colorado River as you cruise along paved Highway 128. Or cut through Castle Valley where incredible rock formations like Castle Rock and Priest and Nuns have served countless times as backdrops for many popular western movies. For some, just cruising paved La Sal Mountain Loop Road will satisfy the need to get away.

Looking west at South Mountain from the east side of La Sal Pass (Trail #41).

Onion Creek is usually just a trickle but can become deep after a heavy rain.

Onion Creek Road crosses open rangeland. Take your time and watch for cattle.

Looking south from Hwy. 128 at Fisher Towers, La Sal Mountains, and Colorado River.

Onion Creek, Fisher Towers 36

Location: Northeast of Moab, southeast of Highway 128.

Difficulty: Easy. Onion Creek Road is a well-maintained road but susceptible to washouts along numerous crossings of Onion Creek. This creek is usually just a trickle but can be deep following heavy rains. The upper section can be slippery and dangerous when wet. The road to Fisher Towers is suitable for passenger cars. Route-finding is extremely easy on both roads.

Features: Onion Creek Road is a relaxing drive through a beautiful deep-cut canyon. Great camping spots are designated along the route. Portable toilets are required in these spots. Please carry out all trash. Fisher Towers is a popular tourist attraction with spectacular red rock towers reaching 900 ft. in height.

Time & Distance: Onion Creek Road as described here is about 10 miles one way. Fisher Towers is about 2 miles one way. Allow 2 hours round-trip driving time for Onion Creek and about 30 minutes for Fisher Towers. With stops for hikes and picnics, you can easily spend a full day in the area.

To Get There: From Highway 191 north of Moab, drive 20.2 miles northeast on Highway 128 following the Colorado River. Turn right on a wide gravel road marked by a sign for Taylor Ranch. After you turn, you'll see a small sign for Onion Creek. For Fisher Towers, stay on 128 another 0.8 miles and turn right at mile post 21.

Trail Description: Reset your odometer as you turn right off Highway 128 onto Onion Creek Road [01]. You'll pass a parking area before the first creek crossing within the first mile. Many more creek crossings follow. This is open range so watch for cattle on the road. I ran into a cattle drive on one of my trips (see photo at left). Cross a small picturesque bridge at 3.6 miles. Prior to the construction of this bridge, the road actually followed the narrow creek under the bridge.

    Your nose will tell you when you pass by Stinking Spring, a sulphur-based natural spring. Soon a sign indicates you are leaving the Colorado River Recreation Area. You'll begin to climb out of the canyon on a winding road. Be careful here; this part of the road can be very slippery when wet. Continue as long as you feel comfortable, as Onion Creek Road changes to Fisher Valley Road. Make sure you leave all gates as you find them. At 9.4 miles Cottonwood Canyon Trail goes left [02]. This is part of

Kokopelli's Bike Trail. It is also the way to difficult Rose Garden Hill (Trail #38). Thompson Canyon (Trail #39) goes left in another mile [03]. Right eventually dead-ends at private property.

Return Trip: To stay on easy terrain, turn around and head back to Highway 128. From there, turn right to visit Fisher Towers. If you are equipped for moderate terrain, you may proceed up through Thompson Canyon (Trail #39) under dry conditions. (This book describes the trail in the opposite direction.) If you are equipped for very difficult terrain, proceed up Cottonwood Canyon to Rose Garden Hill (Trail #38). This is a long trip and eventually takes you back to 128 near the Dewey Bridge.

Services: Onion Creek Road has no toilet facilities. If you camp along Onion Creek Road, you are required to bring your own portable toilet. There are many vault toilets along Highway 128 back to Moab. Fisher Towers has a small, 5-site fee campground with tables, grills, and a vault toilet.

Maps: Latitude 40°, Inc. *Moab East* Biking Map and USGS 7.5 minute maps Fisher Towers 38109-F3 and Fisher Valley 38109-F2.

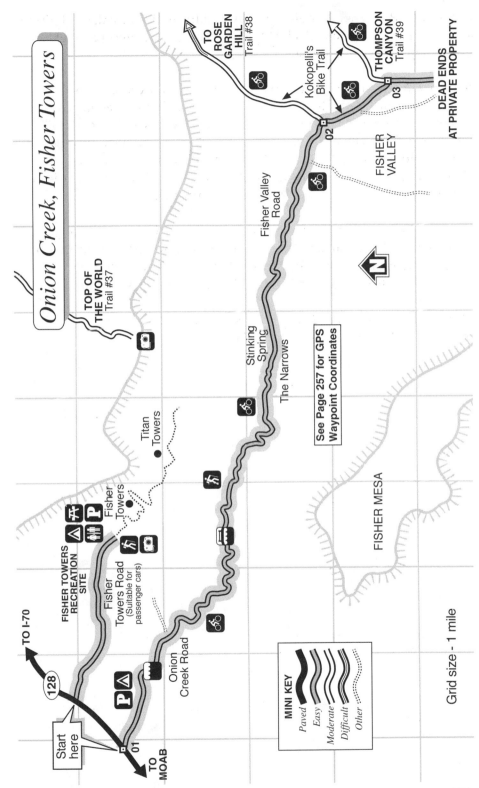

Onion Creek, Fisher Towers

TO ROSE GARDEN HILL Trail #38

THOMPSON CANYON Trail #39

Kokopelli's Bike Trail

DEAD ENDS AT PRIVATE PROPERTY

FISHER VALLEY

03

02

Fisher Valley Road

TOP OF THE WORLD Trail #37

N

Stinking Spring

The Narrows

See Page 257 for GPS Waypoint Coordinates

Titan Towers

FISHER MESA

FISHER TOWERS RECREATION SITE

Fisher Towers

Fisher Towers Road (Suitable for passenger cars)

TO I-70

128

Onion Creek Road

Start here

01

TO MOAB

MINI KEY

Paved
Easy
Moderate
Difficult
Other

Grid size - 1 mile

181

Recent rains filled this stream crossing on Entrada Bluffs Road with more water than usual.

Typical rock ledge on upper part of trail requires careful tire placement for stock vehicles.

View looking west from the Top of the World .

Photo by Robert Omer

Top of the World

Location: Northeast of Moab, southeast of Highway 128 at the Dewey Bridge.

Difficulty: Moderate. A rocky climb over several challenging ledges. Stock, high-clearance vehicles can manage this trail, but careful tire placement is necessary. Previous off-highway driving experience and skid plates are recommended. A great trail for SUV owners ready for more challenge. Route-finding is fairly easy.

Features: The trail culminates at one of the most dramatic overlooks in the Moab area. On a clear day you can see Titan and Mystery Towers, the La Sal Mountains, the Priest and Nuns rock formation in Castle Valley, Arches National Park, and western Colorado.

Time & Distance: Allow adequate time to reach the start of the trail. It's about 30 miles northeast of Moab on scenic but winding paved Utah Highway 128. From there, you'll drive 9.6 miles one-way to the top of the trail. You must go very slowly near the top. Allow 3 to 4 hours for the round trip once on Entrada Bluffs Road.

To Get There: From the intersection of Highways 191 and 128 north of Moab, drive 29.8 miles northeast on Highway 128 to the Dewey Bridge. Turn right just before the bridge on Entrada Bluffs Road—a wide gravel county road at this point. You are now traveling on Kokopelli's Trail.

Trail Description: Reset your odometer as you turn off 128 [01]. Entrada Bluffs Road heads east then gradually swings south. Continue straight across a small water crossing at 2.0 miles. It may be muddy and deep in the spring. A road goes right at 4.6 miles but don't turn yet. At 5.3 miles [02] turn right on a smaller red sandy road (You are now leaving Kokopelli's Trail). Immediately turn right again at a 4-way intersection. Pass through a gate at 5.7 miles. Continue straight as you begin to encounter rockier sections. There is some slickrock but the trail is discernable. Bear right at a fork at 8.6 miles [03]. The trail will loop around and come back to this point later. Another section of slickrock is encountered at 9.1. Watch for signs of the trail, which goes just a little right across the slickrock. You'll reach the top of a ridge at 9.6 miles [04]. Park on the slickrock just before the ridge. Walk to the edge for an outstanding view. Be careful—there are no hand rails at the cliff edge. Children should be closely supervised. This is a great spot for lunch.

Reset your odometer at the top [04]. Head back down east of where you came up. There are a couple of rough spots at 0.4 and 0.6 miles. Take your time and watch your tire placement. Use a spotter if necessary. At 1.1 miles the loop is completed as you return to the intersection mentioned earlier [03]. Turn right and retrace your steps back to Entrada Bluffs Road.

Return Trip: Turn left on Entrada Bluffs Road back to Highway 128. From there, turn left for Moab or right for Cisco and Interstate 70.

Services: Cowskin Campsite along Entrada Bluffs Road has a vault toilet. There is a larger campground with vault toilets near the Dewey Bridge. Many other campgrounds and recreation sites are located along Highway 128 on the way back to Moab. Natural spring water is available at Matrimony Springs on the south side of 128 just east of 191. For all other services you must return to Moab.

The Dewey Bridge: If you are not familiar with the history of the old Dewey Bridge, take a few moments to read the sign at the start of Entrada Bluffs Road. The old bridge, completed in 1916, was replaced in the 1980s by a more modern concrete structure. Foot and bicycle traffic are allowed on the old bridge. (Note: At the time of this writing, the old bridge was closed for refurbishing as part of Grand County's 100-year statehood project. It will be reopened when refurbishing is completed.)

Maps: Latitude 40°, Inc. *Moab East* Biking Map and USGS 7.5 minute maps Dewey 38109-G3, Blue Chief Mesa 38109-G2, Fisher Towers 38109-F3, and Fisher Valley 38109-F2.

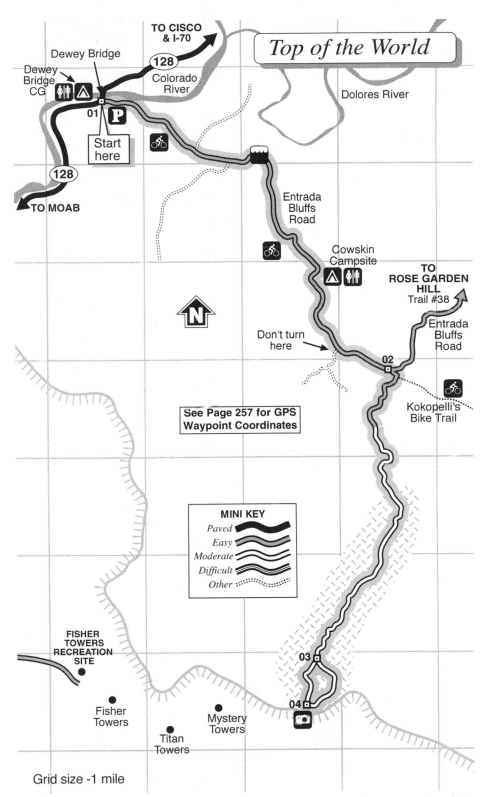

Top of the World

TO CISCO & I-70

128

Colorado River

Dewey Bridge

Dewey Bridge CG

01

P

Start here

128

TO MOAB

Dolores River

Entrada Bluffs Road

Cowskin Campsite

TO ROSE GARDEN HILL
Trail #38

Entrada Bluffs Road

Don't turn here

02

Kokopelli's Bike Trail

N

See Page 257 for GPS Waypoint Coordinates

MINI KEY
Paved
Easy
Moderate
Difficult
Other

FISHER TOWERS RECREATION SITE

Fisher Towers

Titan Towers

Mystery Towers

03

04

Grid size -1 mile

Starting up Rose Garden Hill. It gets steeper and more difficult near the top.

Cottonwood Canyon Trail.

Photos don't capture steepness of hill.

Rose Garden Hill 38

Location: Northeast of Moab, southeast of the Dewey Bridge on Hwy. 128.

Difficulty: Difficult. Rose Garden Hill—a quarter mile of steep, loose rock mixed with high ledges—is the featured obstacle on this trail and is a challenge for any hard-core vehicle. In addition, there are several tough spots above the hill including one very tippy spot. Under wet conditions, the easy parts of the trail can become a quagmire so it is recommended that you drive this trail when it is dry. Lockers and high ground clearance are a must. Don't drive this trail alone.

    The trail is well defined with no confusing slickrock. Junctions above Rose Garden Hill can be confusing so pay close attention to directions. Please stay on designated roads at all times.

Features: Obviously, for hard-core four-wheelers, the main attraction of this trail is Rose Garden Hill. The trail sees little use by four-wheelers except during the Easter Jeep Safari. Although this trail is part of Kokopelli's Bike Trail, it sees only light use by bikers much of the time. It's a great place to enjoy some beautiful secluded backcountry. The day our group drove the trail, we didn't see a single person between Onion Creek Road and Entrada Bluffs Road.

Time & Distance: The entire backcountry portion of the trip from Highway 128 at Onion Creek to the Dewey Bridge is 29.4 miles. Allow 4 to 5 hours for a small, capable group.

To Get There: From Highway 191 north of Moab, drive 20.2 miles northeast on Highway 128 following the Colorado River. Turn right on a wide gravel road marked by a sign for Taylor Ranch. After you turn, you'll see a small sign for Onion Creek. Follow Onion Creek Road southeast 9.4 miles and turn left on a single-lane road into Cottonwood Canyon. You are now on Kokopelli's Trail.

Trail Description: *Reset your odometer as you turn off Onion Creek Road into Cottonwood Canyon* [01]. At 0.4 miles bypass an area frequently washed out by rainstorms. When our group passed through here, the entire road was gone. Apparently it had been washed out for some time because a new road had formed around the bad spot. Under very wet conditions, this spot could be impassable. After this spot bear left.

    At mile 2.0 bear left as a lesser spur goes right. You'll soon reach the base of Rose Garden Hill at 3.1 miles [02]. You may want to inspect the hill before you start up. One member of our group broke an axle on the hill and we spent half the night winching the vehicle back down. The top of the hill is reached at 3.4 miles. Use caution at 5.2 miles [03] where you ascend a steep section of undulating terrain. It's narrow and a misplaced tire could result in a rollover. Other challenges follow as the road twists through several tight spots. Go straight at 5.9 miles as spurs go left and right [04].

You reach a major 4-way intersection at 6.7 miles [05]. Go straight again. Right goes to the Dolores River overlook. Road conditions improve and four-wheel-drive soon becomes unnecessary. Go straight at 7.5 as a lesser road joins on the left. At 10.6 miles go straight as Kokopelli's Bike Trail goes left. You'll rejoin it later. Bear left at the bottom of the canyon at 12.6 miles [06]. The road to the right dead ends. This is where Entrada Bluffs Road begins. You pass the turn-off for Top of the World (Trail #37) on the left at 14.8 miles [07] before reaching Highway 128 at 20.0 miles.

Return Trip: Turn left for Moab or right for Cisco and Interstate 70.

Services: The Dewey Bridge Campgrounds at Highway 128 has vault toilets. More toilets are available at various campgrounds and recreation sites along Highway 128 back to Moab. Natural spring water is available at Matrimony Springs on the south side of 128 just east of 191. For all other services, you must return to Moab.

The Dewey Bridge: If you are not familiar with the history of the old Dewey Bridge, take a few moments to read the sign where Entrada Bluffs Road reaches Highway 128. The old bridge, completed in 1916, was replaced in the 1980s by a more modern concrete structure. Foot and bicycle traffic are allowed on the old bridge. (Note: At the time of this writing, the old bridge was closed for refurbishing as part of Grand County's 100-year statehood project. It will be reopened when refurbishing is completed.)

Maps: Latitude 40°, Inc. *Moab East* Biking Map and USGS 7.5 minute maps Blue Chief Mesa 38109-G2 and Fisher Valley 38109-F2.

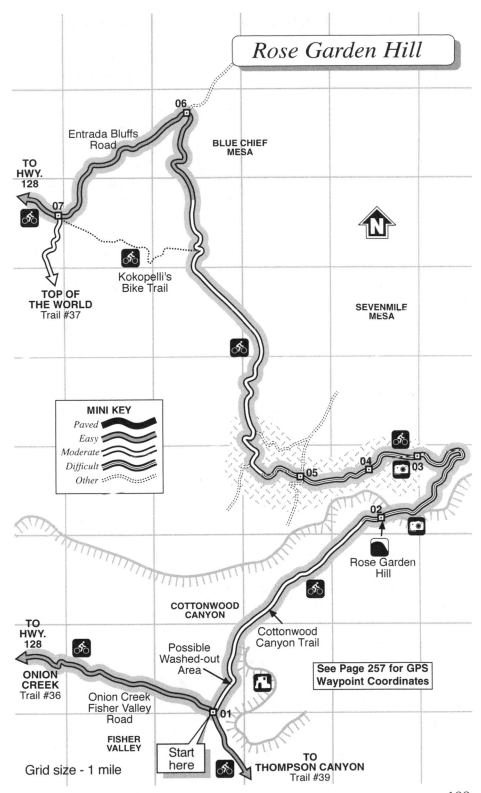

Rose Garden Hill

06

Entrada Bluffs
Road

**BLUE CHIEF
MESA**

TO
HWY.
128

07

N

Kokopelli's
Bike Trail

**TOP OF
THE WORLD**
Trail #37

**SEVENMILE
MESA**

MINI KEY
Paved
Easy
Moderate
Difficult
Other

04 **03**
05

02

Rose Garden
Hill

**COTTONWOOD
CANYON**

Cottonwood
Canyon Trail

TO
HWY.
128

**See Page 257 for GPS
Waypoint Coordinates**

**ONION
CREEK**
Trail #36

Possible
Washed-out
Area

Onion Creek
Fisher Valley
Road

01

**FISHER
VALLEY**

Start
here

**TO
THOMPSON CANYON**
Trail #39

Grid size - 1 mile

Fisher Valley as seen from Castleton Gateway Road from above 8,000 feet.

Much of this trail is easy with time to enjoy scenes like this.

Several places are rocky and steep.   One final descent into Fisher Valley.

Thompson Canyon 39

Location: East of Moab and Castle Valley.

Difficulty: Moderate. When dry, most of this trail is easy except for a few moderately steep, rocky sections. Wet conditions can make the trail difficult and even impassable. One section of shelf road can become slippery and dangerous when wet. Suitable for stock, high-clearance, four-wheel-drive vehicles when dry. Route-finding is easy.

Features: This trail provides respite from Moab's hot summer temperatures as it climbs over 8,000 feet into the La Sal Mountains. The scenic drive through Castle Valley is enhanced when viewed from high in the mountains. Once on the trail, enjoy scenery reminiscent of Colorado. This trail is part of Kokopelli's Bike Trail so watch for bikers.

Time & Distance: The entire round trip from the north side of Moab and back is about 80 miles. Allow about 5 hours driving time plus stops.

To Get There: Reset your odometer at Highway 191 and 128 north of Moab and follow Highway 128 northeast along the Colorado River 15.5 miles. Turn right on Castle Valley Road (also marked as La Sal Mountain Loop Road). Go straight on Castleton Gateway Road at 26.1 miles where the La Sal Mountain Loop Road goes right. Turn left at 33.9 miles on F.S.33, following signs for Kokopelli's Bike Trail. Turn left on lesser Forest Service road 605 at 38.1 miles. If you're driving the trail in the opposite direction, see Onion Creek, Fisher Towers (Trail #36).

Trail Description: Reset your odometer at the start [01]. Head north on F.S. 605. The road narrows and becomes rockier within the first mile. At 1.7 miles you'll exit the forest at a gate. If wet, it can be quite muddy at this point. As you begin to descend at 3.3 miles, shift into low range and use engine compression to brake. At some point, the bike trail splits off to the right as the main road goes left along the edge of Hideout Canyon. (These two roads join up again soon.) You'll begin a gradual descent into Thompson Canyon, which can be seen on the right. The trail is well defined. At 6.6 miles a rougher downhill section is encountered. There's a small rock ledge at 7.9 followed by another steep downhill spot at 8.5. You can shift into two-wheel-drive at 8.7 miles as the road smooths out across a stretch of soft red sand. Go straight at 9.2 miles where a road to Hideout Campsite goes left [02]. At 10.0 shift back into four-wheel-drive to climb a narrow shelf road over one last ridge. This section can be very slippery and dangerous if wet. At the top of the ridge at 10.2 miles [03], you'll pass through a gate and start a gentle descent with a great view of the La Sal Mountains ahead. At 10.9 miles [04] turn right as the trail intersects with Onion Creek/ Fisher Valley Road. *Reset your odometer.*

Return Trip: Rose Garden Hill (Trail #38) goes right at 1.0 miles. Continue left past this point 9.4 miles to Highway 128 where a left turn takes you back to Moab in 20.2 miles.

Trail Description (*In reverse direction starting at Onion Creek*): Follow directions for Onion Creek, Fisher Towers (Trail #36). Thompson Canyon goes left 10.4 miles east on Onion Creek Road [04]. Climb to a gate and descend a narrow shelf road at 0.7 miles [03]. This area can be slippery and dangerous when wet. At 1.7 miles pass a side road on the right to Hideout Campsite [02]. Climb rocky sections at 2.4, 3.0, and 4.3 miles. Pass along the edge of Hideout Canyon at 7.3 miles, then begin climbing before reaching a range gate at 9.2. This area can get muddy after a rain. When you reach F.S. 33 at 10.9 miles [01], turn right. (A left here would take you to Polar Mesa.) In another 4.2 miles turn right on Castleton Gateway Road. Descend to Castle Valley Road and continue northeast to Highway 128 where a left turn takes you back to Moab.

Services: Vault toilets are located at various campgrounds and recreation sites along Highway 128. Natural spring water is available at Matrimony Springs on the south side of 128 just east of 191. Otherwise, return to Moab.

Maps: Latitude 40°, Inc. *Moab East* Biking Map and USGS 7.5 minute map Fisher Valley 38109-F2.

Thompson Canyon

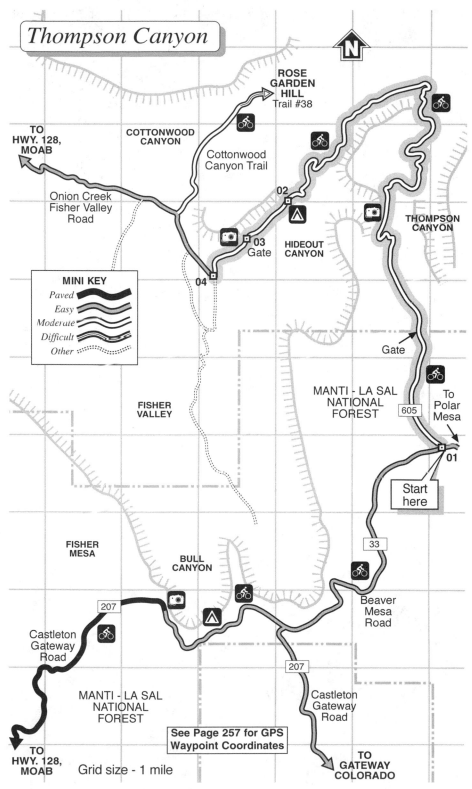

N

ROSE GARDEN HILL
Trail #38

COTTONWOOD CANYON

TO HWY. 128, MOAB

Cottonwood Canyon Trail

Onion Creek Fisher Valley Road

THOMPSON CANYON

02

HIDEOUT CANYON

03 Gate

04

MINI KEY
Paved
Easy
Moderate
Difficult
Other

Gate

FISHER VALLEY

MANTI - LA SAL NATIONAL FOREST

605

To Polar Mesa

01

Start here

FISHER MESA

BULL CANYON

33

207

Castleton Gateway Road

Beaver Mesa Road

207

Castleton Gateway Road

MANTI - LA SAL NATIONAL FOREST

See Page 257 for GPS Waypoint Coordinates

TO HWY. 128, MOAB

Grid size - 1 mile

TO GATEWAY COLORADO

193

Geyser Pass at 10,600 ft. is heavily treed with some nice camping spots but no views.

Much of the road is open rangeland. Watch for cattle crossing road.

Mt. Peale is the highest peak in the La Sals.   Aspens are seen at higher elevations.

Geyser Pass 40

Location: East of Moab in the La Sal Mountains.

Difficulty: Easy. The west side of the pass is a wide, smooth gravel road suitable for most passenger cars when dry. The east side is narrower and rockier but suitable for any stock sport utility vehicle. Roads are well marked and route-finding is easy.

Features: A relaxing and pretty drive through the La Sal Mountains. Hike or mountain bike in the area or just enjoy a relaxing picnic. Great views of Spanish Valley from the west side and Mt. Peale from the east side. Mt. Peale is the highest peak in the La Sal Mountains at 12,721 ft.

Time & Distance: From La Sal Mountain Loop Road to Highway 46 is 25.1 miles as described here. Allow about 2 hours one way. With transit time to and from the trail, this drive can easily fill a morning or afternoon.

To Get There: Head south on Highway 191 from Moab. About 7.1 miles south of town turn left, following signs for the La Sal Mountain Loop Road at mile post 118. Pass by a gravel operation and turn right on Spanish Valley Drive. Stay on this paved road as it eventually turns north and becomes the La Sal Mountain Loop road marked as County Road 126. The turn for Geyser Pass is about 21 miles from Moab. Watch for a well-marked, wide gravel road on the right. Don't go too far; there's another turn farther north that goes to Oowah Lake.

Trail Description (West to East): *Reset your odometer as you turn off La Sal Mountain Loop Road* [01]. Follow a wide gravel road as it begins a gradual climb toward Geyser Pass. There's a hiking and biking trail at 2.9 miles with a small place to park and a nice view. A much larger parking area with modern vault toilets is reached at 4.5 miles [02]. Bear left at 5.5 as Gold Basin Road goes right. The forest thickens as views become less frequent. By the time you reach Geyser Pass at 7.8 miles [03], there are no views at all. Bear right at the pass. At 8.4 miles bear right again as a spur goes left to Blue Lake. At 11.9 bear left as a lesser road goes right. Bear right at 13.2. At 13.3 [04] you intersect with Dark Canyon Lake Road F.S. 129. Bear right; the lake is left. Continue straight at 16.7 [05] as an equal size road joins on the right. Turn right when you reach F.S. 208 at 20.6 miles [06].

　　At 23.2 miles La Sal Pass (Trail #41) goes right. You can return to Moab this way, but be aware that the west side descent is rated moderate. It is rockier and narrower than Geyser Pass Road. At one point, you must traverse a shelf road across a loose talus slope.

At 23.6 miles a road goes left to Paradox. Bear right staying on F.S. 208 to reach Highway 46 at 25.1 miles [07].

.

Return Trip: To reach Moab, turn right on Highway 46. When it intersects with Highway 191, turn right again.

Trail Description (East to West): These directions are intended for use as a return route for La Sal Pass (Trail #41). If not driving La Sal Pass, take Highway 191 south from Moab and Highway 46 east to County Road 154 [07].

Reset your odometer at Highway 46 and County Road 154. Drive 4.5 miles north on C.R. 154 and turn left [06] onto Dark Canyon Road F.S. 129. Bear right at an unmarked fork at 8.3 miles [05]. At 11.7 [04] bear left as 129 goes right to Dark Canyon Lake. Bear left again at 11.8 and right at 12.9. At 16.6 miles, where a road goes right to Blue Lake, you stay left. Bear left again at Geyser Pass at 17.2 miles [03].

The road quickly improves and widens as you descend. At 20.6 pass a large parking area and vault toilet on the right [02]. Note the hiking and biking trail at 22.1 miles. Turn left for Moab when you reach La Sal Mountain Loop Road at 25.1 miles [01]. Moab is about 21 miles from this point.

Services: Just one vault toilet on the west side of the pass. Return to Moab for all other services.

Maps: Latitude 40°, Inc. *Moab East* Biking Map and USGS 7.5 minute maps Mt. Peale 38109-D2, La Sal East 38109-C2, and Mt.Tukuhnikivatz 38109-D3.

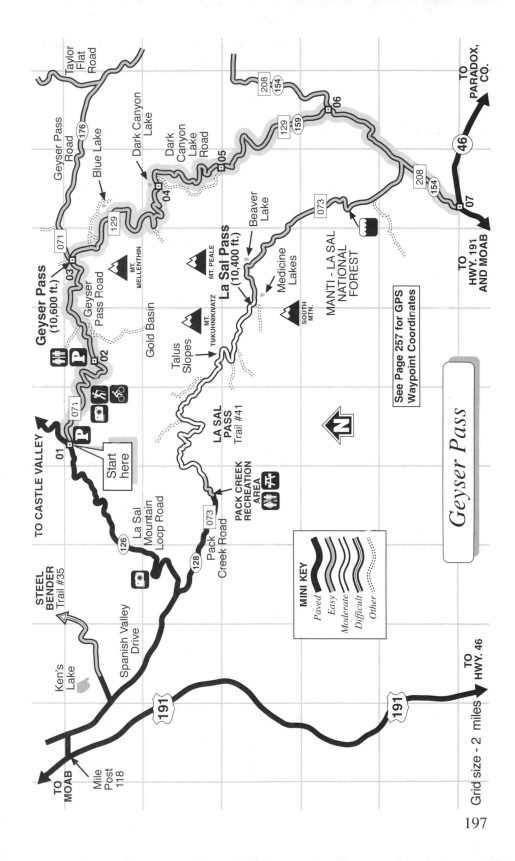

Geyser Pass

Ledge portion of the trail on the west side.   Approaching Mt. Tukuhnikivatz.

Proceed slowly across this talus slope and stay centered on the trail.

La Sal Pass looking north to Mt. Peale. The east side descent gets easier from this point.

La Sal Pass

41

Location: East of Moab in the La Sal Mountains.

Difficulty: Moderate. This trail is suitable for stock high-clearance vehicles when dry but it is steep, rocky, and narrow in places on the west side. Brush comes in contact with sides of vehicle. Wide vehicles may be scratched. Several places along the trail are often muddy even during periods of dry weather. Do not drive this trail after a prolonged period of wet weather. One talus slope is quite rocky but manageable if you drive slowly. Stay in the middle of the trail and do not disturb the talus slope. The east side is easy and suitable for most passenger cars when dry. Route-finding is easy.

Features: A great drive for sport utility owners looking for some challenge. La Sal Pass offers close-up views of Mt. Peale, the highest peak in the La Sal Mountains at 12,721 ft. Spur roads take you to Medicine and Beaver Lakes.

Time & Distance: The trail, as described here, is 18.1 miles. Progress is slow on the west side so allow about 3 hours one way. Add transit time to and from the trail. To minimize driving on paved roads, return via Geyser Pass (Trail #40).

To Get There: Head south on Highway 191 from Moab. About 7.1 miles south of town turn left, following signs for the La Sal Mountain Loop Road at mile post 118. Pass by a gravel operation and turn right on Spanish Valley Drive. Stay on this paved road 4.8 miles and turn right on Pack Creek Road, marked as County Road 128. It becomes F.S. 73. The pavement ends at the Pack Creek Recreation Area in 2.7 miles.

Trail Description (West to East): Reset your odometer where the pavement ends [01]. Drive through a picnic area and past a vault toilet. Turn left uphill at 0.2 miles. The road dead ends if you go straight. At 0.3 miles the trail appears to end at a wide place where you can turn around. Just around the corner, the trail continues. The road narrows and quickly shows signs of low maintenance. You'll want to shift into low gear as it gets steeper. Some of these steeper sections can become very slippery under wet conditions. Pass through a narrow area of dense scrub oak. Be careful not to scratch your paint. After passing through a scenic section of forest, bear right at 5.6 miles.

Bear left uphill at 6.1 miles [02] as the trail becomes quite narrow. Watch for range cattle in the middle of the trail. They can appear suddenly with no room to move out of your way. Be patient and quiet until there is room for them to step aside.

Bear right at 6.5 miles at a juncture with F.S. Road 700. Left is overgrown from disuse. You're greeted by a daunting talus slope at 6.9 miles. It is manageable at a slow pace. Stay in the center to avoid disturbing any rocks along the side of the trail. Although rare, rock slides are possible. The road crosses a small stream and climbs up a couple of switchbacks before reaching a fork at 7.6 miles [03]. Bear left at the fork. The road can be muddy through this section before crossing a cattle guard at 8.4.

La Sal Pass is reached at 9.4 miles [04], identified by a sign for Mt. Peale on the left. The road widens and, when dry, is suitable for two-wheel drive the rest of the way. Bear left at 9.7 as a spur goes right to Medicine Lakes. A spur to Beaver Lake goes left at 10.6 miles [05]. You go right. Cross a stream at 14.5 before reaching County Road 154 at 16.5 miles [06]. Turn right, followed by another right at 16.9 before reaching paved Highway 46 at 18.4 miles [07].

Return Trip: Turn right on Highway 46 to return to Moab. When you get to Highway 191 turn right again. A more interesting return route is to head north on C.R. 154 then west over Geyser Pass (Trail #40).

Trail Description (East to West): These directions are intended for use as a return route for Geyser Pass (Trail #40). If not driving Geyser Pass, take Highway 191 south from Moab and Highway 46 east to C.R. 154.

Reset your odometer as you turn off 46 [07] and drive 1.8 miles north on C.R. 154. Turn left on well-marked La Sal Pass Road [06]. At 7.8 miles bear left where Beaver Lake goes right [05]. Continue west over La Sal Pass at 9.0 miles [04]. Continue straight as a road joins on the left at 10.8 miles [03], then follow switchbacks downhill. Cross a talus slope at 11.4 and bear left at 11.9. Bear right at 12.3 [02] as a road joins on the left. Continue straight at 12.8. At 18.2 turn right and pass through a picnic area [01]. Follow Pack Creek Road and Spanish Valley Drive northwest back to Moab.

Services: There's a vault toilet at the start of the trail at the Pack Creek Recreation Area and one on the west side of Geyser Pass. There's also a nice rest stop on Highway 191 back to Moab.

Maps: Latitude 40°, Inc. *Moab East* Biking Map and USGS 7.5 minute maps Mt. Peale 38109-D2, La Sal East 38109-C2, and Mt.Tukuhnikivatz 38109-D3.

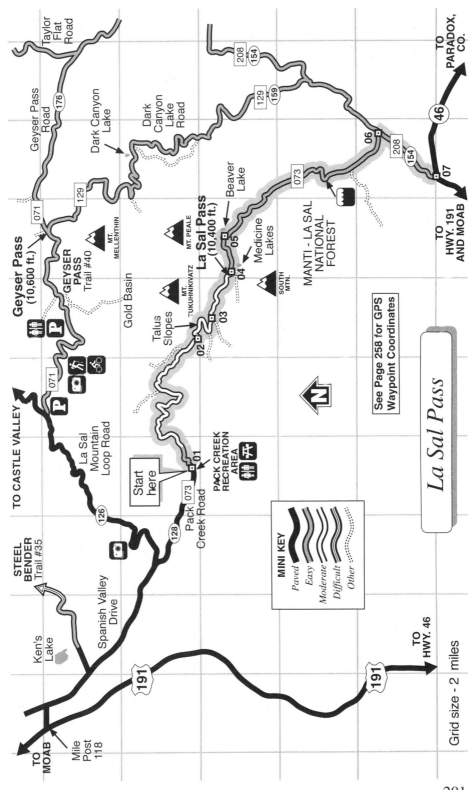

TO PARADOX, CO.

Taylor Flat Road

Geyser Pass Road

176

129

071

Dark Canyon Lake

Dark Canyon Lake Road

208
154

129
159

073

06

208
154

46

07

TO HWY. 191 AND MOAB

Beaver Lake

MT. MELLENTHIN

MT. PEALE

La Sal Pass (10,400 ft.)

05

04

Medicine Lakes

SOUTH MTN.

MANTI - LA SAL NATIONAL FOREST

Geyser Pass (10,600 ft.)

GEYSER PASS Trail #40

Gold Basin

MT. TUKUHNIKIVATZ

Talus Slopes

02

03

071

P

P

See Page 258 for GPS Waypoint Coordinates

N

La Sal Mountain Loop Road

TO CASTLE VALLEY

01

Start here

Pack Creek Road

073

PACK CREEK RECREATION AREA

126

128

STEEL BENDER Trail #35

Spanish Valley Drive

Ken's Lake

MINI KEY

Paved
Easy
Moderate
Difficult
Other

La Sal Pass

191

TO MOAB

Mile Post 118

191

TO HWY. 46

Grid size - 2 miles

AREA 4

Southwest Moab & Canyonlands National Park

42. Shafer Trail
43. Lathrop Canyon
44. White Rim
45. Chicken Corners
46. Lockhart Basin
47. Colorado River Overlook
48. Elephant Hill
49. Salt Creek/ Horse Canyon
50. Lavender Canyon

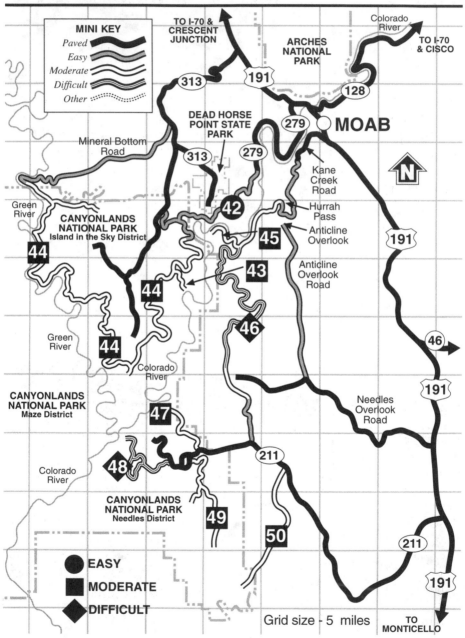

MINI KEY

Paved
Easy
Moderate
Difficult
Other

TO I-70 &
CRESCENT
JUNCTION

Colorado River

ARCHES NATIONAL PARK

TO I-70 & CISCO

313

191

128

DEAD HORSE POINT STATE PARK

279

MOAB

279

Mineral Bottom Road

313

Kane Creek Road

Green River

CANYONLANDS NATIONAL PARK
Island in the Sky District

42

Hurrah Pass

Anticline Overlook

44

45

191

43

Anticline Overlook Road

44

44

46

Green River

Colorado River

46

CANYONLANDS NATIONAL PARK
Maze District

Needles Overlook Road

191

47

Colorado River

48

211

211

191

CANYONLANDS NATIONAL PARK
Needles District

49

50

N

● **EASY**

■ **MODERATE**

◆ **DIFFICULT**

Grid size - 5 miles

TO MONTICELLO

Southwest Moab & Canyonlands National Park

All the trails in this area are near or inside stunning Canyonlands National Park, one of few national parks with an extensive backcountry roads program. Most of the trails are rated easy to moderate and are ideally suited for modern sport utility vehicles. Serious four-wheelers who overlook these trails are missing out on some of the best backcountry experiences imaginable. Don't be mislead—these trails take you to remote locations where Mother Nature is in control. You must be prepared to handle emergencies because you are often alone and many miles from any services. This realization occurs when hours go by without seeing another person, when you can't tune in a single station on your radio, and when your cell phone blinks "no service." For this reason, I highly recommend you travel with another vehicle, especially on longer trails like White Rim (#44), Lockhart Basin (#46, not in the park) and Lavender Canyon (#50). Some trails require pre-planning (permits, fees, reservations, etc.). When you see what you get for your minimal efforts—mile upon mile of secluded, breathtaking adventure roads—you'll be immensely satisfied.

The White Rim (Trail #44) in Canyonlands National Park—you'll never forget it.

Shafer Trail as seen from Dead Horse Point Overlook.

The butte across the Colorado River is an extension of land north of the Gooseneck.

A portion of the Shafer Switchbacks, fairly easy despite a terrifying appearance.

204

Shafer Trail 42

Location: Immediately south of Dead Horse Point State Park between Moab and the northeast corner of Canyonlands National Park.

Difficulty: Easy. A well-maintained road suitable for stock high-clearance four-wheel-drive vehicles. Possible muddy conditions in spots during wet periods. One brief, narrow shelf road crosses high above the Colorado River north of the Gooseneck. The trail concludes with a breath-taking but relatively easy climb up the Shafer Switchbacks. Route-finding is easy. Carry at least one gallon of drinking water per person. Summers are hot and dry. Best if driven in spring and fall.

Features: This trail enters Canyonlands National Park. Visit the Moab Information Center (at the corner of Main Street and Center Street) in advance to become familiar with park features, regulations, fees, camping permits, and possible road closures.

   The drive to the trail is very scenic with well-marked Indian petroglyphs, hiking trails, and arches. Once on the trail, you'll be treated to incredible views of the Colorado River as it meanders around the perimeter of Canyonlands National Park. Once inside the park, no pets, firearms, or wood campfires are allowed.

Time & Distance: From the end of the pavement on Highway 279 to the paved road inside Canyonlands National Park is 18.2 miles. Allow about 2 hours driving time.

To Get There: Drive north from Moab on Highway 191. About 1.5 miles north of the Colorado River, turn left on Potash Road Highway 279. Continue south 16.5 miles where the pavement ends at the potash plant.

Trail Description: Reset your odometer where the pavement ends [01]. Go by a boat ramp and parking area on the left. The road gradually climbs high above the river but is still well below the high cliffs of Dead Horse Point State Park. The aerial-like photo at left was taken from Dead Horse Point Overlook. Continue straight at a stop sign at 2.2 miles [02]. Watch for vehicles crossing from the potash plant. Bear right as a private road goes left at 2.4 miles. Follow a chain-link fence around blue and gray evaporation ponds. At 5.8 miles [03] continue straight as a lesser road goes left to an overlook west of Pyramid Butte. A gate at 6.7 should be closed after passing through. Stay on the main road as spurs depart along the way. After passing through a fence at 8.6, the main road swings right. Before you continue, get out of your vehicle and explore the area to the left where you'll find several great views of the river below. There's a dramatic shelf road at 9.6. If heights make you squeamish, you'll feel uncomfortable through this short stretch.

At 11.2 miles [04], enter Canyonlands National Park. Bear right at 11.8 as a lesser road goes left before reaching Shafer Campsite at 12.0 (permit required). Turn right a mile later at a T intersection [05]. Left takes you on the White Rim Trail #44; right up the Shafer Switchbacks to Canyonlands Island in the Sky. Don't be intimidated by the switchbacks. Shift into four-wheel-drive, take your time, and before you know it, you'll be at the top. A paved road is reached at 18.2 miles [06].

Return Trip: A left turn at the paved road takes you to Island in the Sky Visitor Center. Right goes to Moab. If you haven't already purchased a pass, you'll pay on the way out. A vehicle pass is good for seven days and gives you an opportunity to come back as often as you like during that period. It's good at both Island in the Sky and Needles Districts.

You'll run into Highway 313 in about 5 miles. Straight connects to Highway 191 in another 14 miles. Right goes to Dead Horse Point State Park and Long Canyon (Trail #17). Long Canyon is an exciting and scenic drive which intersects with Potash Road at Jug Handle Arch.

Services: There are vault toilets at the boat ramp at the start of the trail, at Shafer Campsite inside the park, and at the T intersection where Shafer Trail connects to the White Rim Trail. There are no services inside the park other than modern vault toilets at Island in the Sky Visitor Center. Gas is available where 313 intersects 191.

Side note: You may be wondering why some of the potash evaporation ponds are a dark blue color. Dye has been added to the water to speed the evaporation process. Gray ponds have already evaporated. Before 1964, potash was mined underground. After a major explosion killed 18 miners, the process was converted to solution mining. Water is pumped into the massive salt deposits beneath Shafer Basin and forced to the surface into the evaporation ponds. Processing converts the final residue to potash and industrial salt. Potash is a major ingredient in fertilizer and the salt is used on our highways.

Maps: Canyonlands Official Map and Guide, Latitude 40°, Inc. *Moab West Biking Map*, Trails Illustrated Canyonlands National Park #210, and USGS 7.5 minute maps Shafer Basin 38109-D6 and Musselman Arch 38109-D7.

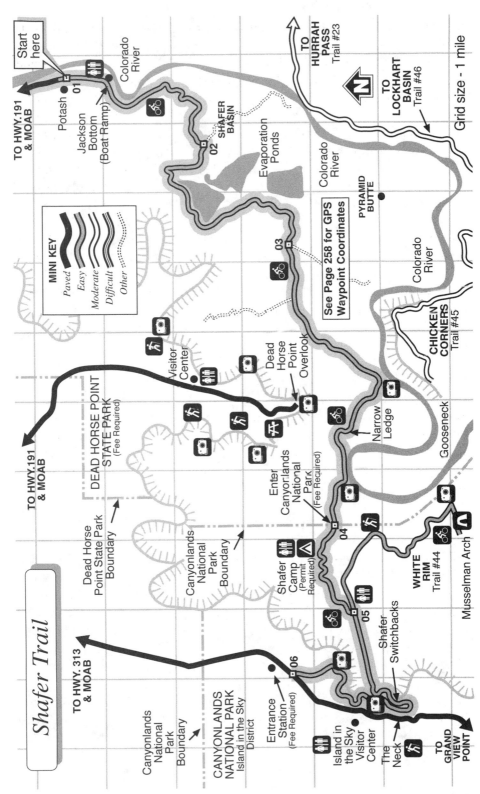

Shafer Trail

Start here

TO HWY.191 & MOAB

TO HWY.191 & MOAB

TO HWY. 313 & MOAB

TO GRAND VIEW POINT

Potash

Jackson Bottom (Boat Ramp)

Colorado River

01

SHAFER BASIN

02

Evaporation Ponds

Colorado River

TO HURRAH PASS Trail #23

TO LOCKHART BASIN Trail #46

N

Grid size - 1 mile

PYRAMID BUTTE

Colorado River

03

See Page 258 for GPS Waypoint Coordinates

MINI KEY

Paved
Easy
Moderate
Difficult
Other

Visitor Center

Dead Horse Point Overlook

Narrow Ledge

Gooseneck

CHICKEN CORNERS Trail #45

DEAD HORSE POINT STATE PARK
(Fee Required)

Dead Horse Point State Park Boundary

Canyonlands Park Boundary

Enter Canyonlands National Park
(Fee Required)

04

Shafer Camp (Permit Required)

WHITE RIM Trail #44

Musselman Arch

05

Shafer Switchbacks

Canyonlands National Park Boundary

CANYONLANDS NATIONAL PARK
Island in the Sky District

Entrance Station
(Fee Required)

06

Island in the Sky Visitor Center

The Neck

207

You'll have to get out of your vehicle for a good look at Musselman Arch.

Lathrop Canyon is a great adventure. Be aware that conditions are subject to change.

There's a small picnic area at the end of the trail. You'll need insect repellent in the summer.

Lathrop Canyon 43

Location: In the northeast corner of Canyonlands National Park.

Difficulty: Moderate. Minor rock challenges and narrow sections. Suitable for stock high-clearance vehicles under normal conditions. Check at visitor center for possible rock slides or trail blockages. Route-finding is very easy. Carry at least one gallon of drinking water per person. Summers are hot and dry. Best driven in spring and fall.

Features: This is a fee area inside Canyonlands National Park. Before you drive the trail, stop at the Islands in the Sky Visitor Center where you will learn about park features, regulations, fees, camping permits, and possible road closures. No pets, wood campfires, or firearms are allowed in the backcountry of Canyonlands National Park.

Access to this trail is via the White Rim (Trail #44), which typically takes more than a day to drive. Lathrop Canyon makes a convenient day trip. It is also slightly more difficult than the White Rim as it descends all the way to the Colorado River. The trail features the Gooseneck Hiking Trail, a spur to an overlook of the Colorado River, and a side trip to Musselman Arch. This trip can also be driven as an extension of the Shafer Trail (#42). This is a very popular biking trail so watch for bikers at all times.

Time & Distance: The drive is about 20 miles one way. Allow about 4 hours for the round trip plus stopping time.

To Get There: Drive 9 miles north from Moab on Highway 191. Turn left on Highway 313 and follow signs to Canyonlands National Park. Continue straight where 313 goes left to Dead Horse Point State Park. The entrance booth to Canyonlands is about 20 miles from Highway 313. At 0.2 miles after the entrance booth turn left on a wide gravel road to the Shafer Trail. The visitor center is 1.2 miles beyond the entrance booth.

Trail Description: Reset your odometer at the start. [01]. The road meanders along the top for a couple of miles before beginning to descend the Shafer Switchbacks. Although an intimidating sight to some, the switchbacks are easy to drive in good weather with a safe vehicle. Before you start down, shift into low range and avoid using your brakes as much as possible.

At 5.3 miles [02] Shafer Trail (#42) departs to the left back to Potash Road and Moab. A vault toilet marks this location. Continue straight. You are now officially on the White Rim (Trail #44). You'll pass the Gooseneck

Hiking Trail on the left at 6.4 miles. At 8.2 [03] there's a short side trip to an overlook of the Colorado River on the left. This is a great view and only takes a few extra minutes. As you continue on the White Rim, you reach the turn for Musselman Arch at 8.4 on the left. (I'm not counting mileage for side trips.) Again this is a short, worthwhile side trip. From here the road gets a little rockier.

The Lathrop Canyon Hiking Trail meets the White Rim on the right just before the turn for Lathrop Canyon at about 16.6 miles [04]. Turn left and start the descent into the canyon. There's a tight switchback at the beginning that's probably the toughest spot. Weather can have a great bearing on the condition of the trail. Heavy rains can loosen boulders and possibly block the trail. You have to decide for yourself if conditions are suitable for your vehicle. Bear left at 19.7 before reaching the bottom at 20.1 miles [05]. Walk down to the river's edge or enjoy a picnic on the tables provided. (Expect insects whenever near water during the summer.)

Return Trip: Return the way you came.

Services: Gas is available near the intersection of Highways 191 and 313. Vault toilets are available at the visitor center, below the Shafer Switchbacks, and at the bottom of Lathrop Canyon next to the river.

Maps: Canyonlands Official Map and Guide, Latitude 40°, Inc. *Moab West Biking Map*, Trails Illustrated Canyonlands National Park #210, and USGS 7.5 minute maps Musselman Arch 38109-D7 and Monument Basin 38109-C7.

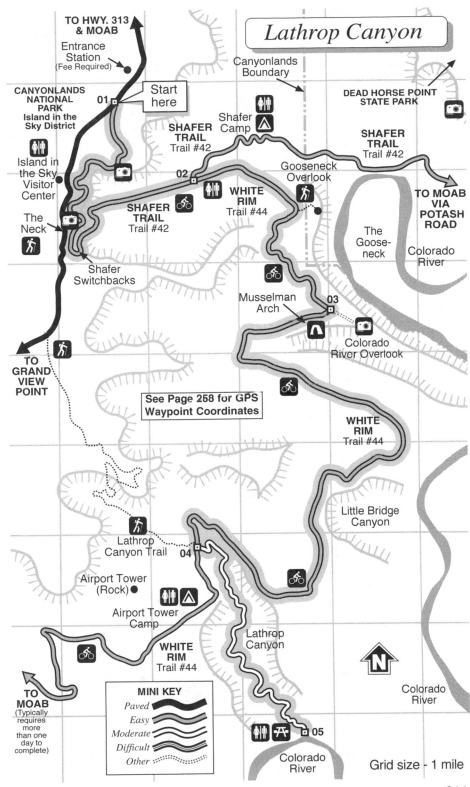

Lathrop Canyon

TO HWY. 313 & MOAB

Entrance Station
(Fee Required)

01 Start here

CANYONLANDS NATIONAL PARK
Island in the Sky District

Canyonlands Boundary

Shafer Camp

SHAFER TRAIL
Trail #42

DEAD HORSE POINT STATE PARK

SHAFER TRAIL
Trail #42

Island in the Sky Visitor Center

02

SHAFER TRAIL
Trail #42

WHITE RIM
Trail #44

Gooseneck Overlook

TO MOAB VIA POTASH ROAD

The Neck

Shafer Switchbacks

The Gooseneck

Colorado River

TO GRAND VIEW POINT

Musselman Arch

03

Colorado River Overlook

See Page 258 for GPS Waypoint Coordinates

WHITE RIM
Trail #44

Little Bridge Canyon

Lathrop Canyon Trail **04**

Airport Tower (Rock)

Airport Tower Camp

WHITE RIM
Trail #44

Lathrop Canyon

N

TO MOAB
(Typically requires more than one day to complete)

MINI KEY
Paved
Easy
Moderate
Difficult
Other

05

Colorado River

Colorado River

Grid size - 1 mile

211

A portion of the White Rim Trail (in foreground) as seen from Grandview Point.

The trail closely follows the rim in places.

Zeus & Moses at the end of Taylor Canyon.

Part of the Fort Bottom Hiking trail.

Location: Southwest of Moab inside Canyonlands National Park, Island in the Sky District.

Difficulty: Moderate. Most of the trail is easy and relatively flat. Several exceptions include Murphy Hogback and Hardscrabble Hill, both steep, rocky and challenging. You frequently drive near high cliffs and sheer walls. Suitable for stock high-clearance vehicles under normal conditions. Check at the visitor center for possible rock slides or trail blockages. The trail is well marked and easy to follow with few spurs. Watch for mountain bikers.

Special Notes: Summers are hot and dry. Best driven in spring and fall. Carry at least one gallon of water per person per day. No gas or services anywhere in the park. Camp in designated sites only. Permits and fees are required to camp. (Day use requires only an entrance fee.) Reserve sites six months to a year in advance by mail. Permits not reserved in advance will be available for walk-ins. Pets are not allowed in the backcountry of Canyonlands National Park—not even in vehicles. No wood campfires. Pack out all trash. See appendix for phone numbers.

Features: An incredible driving adventure along the edge of countless canyons in the shadow of towering buttes and high cliffs. Descend thrilling switchbacks, visit dramatic arches and rock formations, hike to Indian ruins, and camp quietly far away from others.

Time & Distance: Over 90 miles of slow off-highway driving plus 40 miles of pavement with no services along the way. This mileage does not include side trips to Lathrop and Taylor Canyons. Plan at least 2 days driving and one night of camping. Another good alternative is to drive 2 1/2 days and camp two nights in sites approximately one third of the way around.

Since there's an outside chance that the trail could be blocked by a rock slide or some other act of God, you might be forced to turn around beyond the halfway point. A worst-case scenario could mean driving the trail twice. Keep this in mind when figuring your fuel requirements.

To Get There: Drive 9 miles north from Moab on Highway 191. Turn left on Highway 313 and follow signs to Canyonlands National Park which is another 20 miles. Continue straight where 313 goes left to Dead Horse Point State Park. At 0.2 miles after the entrance booth turn left on a wide gravel road. If you wish to go the the visitor center before starting the trail, con-

Above Hardscrabble Camp driving the trail in a counterclockwise direction.

Looking southeast from atop Murphy Camp at Junction Butte.

Monster Tower.

Take your time across this rough spot.

tinue on the paved road another 1.2 miles past the entrance booth.

Trail Description (Clockwise): *Reset your odometer at the start.* [01].
The road meanders for a couple of miles before descending the Shafer
Switchbacks. Although an intimidating sight, they are easy to drive in good
weather. Before you start down, shift into low range and avoid using your
brakes as much as possible.

At 5.3 miles go straight as Shafer Trail goes left. Consider stops
at the Gooseneck Hiking Trail, Colorado River Overlook, and Musselman
Arch before reaching the turn for Lathrop Canyon (Trail # 43) at 16.6 miles.
Airport Tower Camp is the first designated campsite at 17.4 [02]. There's one
rocky climb on the way to Gooseberry Camp at 28.1 [03]. The next stretch to
White Crack Camp at 36.1 [04] is easier. The campsite is located another 1.4
miles left. Bear right to continue on the White Rim.

Take your time on the next section of road to Murphy Camp. There
are several steep, rocky sections that require patience. In my opinion the
toughest spot on the trail is just before Murphy Camp at 42.9 miles [05]. A
steep shelf road is carved up the side of the hogback. Coming down the
other side is also a challenge. Murphy Camp is very high with great views
and is my personal favorite.

The road gradually improves as you proceed to Candlestick Camp
at 53.2 miles [06] and Potato Bottom Camp at 64.2 [07]. There's a steep section of switchbacks called Hardscrabble Hill at 65.6. Make sure you shift
into low gear before starting up this section.

Fort Bottom Hiking Trail is on the left at 66.2 miles. This 2-hour
round trip hike descends to a narrow ridge then climbs to a high lookout
point with an Indian ruin. Do not touch or go inside the ruin. A metal case
at the ruin holds a sign-in logbook and information on the ruin. The trail
continues to the river below where there's a small cabin. Take plenty of water;
the hike can be strenuous on a hot day. If you enjoy hiking, don't miss this one.

After Fort Bottom, you'll descend along a high ledge to
Hardscrabble Camp at 68.2 miles [08]. Bear right to continue. You'll pass the
Upheaval Dome Hiking Trail before reaching Labyrinth Camp and the spur
to Taylor Canyon on the right at 70.4 [09]. If you have time, drive up Taylor
Canyon to see gigantic Zeus and Moses. The round trip adds 10 miles
and another hour to your journey. Much of the drive follows a dry wash.
Although easy most of the time, it can become boulder strewn and difficult
after a heavy rain.

Not counting the mileage to Taylor Canyon, the park boundary
is crossed at 73.0 miles. This part of the trip can be extremely dusty with
very poor visibility especially with a vehicle in front of you. Allow plenty
of space between vehicles. The trail is narrow and very close to the river in
places. You intersect with Mineral Bottom Road at 76.9 miles [10]. Turn right

and start up the steep switchbacks. The road is very wide and easy when dry. When wet, however, it becomes slippery and dangerous. Wait for the road to dry before going up. Highway 313 is reached at 91.3 miles [11].

Return Trip: Turn left for Moab. When you reach Highway 191 in about 12 miles, turn right. To return to Canyonlands National Park, turn right at Highway 313.

Trail Description (Counterclockwise): Consider driving the trail in this direction if you intend to drive it in a single day. The sun tends to be more in shadow and less glaring. Start very early and plan for a long day. It's best to purchase a park pass at the entrance station in advance. At that time you can ask about trail conditions and possible closures.

Take Highway 191 north from Moab and turn left on 313 following signs to Canyonlands National Park. Turn right on well-marked Mineral Bottom (Horsethief) Road at 11.9 miles just after a cattle guard.

Reset your odometer as you turn off the pavement [11]. Descend the Mineral Bottom Switchbacks at 12.9 miles. If wet, wait until they dry. Turn left at the bottom at 14.4 [10]. Enter the park at 18.3. Pass Labyrinth Camp and bear right where Taylor Canyon goes left at 20.9 [09]. Pass Hardscrabble Camp at 23.1 [08] and climb a high shelf road. Pass the Fort Bottom Hiking Trail then descend steep Hardscrabble Hill at 25.7. Pass Potato Bottom and Candlestick Camps at 27.1 [07] and 38.1 [06]. Prior to Murphy Camp, trail conditions worsen. The hardest part of the trail is before and after Murphy Camp at 48.4 [05]. The stretch between Murphy and White Crack is interesting and challenging. Pass the spur to White Crack Camp at 55.5 [04]. Go by Gooseberry Camp at 63.2 [03] and Airport Tower Camp at 73.9 [02]. The spur to Lathrop Canyon goes right at 74.7. Pass Musselman Arch and the Colorado River Overlook before Shafer Trail (#42) goes right at 86.0. Turn right here to reach Potash Road or continue straight up the Shafer Switchbacks. The paved road at Islands in the Sky is reached at 91.3 miles [01]. Exit the park to the right past the entrance station. Go about 20 miles to Highway 191 and turn right for Moab.

Services: The nearest gas station is north of the intersection of Highways 313 and 191. No gas, water, or food is available anywhere inside the park. Modern vault toilets are available at the visitor center and at all the designated campsites.

Maps: Canyonlands Official Map and Guide, Latitude 40°, Inc. *Moab West Biking Map*, Trails Illustrated Canyonlands National Park #210. For GPS purposes use the USGS 1 x 2 degree series 1:250,000 scale Moab 38108-A1.

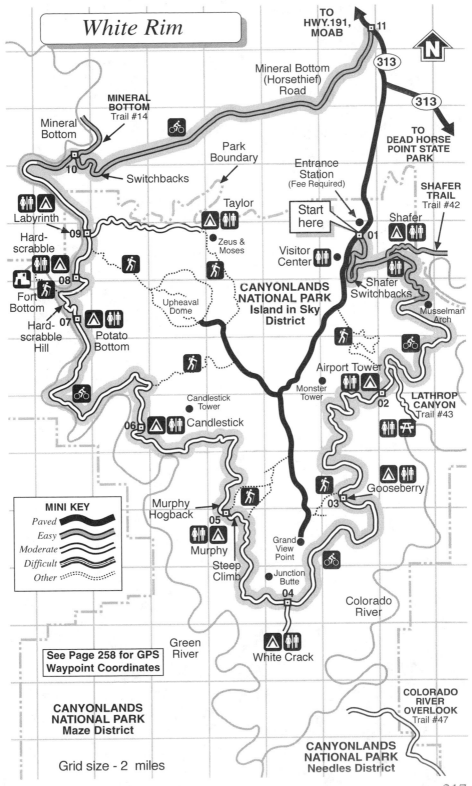

White Rim

TO HWY.191, MOAB

11

313

313

N

TO DEAD HORSE POINT STATE PARK

Mineral Bottom (Horsethief) Road

MINERAL BOTTOM Trail #14

Mineral Bottom

10

Switchbacks

Park Boundary

Taylor

Entrance Station (Fee Required)

SHAFER TRAIL Trail #42

Shafer

Start here

01

Labyrinth

Zeus & Moses

Visitor Center

Shafer Switchbacks

Hard-scrabble

09

CANYONLANDS NATIONAL PARK Island in Sky District

Musselman Arch

08

Fort Bottom

Upheaval Dome

Hard-scrabble Hill

07

Potato Bottom

Airport Tower

Monster Tower

02

LATHROP CANYON Trail #43

Candlestick Tower

06 Candlestick

Gooseberry

03

Murphy Hogback

05

Grand View Point

Murphy

Steep Climb

Junction Butte

04

Colorado River

MINI KEY

Paved
Easy
Moderate
Difficult
Other

See Page 258 for GPS Waypoint Coordinates

Green River

White Crack

CANYONLANDS NATIONAL PARK Maze District

COLORADO RIVER OVERLOOK Trail #47

Grid size - 2 miles

CANYONLANDS NATIONAL PARK Needles District

The trail starts down this rocky shelf road on the west side of Hurrah Pass.

This is the toughest spot on the trail. Make a sharp right here and head uphill out of the wash.

Chicken Corners above the Colorado River—an intimidating sight but not that tough.

Chicken Corners

Location: Southwest of Moab and Kane Creek Road. South of Dead Horse Point State Park and the Colorado River.

Difficulty: Moderate. Just a few rough spots on this predominantly easy trail. At one point, you're forced near the edge of a high cliff above the Colorado River. This spot is intimidating but easy (see photo at left). Suitable for stock, high-clearance vehicles under normal conditions. Water crossings along Kane Creek Road can be deep in early spring or after heavy rains. Best driven in late spring and fall. Hot in summer.

Features: Descend from Hurrah Pass on the more remote west side to the scenic Colorado River gorge. See Dead Horse Point State Park and Pyramid Butte across the river. Experience the thrill of Chicken Corners. Please stay on the trail at all times. This area has been heavily tracked by irresponsible drivers. Continued abuse could result in the area being closed.

Time & Distance: It's 11.5 miles from the top of Hurrah Pass to the end of the trail. Allow about 4 hours for the round trip plus an additional hour to reach Hurrah Pass.

To Get There: *Reset your odometer.* From the south side of Moab at the McDonald's Restaurant on Main Street, take Kane Creek Road west. Bear left at the first fork and head south along the Colorado River. The pavement ends at 4.7 miles where the road swings left away from the river. Continue on a wide gravel road cut across high canyon walls, then descend south to the valley floor. Follow the main road until it crosses Kane Creek. Swing right after this crossing at 11.0 miles and begin the gradual climb to Hurrah Pass, reached at 14.4 miles (Elevation 4,780 ft).

Trail Description: *Reset your odometer at Hurrah Pass.* [01]. Start down the west side on a rocky, winding ledge road. At 2.5 miles [02] bear left uphill where lesser Jackson Hole Trail goes right. Trail conditions worsen as you drop into a dry wash. Negotiate a rocky challenge at 2.8 then bear sharply right uphill. The road flattens out as you head southwest. This is open range so watch for cattle on the road. Bear right at 4.2 as a lesser road goes left. At 4.4 [03] another road goes left to Dripping Spring; bear right following a sign to Lockhart Basin. The road gets rocky again and narrows to a single lane as it winds closer to the river in places.

    You'll pass through a barbed wire gate (close it after passing through) before reaching a key fork at 6.8 miles [04]. A sign should indicate Lockhart Basin left. Sometimes this sign is knocked down or removed by vandals. Bear right, climbing out of a dry, rocky wash. From here the trail is well defined as it crosses a broad, flat area with several easy rocky sections. Gradually a high wall on the left forces you closer to a cliff edge overlooking the river. The narrowest point at 10.0 miles [05] is the driveable Chicken Corner. It's easy but may be intimidating to some. The road continues another 1.5 miles where it comes to an abrupt end at a remote overlook [06]. (From here, you'll see a hiking trail that continues around a terrifying point. This is the real Chicken Corner.) Dead Horse Point Overlook is directly north across the river. (Note: The final scene from the movie *Thelma and Louise* was shot across the river near this location. If you saw the movie, you'll remember the two fleeing women deliberately drove their speeding convertible off the edge of one of these high cliffs.)

Return Trip: Return the way you came or via Lockhart Basin (Trail #46). This trail is a full-day trip and is much more difficult than Chicken Corners. Although both trails can be done in one very long day, it's more enjoyable if you take an extra day and camp overnight.

Services: None. Return to Moab. Make sure you carry a least a gallon of drinking water per person per day. Camping is restricted to campgrounds while in the Colorado Riverway along Kane Creek.

Maps: Latitude 40°, Inc. *Moab West* Biking Map and USGS 7.5 minute maps Trough Springs Canyon 38109-D5 and Shafer Basin 38109-D6.

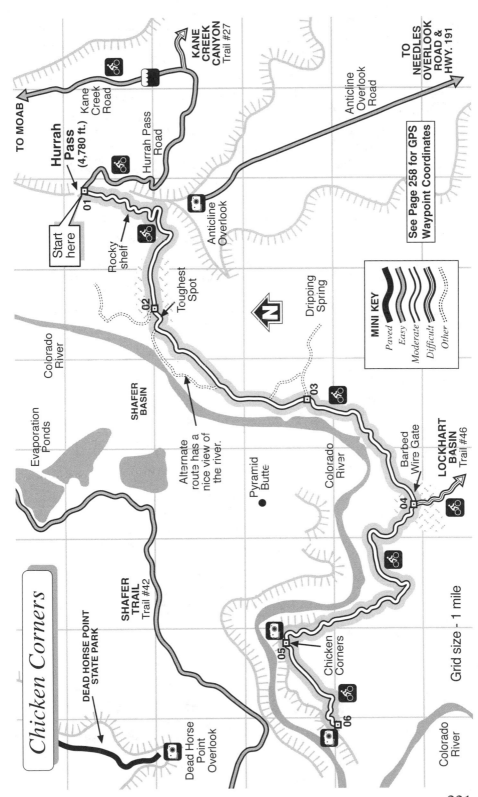

Chicken Corners

TO MOAB

KANE CREEK CANYON Trail #27

Kane Creek Road

Hurrah Pass (4,780 ft.)

Hurrah Pass Road

TO NEEDLES OVERLOOK ROAD & HWY. 191

Anticline Overlook Road

Anticline Overlook

See Page 258 for GPS Waypoint Coordinates

01

Start here

Rocky shelf

02

Toughest Spot

Dripping Spring

Colorado River

SHAFER BASIN

Alternate route has a nice view of the river.

MINI KEY

Paved
Easy
Moderate
Difficult
Other

N

03

Barbed Wire Gate

LOCKHART BASIN Trail #46

Evaporation Ponds

Pyramid Butte

Colorado River

04

SHAFER TRAIL Trail #42

DEAD HORSE POINT STATE PARK

05

Chicken Corners

06

Dead Horse Point Overlook

Grid size - 1 mile

Colorado River

221

If you reach this point, back up—You've just missed an important turn.

Not enough ground clearance for this SUV.

You must pass through this canyon.

The trail is extremely remote. Travel with another vehicle and carry plenty of water.

Lockhart Basin ◆46◆

Location: East of Canyonlands National Park in the Canyon Rims Recreation Area.

Difficulty: Difficult. You must pass through a difficult canyon at the start of the trail. Only the most capable of stock vehicles can get through. You'll need high ground clearance and excellent driving skill to avoid body damage. I encountered a full-size Suburban attempting to enter the canyon (see photo at left). He quickly became high centered on his low-slung running boards. South of this canyon, conditions range from easy to moderate with few difficult spots. The last 15 miles are easy unless Indian Creek is high. Best driven in late spring and fall. Hot in summer.

　　　Route-finding is easy after you locate the entry point through the initial canyon. Follow directions carefully.

Features: A vast, remote area where vehicle failure is a serious matter. Do not drive this trail alone.

Time & Distance: The drive from Moab to the start of the trail, as described here, is about 21 miles and takes about 3 hours. Add another 6 hours for the 37 miles of the trail. It is more enjoyable to drive it over a two-day period.

To Get There: Follow directions to Chicken Corners (Trail # 45). Turn left 6.8 miles southwest of Hurrah Pass where a sign indicates Lockhart Basin left and Chicken Corners right. (Lockhart Basin can also be reached from the easier southern end, starting at Highway 211 east of the Needles District entrance.)

Trail Description: Reset your odometer at the sign where Chicken Corners goes right at 6.8 miles [01]. Bear left following a wide wash. Bear left again almost immediately at 0.1 miles into a smaller wash. It's marked with cairns but they are not obvious. If you miss this turn, the trail soon splits at a rock wall (see top photo previous page). Back up and turn left at the smaller wash.

　　　As you start up the smaller wash, you'll maneuver over large rock slabs and begin to climb. The canyon quickly narrows and becomes more difficult. Within a mile, conditions improve but are by no means easy. At 4.7 miles [02] cross a high picturesque ridge from which you can see Islands in the Sky Mesa to the west, the La Sal Mountains to the east, and the Canyonlands Needles District to the south. You'll head south from here along the irregular western side of Hatch Point. Drive in high range much of the time as you cross wide areas of rocky terrain interrupted by numerous small washes. Some may be difficult depending upon recentness of any rain storms.

At 13.9 miles [03] bear left at an unmarked fork. Gradually climb to a high ridge then descend to a wide, easy road at 21.8 [04]. A hard right here goes to Lockhart Canyon in another 10.8 miles. Continue straight as the road swings south and is interrupted by several gates. Go straight at 28.0 miles [05] where a spur goes right to a landing strip. After a stretch of shelf road, round a corner and look for Indian ruins above the road on the right. Descend to Indian Creek at 34.2 miles [06]. The road reverses direction at the bottom of the hill, then turns left and crosses the creek. It's normally shallow but can be deep in the spring or after a heavy rain. Pass by Hamburger Rock Campground before reaching Highway 211 at 37.1 miles [07].

Return Trip: Moab is 29 miles east on Highway 211 and another 39 miles north on 191. View outstanding petroglyphs along Highway 211 at Newspaper Rock.

A right turn on 211 takes you to the Needles District of Canyonlands National Park. The Colorado River Overlook (Trail #47), Elephant Hill (Trail #48), and Salt Creek/Horse Canyon (Trail # 49) are in this area.

Services: Vault toilets at Hamburger Rock Campground, Newspaper Rock, and a rest stop south of Moab. Lockhart Basin is in the Canyon Rims Recreation Area where use of portable toilets is encouraged. No water anywhere. Make sure you carry at least a gallon of drinking water per person per day.

After completing the trail, you can turn right on Highway 211 and drive west where you'll see signs for the Needles Outpost on the right before reaching the entrance booth to Canyonlands National Park. There is a general store and campground at this location. (It is privately owned and not associated with the park.) They sell fuel, bottled water, camping spots (no hook-ups), and supplies. Flush toilets and showers are available. It is a seasonal business and not always open, so call ahead if you're low on fuel. (See telephone number in Appendix.)

Maps: Trails Illustrated Canyonlands National Park #210 and USGS 30 x 60 minute series 1:100,000-scale La Sal 38109-A1.

Note: At the time of this writing, Canyonlands National Park was under consideration for expansion. If this occurs, Lockhart Basin will likely become part of the park.

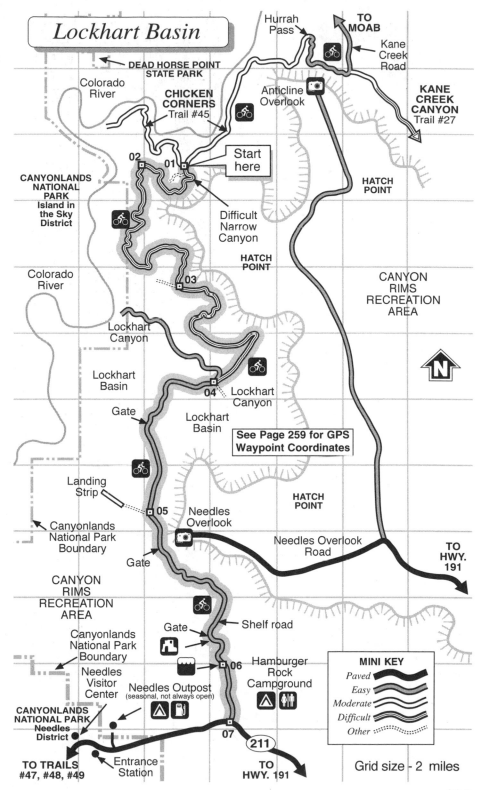

Lockhart Basin

TO MOAB

Hurrah Pass

Kane Creek Road

DEAD HORSE POINT STATE PARK

Colorado River

CHICKEN CORNERS Trail #45

Anticline Overlook

KANE CREEK CANYON Trail #27

Start here

02   01

CANYONLANDS NATIONAL PARK Island in the Sky District

Difficult Narrow Canyon

HATCH POINT

HATCH POINT

Colorado River

03

CANYON RIMS RECREATION AREA

Lockhart Canyon

Lockhart Basin

04   Lockhart Canyon

Gate

Lockhart Basin

See Page 259 for GPS Waypoint Coordinates

N

HATCH POINT

Landing Strip

05   Needles Overlook

Canyonlands National Park Boundary

Gate

Needles Overlook Road

TO HWY. 191

CANYON RIMS RECREATION AREA

Canyonlands National Park Boundary

Shelf road

Gate

Needles Visitor Center

Needles Outpost (seasonal, not always open)

Hamburger Rock Campground

06

MINI KEY

Paved
Easy
Moderate
Difficult
Other

CANYONLANDS NATIONAL PARK Needles District

07   211

TO TRAILS #47, #48, #49

Entrance Station

TO HWY. 191

Grid size - 2 miles

225

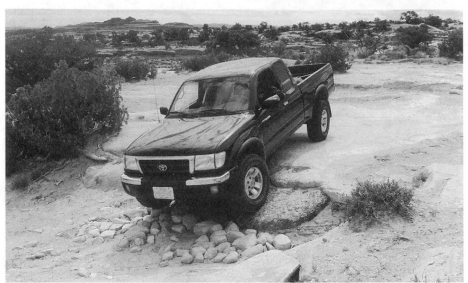

The park has filled-in some of the bigger holes to make the trail a little easier.

The last part of the trail is mostly undefined slickrock. Watch for cairns marking the trail.

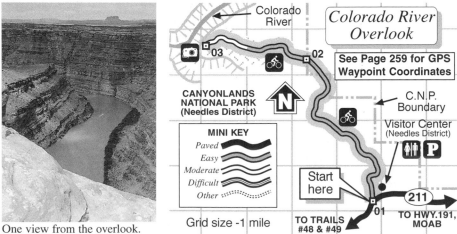

One view from the overlook.

Colorado River Overlook 47

Location: Directly northwest of the Needles District Visitor Center in Canyonlands National Park.

Difficulty: Moderate. Just a few challenging rocky spots near the end. Suitable for stock high clearance vehicles. Skid plates recommended. Easy if you walk the last mile. Route-finding is easy.

Features: A short drive with a great view at the end. If you've been reluctant to try a moderate trail, this is a good opportunity. Walk part if necessary.

Time & Distance: It's 7.3 miles one way. Allow 2 hours for the round trip. The drive from Moab takes about 1.5 hours.

To Get There: Drive south on Highway 191 about 40 miles and turn right on Highway 211, following signs to Canyonlands National Park Needles District. After 34 miles, pay a fee at the entrance station and continue a short distance to the visitor center. Although not required, it's a good idea to ask about trail conditions and park regulations in the visitor center. The trail may be closed if it is too wet.

Trail Description: Reset your odometer at the visitor center [01]. Head north from the visitor center. (Do not get back on the main road.) Pass through a gate and follow a dirt road. Follow Jeep signs through an intersection at 2.7 miles. At 3.3 it starts getting rocky. Swing left uphill at 4.5 [02] as a road joins on the right. At 6.2 miles a tougher spot begins the moderate portion of the trail. Many stock vehicles manage the entire length of the trail, but if you're worried about damaging your vehicle, you can walk from here. This is a great place to practice your off-highway driving skills. Follow cairns across slickrock to the end of the trail at 7.3 miles [03]. Walk a short distance west to see the Colorado River. There are no handrails so keep an eye on the kids.

Return Trip: Return the way you came.

Services: The visitor center has flush toilets and water. Water is also available at the Squaw Flat Campgrounds. Gas and supplies are available at the Needles Outpost seasonally or when open. Otherwise return to Moab.

Maps: Trails Illustrated Canyonlands National Park #210 and USGS 7.5 minute map The Loop 38109-B7.

Starting up Elephant Hill.

Steep descent down the back side.

Heading north on Devils Lane. Needles North in the distance.

228

Elephant Hill ◀48▶

Location: Canyonlands National Park, Needles District.

Difficulty: Difficult. Steep, narrow, rocky ascents and descents. The switchbacks on Elephant Hill require backing. Although Canyonlands National Park tries to maintain the trail for stock vehicles, constant deterioration makes this difficult. If you drive a stock vehicle, ask at the visitor center for latest conditions. This is not a trail for beginners; experience is necessary. High ground clearance, skid plates, and rocker panel protection are recommended to avoid body damage. The trail is well marked and easy to follow.

Features: Beautiful scenery combined with just the right amount of challenge. This one-way loop is one of the most enjoyable trails I've ever driven. Take the spur to the Confluence Overlook to see the point where the Colorado and Green Rivers converge. No permit is required to drive the trail although one is required to camp overnight. No pets or firearms. Pack out all trash. Carry at least one gallon of water per person per day.

Time & Distance: The round trip, as described here including the Confluence Overlook spur, is 15.2 miles and takes 3 to 4 hours.

To Get There: Drive south on Highway 191 about 40 miles and turn right on Highway 211, following signs to Canyonlands National Park Needles District. After 34 miles, pay a fee at the entrance station and continue into the park. Check at the visitor center for trail conditions. Continue west past the visitor center, following signs to Elephant Hill. Bear right when the road splits. Turn left soon after the roads come back together. Go right on another paved road, then right again on a dirt road just before a camping area. Continue 2.7 miles on the dirt road until reaching a parking and picnic area. The trail is on the right at the end of the parking area.

Trail Description: Reset your odometer at the start of the trail [01]. Check to make sure no one is coming down, then begin climbing the steep, narrow switchbacks. Pull-outs are provided to assist in making the tight turns. The trail is very rough so take your time. It levels out for a short distance before coming back down at 0.6 miles. Although the descent is severe, traction is excellent on the slickrock surface. The switchbacks are too tight to make the turns. Signs indicate you should pull forward then back down to the next switchback.

After crossing a dry wash, bear left where the one-way section begins at 1.5 miles [02]. Several rocky challenges follow before reaching a narrow passage between two rock walls at 3.3. It's wider than it looks. At 3.4 [03] bear right to Devils Lane. To the left is Devils Kitchen, a great camping site (permit required). Bear right at 3.9 [04]. Pass an obstacle called the Silver Stairs before reaching the spur to Confluence Overlook at 5.3 miles [05]. I'm including this side trip in my trail description, but it may be skipped by turning right at this point.

To reach the Confluence Overlook, bear left. The road gets easier and you can make good time. Bear right at 7.7 before reaching a picnic area and vault toilet at 8.5 [06]. Park here and hike a short distance to the overlook.

Reset your odometer as you head back. Turn left at 3.1 miles when you get back to the original trail [05]. After a tough downhill section at 3.3, rejoin two-way traffic at 5.2 miles [02]. Turn left and retrace your earlier path over Elephant Hill. You'll reach the start of the trail at 6.7 miles [01].

Return Trip: Return the way you came.

Services: The visitor center has flush toilets and water. Water is also available at the Squaw Flat Campground. There are vault toilets at the start of the trail, Devils Kitchen Campsite, and at the Confluence Overlook picnic area.

Just outside the entrance booth to the park is the Needles Outpost. There is a general store and campgrounds at this location. (It is privately owned and not associated with the park.) They sell fuel, bottled water, camping spots (no hook-ups), and supplies. Flush toilets and showers are available. It is a seasonal business and not always open, so call ahead if you are low on fuel. (See phone number in Appendix.)

Maps: Canyonlands Official Map and Guide, Trails Illustrated Canyonlands National Park #210 and USGS 7.5 minute map The Loop 38109-B7.

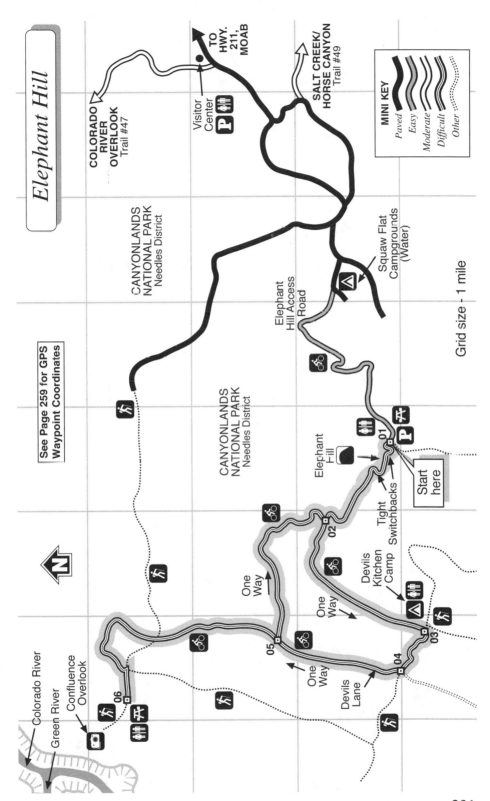

Elephant Hill

See Page 259 for GPS Waypoint Coordinates

MINI KEY

Paved
Easy
Moderate
Difficult
Other

Grid size - 1 mile

N

COLORADO RIVER OVERLOOK
Trail #47

TO HWY. 211, MOAB

SALT CREEK/ HORSE CANYON
Trail #49

Visitor Center
P

Squaw Flat Campgrounds (Water)

Elephant Hill Access Road

CANYONLANDS NATIONAL PARK
Needles District

CANYONLANDS NATIONAL PARK
Needles District

Elephant Hill

01

Start here

Tight Switchbacks

02

Devils Kitchen Camp

03

One Way

One Way

05

04

One Way

Devils Lane

06

Confluence Overlook

Colorado River

Green River

P

231

Much of the trail follows creek bed.

Paul Bunyan's Potty.

Rock art near Peekaboo Camp.

Don't climb up to Tower Ruin.

This maneuver between boulder and overhanging wall is easier than it looks.

Salt Creek/Horse Canyon

49

Location: Canyonlands National Park, Needles District.

Difficulty: Moderate (under low-water conditions). Both trails follow stream beds which can reach unsafe levels during the spring and after heavy rains. Vehicles have been known to get buried up to their windshields, so stay out if heavy rains are predicted. Watch for quicksand and the possibility of flash floods. Sandy conditions may require airing down. Brush may touch sides of vehicle. Horse Canyon has one tight squeeze between a rock overhang and boulder and is very rocky the last quarter mile. Suitable for stock high-clearance vehicles under low-water conditions. Check trail conditions at visitor center before starting your trip. Route-finding is easy.

Features: This area is listed on the National Register of Historic Places. Anasazi Indians inhabited this area for thousands of years, leaving ruins and abundant rock art. There are many arches in the area although hiking is often necessary to see them. One exception is Paul Bunyan's Potty which has its own parking area and vault toilet.

   This trail requires a special permit. Even if you have reservations, you must pick up the permit and a combination to the locked gate at the visitor center. Salt Creek is closed to vehicles beyond Peekaboo Camp. You must hike 20 miles round trip to see Angel Arch. No permit is required to hike but one is required to camp overnight. No pets or firearms. Pack out all trash.

Time & Distance: Horse Canyon is 12. 6 miles including side trips to Peekaboo Camp and Tower Ruin. Add another 8.5 miles to drive out. Allow 3 to 4 hours driving time and additional hiking time.

To Get There: Drive south on Highway 191 about 40 miles and turn right on Highway 211, following signs to Canyonlands National Park Needles District. After 34 miles, pass the entrance station (fee required) and continue to the visitor center. After you've picked up your permit, continue on the main road past the visitor center and turn left where the road splits. Turn left again on a dirt road, following signs to Salt Creek. Turn right in less than a mile and drive to the gate. Make sure you relock the gate after passing through.

Trail Description: Reset your odometer at the start of the trail [01]. You'll pass through tall brush and begin crossing the creek. Soon the creek

233

becomes the trail. When I drove the trail in early May, it contained between 2 and 10 inches of water. I was fortunate not to encounter quicksand. You must use your own judgment as to whether it is safe to proceed. (Read about quicksand on page 33.) Move at a steady pace and avoid stopping in the creek. Stay away from deep places near outer banks. Bear right at 2.2 miles [02], staying on Salt Creek. The four-wheel-drive portion of the trail ends at Peekaboo Camp at 3.3 miles [03]. See rock art where Peekaboo Hiking Trail departs west or take a 20-mile round trip hike to Angel Arch.

Return to waypoint 02 where Horse Canyon Road branches off to the right. Don't confuse an arch at 4.9 miles with Paul Bunyan's Potty. That is reached at 5.5 miles [04]. A parking area and vault toilet mark this location. The road gets sandier as you proceed south. Air down your tires if necessary. At 6.5 miles [05] turn left to visit the Tower Ruin. The ruins are located in a cave high on a cliff (see photo) and must be viewed from below. Return to the main trail and turn left. Brush closes in along the trail before reaching a rock overhang at 12.0 miles. I had no trouble squeezing through, but larger vehicles might find this spot a challenge. At 12.4 miles [06] the hiking trail to Castle Arch departs to the right. It's a short hike to see the arch. You can continue past Castle Arch but the trail gets rocky and difficult. I'd recommend you walk the last quarter mile to see Fortress Arch.

Return Trip: Return the way you came.

Services: The visitor center has flush toilets and water. There are vault toilets at Peekaboo Camp and Paul Bunyan's Potty.

Just outside the entrance booth to the park is the Needles Outpost. There is a general store and campgrounds at this location. (It is privately owned and not associated with the park.) They sell fuel, bottled water, camping spots (no hook-ups), and supplies. Flush toilets and showers are available. It is a seasonal business and not always open, so call ahead if you are low on fuel. (See phone number in Appendix.)

Maps: Canyonlands Official Map and Guide, Trails Illustrated Canyonlands National Park #210 and USGS 7.5 minute maps The Loop 38109-B7, Druid Arch 38109-A7, and South Six-Shooter Peak 38109-A6.

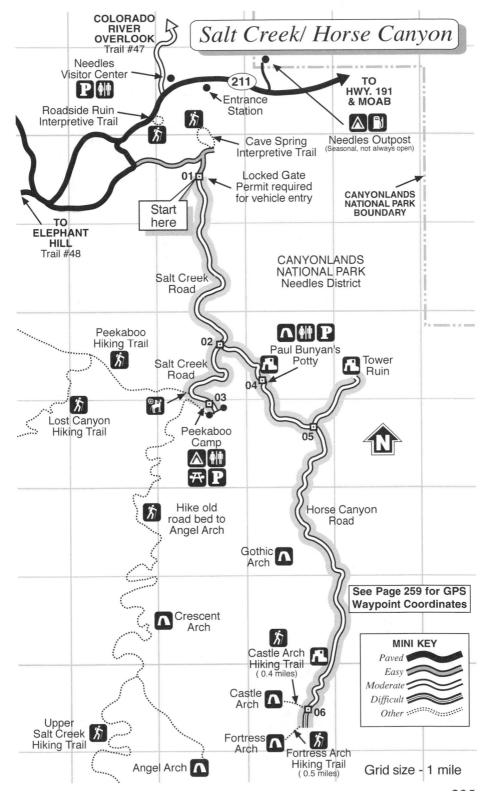

COLORADO RIVER OVERLOOK
Trail #47

Salt Creek/ Horse Canyon

Needles Visitor Center

🅿 🚻

Roadside Ruin Interpretive Trail

211

Entrance Station

TO HWY. 191 & MOAB

🏕 ⛽

Cave Spring Interpretive Trail

Needles Outpost
(Seasonal, not always open)

01

Locked Gate
Permit required for vehicle entry

CANYONLANDS NATIONAL PARK BOUNDARY

Start here

TO ELEPHANT HILL
Trail #48

CANYONLANDS NATIONAL PARK
Needles District

Salt Creek Road

Peekaboo Hiking Trail

02

🏕 🚻 🅿

Paul Bunyan's Potty

Tower Ruin

Salt Creek Road

04

03

Lost Canyon Hiking Trail

05

Peekaboo Camp

🏕 🚻
⛱ 🅿

N

Hike old road bed to Angel Arch

Horse Canyon Road

Gothic Arch

See Page 259 for GPS Waypoint Coordinates

Crescent Arch

Castle Arch Hiking Trail
(0.4 miles)

MINI KEY	
Paved	
Easy	
Moderate	
Difficult	
Other	

Castle Arch

06

Upper Salt Creek Hiking Trail

Fortress Arch

Fortress Arch Hiking Trail
(0.5 miles)

Angel Arch

Grid size - 1 mile

Typical conditions when water is low. Be aware that flash floods are possible.

Handhold Arch.

The gate at the boundary to Canyonlands National Park.

Lavender Canyon closes in.

Cleft Arch near the end of the trail.

Lavender Canyon

50

Location: Canyonlands National Park, southern tip of Needles District.

Difficulty: Moderate (under low-water conditions). Follows the broad, sandy floor of Lavender Canyon. When dry, the sand can be difficult. Air down if necessary. Stay out of the canyon in the spring and after heavy rains when high water is likely. If heavy thunderstorms are predicted, plan your trip another day. If a flash flood should occur when you're in the canyon, get out of your vehicle and climb to higher ground. The trail includes two crossings of Indian Creek, which can also be deep at times. This is an extremely remote area; travel with another vehicle. Suitable for stock vehicles under ideal conditions. Carry at least one gallon of drinking water per person per day. The route is fairly obvious as it follows a natural stream bed, but side canyons can be confusing. Watch your mileage and follow directions carefully.

Features: See Six-Shooter Peaks, Cleft and Caterpillar Arches, and the high colorful walls of Lavender Canyon. Enjoy solitude in an area where you seldom see another vehicle. There are Indian ruins along the base of the canyon walls. Stop periodically to hike and search for them. This trail requires a special permit. Even if you have reservations, you must pick up the permit and a combination to the locked gate at the visitor center. No permit is required to hike but one is required to camp overnight. No pets or firearms. Pack out all trash.

Time & Distance: It's 14.5 miles to the gate at the boundary to Canyonlands National Park. You can drive another 3 to 4 miles into the park. Allow about 4 hours for the round trip.

To Get There: Drive south on Highway 191 about 40 miles and turn right on Highway 211, following signs to Canyonlands National Park Needles District. After 26 miles, watch for a sign to Lavender Canyon on the left. Before starting the trail, continue on Highway 211 to the Needles Visitor Center to pick up your permit and gate combination.

Trail Description: Reset your odometer when you pull off Highway 211 [01]. Pass through a large metal gate and close it. Bear right at 0.6 miles. The trail meanders and crosses dry creek beds. Bear left at 1.5 and pass through a barbed wire gate at 1.8 miles [02]. Turn right after going through the gate towards Davis Canyon. At 3.5 miles [03] turn left out of a dry wash onto a lesser road marked to Lavender Canyon. Within a mile, you'll see Indian Creek on your left. Cross it at 4.9 miles and bear left as you come out. Cross a cattle guard at 5.0 miles [04]. At 5.2 cross Indian Creek again. From there, the trail heads south into Lavender Canyon following a sandy creek bed. Do your best to stay on the main part of the trail heading south-south-west. At 12.9 miles [05], bear right as Dry Fork Canyon goes left. At 13.8 bear left as a lesser road goes right up a side canyon. Finally, you reach the locked gate to Canyonlands National Park at 14.5 miles [06].

Relock the gate after passing through. Watch for Caterpillar Arch on the right. At 15.1 miles a spur goes right to a side canyon. You can explore this 2-mile spur later. Bear left and continue up the main canyon. The trail becomes very narrow at times then widens again. It disappears for awhile, then reappears. I finally shifted into low gear at 15.7 miles as conditions worsened. At 18.3 miles look to the right for gigantic Cleft Arch. I turned around at 18.4 miles [07].

Return Trip: Return the way you came.

Services: No services of any kind along the trail. The visitor center, 8 miles west on Highway 211, has flush toilets and bottled water in vending machines. There are toilets at Newspaper Rock east on 211.

After completing the trail, you can turn left on Highway 211 and drive west, where you'll see signs for the Needles Outpost on the right before reaching the entrance booth to Canyonlands National Park. There is a general store and campground at this location. (It is privately owned and not associated with the park.) They sell fuel, bottled water, camping spots (no hook-ups), and supplies. Flush toilets and showers are available. It is a seasonal business and not always open, so call ahead if you're low on fuel. (See telephone number in Appendix.)

Maps: Canyonlands Official Map and Guide, Trails Illustrated Canyonlands National Park #210, and USGS 7.5 minute maps North Six-Shooter Peak 38109-B6, South Six-Shooter Peak 38109-A6, and Harts Point South 38109-A5.

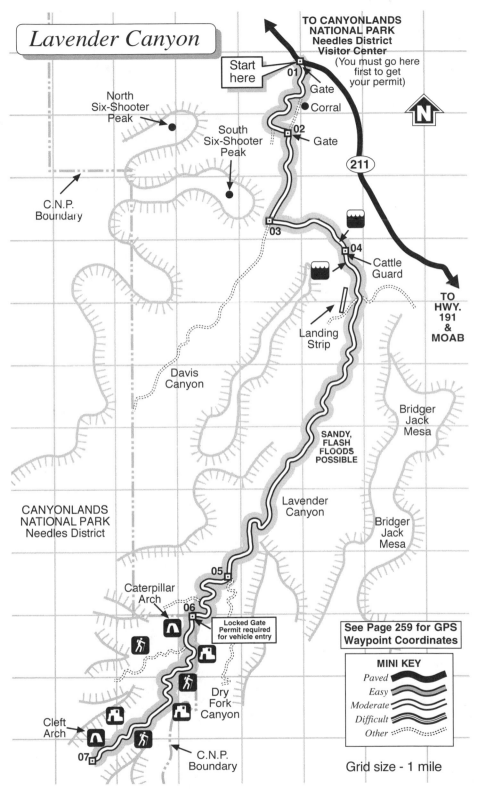

Lavender Canyon

TO CANYONLANDS NATIONAL PARK Needles District Visitor Center (You must go here first to get your permit)

Start here

01 Gate

Corral

02 Gate

211

North Six-Shooter Peak

South Six-Shooter Peak

C.N.P. Boundary

03

04 Cattle Guard

TO HWY. 191 & MOAB

Landing Strip

Davis Canyon

SANDY, FLASH FLOODS POSSIBLE

Bridger Jack Mesa

Lavender Canyon

Bridger Jack Mesa

CANYONLANDS NATIONAL PARK Needles District

05

Caterpillar Arch

06 Locked Gate Permit required for vehicle entry

Dry Fork Canyon

Cleft Arch

07

C.N.P. Boundary

See Page 259 for GPS Waypoint Coordinates

MINI KEY
Paved
Easy
Moderate
Difficult
Other

Grid size - 1 mile

239

Lion's Back & Potato Salad Hill

Lion's Back and Potato Salad Hill are obstacles, not trails. Because they are so popular, this book would not be complete without mentioning them. Lion's Back became famous years ago when a vehicle, having lost its brakes, careened off the side. The driver survived. The event was caught on video tape and was shown on several television programs. Potato Salad Hill draws crowds by the hundreds during the Jeep Safari. Rollovers are common. Pictures don't capture the steepness of either obstacle. They are both extremely dangerous. Potato Salad Hill is technically more challenging than Lion's Back but a mistake on Lion's Back can have more dire consequences.

To reach Lion's Back, take Sand Flats Road east out of town 1.4 miles from the stop sign by the cemetery. Turn left into a parking area at a private campground. There's a fee to drive Lion's Back but not to watch.

To reach Potato Salad Hill, take Sand Flats Road east out of town 1.0 miles past the stop sign near the cemetery. Turn right, following signs to America's Most Beautiful Dump. Go about a mile south on a moderate four-wheel-drive road to a flat area. Potato Salad Hill is out of view on the right. To drive it, bear left, then swing right to the bottom of the hill. To watch, park in this open area and walk west.

Lion's Back

Potato Salad Hill

APPENDIX

Pine Tree Arch inside Arches National Park.

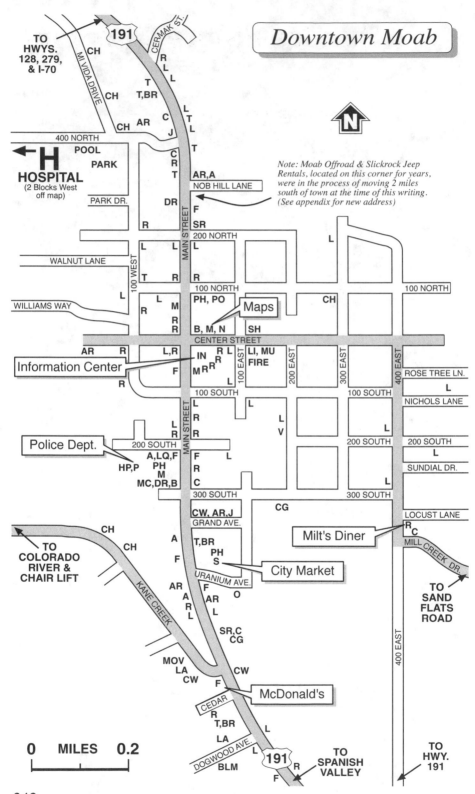

Downtown Moab

TO HWYS. 128, 279, & I-70

191

CERMAK ST.

MI VIDA DRIVE

CH
CH
CH

T
T,BR
AR

R
L
L
L
T
L
C
J
L
T
L
T
C
R
T

N

Note: Moab Offroad & Slickrock Jeep Rentals, located on this corner for years, were in the process of moving 2 miles south of town at the time of this writing. (See appendix for new address)

400 NORTH

POOL
PARK

H
HOSPITAL
(2 Blocks West off map)

PARK DR.

DR

AR,A
NOB HILL LANE

F
SR

R

200 NORTH

L

L
L
R

L

WALNUT LANE

100 WEST

T
R

L
R

100 NORTH

L

100 NORTH

CH

WILLIAMS WAY

L

L
R
M
R
R

PH, PO

B, M, N

SH

Maps

CENTER STREET

AR
R
R

L,R

IN
M
R
R
R
L
R

LI, MU
FIRE

100 EAST

200 EAST

300 EAST

400 EAST

Information Center

F

L

100 SOUTH

100 SOUTH

ROSE TREE LN.

L

NICHOLS LANE

L

L
R
R

L
R
R

L

L V

L

200 SOUTH

SUNDIAL DR.

Police Dept.

200 SOUTH

A, LQ, F
PH
M
MC, DR, B

HP, P

F
R
C

L

L

200 SOUTH

300 SOUTH

300 SOUTH

CG

LOCUST LANE

CW, AR, J
GRAND AVE.

R
C

Milt's Diner

TO COLORADO RIVER & CHAIR LIFT

CH

CH

KANE CREEK

A

F

AR
AR
R
L

T,BR
PH
S

F
AR
L

O

City Market

MILL CREEK DR.

TO SAND FLATS ROAD

SR, C
CG

MOV
LA
CW

CW

F

McDonald's

CEDAR
R
T,BR

LA

DOGWOOD AVE.

BLM

400 EAST

L

L

191

R

F

TO SPANISH VALLEY

TO HWY. 191

0   MILES   0.2

URANIUM AVE.

200 SOUTH

242

Services/Store Directory

CODE	SERVICE
A	Auto Parts
AR	Auto Repair
B	Bank
BLM	Bureau of Land Management
BR	Bicycle Rentals
C	Convenience Store
CG	Campground/RV Park
CH	Church
CW	Car Wash
DR	Doctor
F	Fast Food
FIRE	Fire Department
H	Hospital, Allen Memorial
HP	Highway Patrol
IN	Information Center
J	Jeep Rental
L	Lodging
LA	Laundromat
LI	Library
LQ	Liquor Store
M	Map/Bookstore
MC	Medical Center
MOV	Movie Theatre
MU	Museum
N	Newspaper
O	Optometrist
P	Police Department
PARK	Public Park
PH	Pharmacy
PO	Post Office
POOL	Public Swimming Pool
R	Restaurant
S	Supermarket
SH	Sheriff
SR	Service Station
T	Tours/Expeditions
V	Veterinarian

GPS Basics

Frequently asked Questions:

What is GPS? GPS stands for Global Positioning System. It consists of 27 satellites that circle the earth and broadcast signals to receiving units below. These signals allow you to determine your position on the earth. Five to 12 satellites can be picked up at any one time. A GPS unit with 12-satellite capability has the best chance of determining your position quickly.

Is GPS necessary? No. Some people prefer to rely on instinct, orienteering and map-reading skills. In many areas roads are well defined and easy to follow. You may travel with people who are familiar with the trail or you may prefer hiring a guide. Most of the trails in this book can be driven without the use of GPS.

Then why should I buy a GPS unit? It's the fastest and easiest way to determine your position. Like any new device, you'll wonder how you got along without it.

What kind of GPS unit do I need? There are many brands and models in all price ranges. It depends on your needs. Don't get one with less than 12 parallel satellite channels. I wouldn't buy one without the ability to download data to a computer. New products are coming onto the market everyday. Shop around and educate yourself before buying.

How complicated is it to use a GPS unit? My GPS unit came with a 4˝x 6˝ 100-page user's manual. It took a little time to read but it was simple and easy to understand. After a little practice, using the unit becomes second nature.

What are waypoints and trackpoints? Waypoints are important locations you choose to mark along your route, like where you start, key intersections along the way, and your final destination. Waypoints are recorded when you consciously hit a button. Trackpoints are automatically recorded as you move along. They're often referred to as a breadcrumb trail.

How accurate is GPS? Reasonably close, but not perfect. The government deliberately scrambles the satellite signals for the civilian population. This error is referred to as *selective availability*. Your location can be off by as much as the length of a football field in all directions. This is close enough for most situations, but is a problem when intersections are close together. Still, it's easier to figure out which way to turn when you know the direction of your destination. GPS is a poor way to determine altitude.

244

Do I need a computer to use a GPS unit? No, but if you have a computer, you'll be able to do a lot more. You can download waypoints and trackpoints to your home computer onto digital maps and see exactly where you went. You can print maps showing your exact route. You can save a large number of routes to upload to your GPS unit anytime you want. You can exchange routes and maps with friends. You can store many detailed maps in the computer at a very low cost per map. You can see a much bigger picture of a map than what you see on your tiny GPS screen. You can use maps with more detail.

If you use a laptop, you can take it with you and follow your progress on the screen. You can download hundreds of waypoints and trackpoints instantly into your GPS unit and avoid the tedious task of entering them by hand. Most GPS units don't have a keypad, so entering numerical data takes some time.

Is a laptop easy to use in the field? No. It's hard to find a good place to set it up. The screen is hard to see in the sun. It's exposed to damage from dust and vibration. I keep mine in its case much of the time and pull it out when I need it. Despite these drawbacks, it has been indispensible at times and saved me many hours of wandering around aimlessly. I know I'll never get lost when I have it with me.

I already have paper maps. Will a GPS unit help me? Yes. You can plot your GPS location on any map that has tick marks along the edge for latitude/longitude or UTM coordinates. You can get a general idea where you are by sighting across the map. To determine your exact position, you'll need to draw lines and use a template. It's awkward to do in a cramped vehicle but the results are just as good as using a computer. Talk to your local map store for the right templates.

What's UTM (Universal Transverse Mercator)? It's an alternative to using Latitude/Longitude coordinates. Many people prefer it because it's easier to plot on a map. Most topo maps have ruled UTM grid lines. Others argue that UTM is not as accurate as Lat./Long. Some maps may have only one set of coordinates, so you need both. Most GPS units give coordinates both ways. Both are given in this book.

What maps do I need? Again it depends on your needs. The greatest amount of detail is shown on USGS 7.5 minute maps, but many maps are needed to cover a large area. They can be expensive in paper and awkward to carry around. I buy them as Digital Rasterized Graphics images (DRGs) for my computer. For about $35 I was able to buy sixty-four 7.5 maps, which covered all of the trails in this book. I understand you'll soon be able to buy an entire state of 7.5 minute maps for about $100, which would also include the mapping software. I have not seen these products but they sound great. They will be offered by All Topo Maps, Delorme, and Wildflower Productions and will be available by the time you read this.

Most people use vector maps rather than rasterized maps. They have less detail but you can get the entire US on just a few CDs.

What's the difference between rasterized and vector maps? A rasterized image looks like a photograph of the original map. It takes a lot of computer space. When you zoom out you lose detail. Up close, however, it has the best detail. A vector map is a line conversion and looks more like a drawing in flat color. It lacks detail, but looks the same as you zoom in and out. It doesn't require as much computer space and can be downloaded directly into some new GPS units. If you use rasterized maps, you'll need mapping software to manipulate the maps. Vector maps usually have their own mapping software built-in.

What's mapping software do? Among other things, it allows you to manipulate rasterized maps, download and upload your waypoints and trackpoints, save map images and print them out. It finds the next map as you run off the page and switches automatically to the next map when you're moving in your vehicle with your GPS on. This software is made by Fugawi, OziExplorer, All Topo Maps, Delorme, and Wildflower Productions.

What specific equipment and maps do you use, Mr. Wells? I use a Garmin II Plus GPS receiver. I bought two additional accessories— a dash mount and a computer cord. The computer cord is split with one part that goes to my cigarette lighter which powers the GPS unit. I've never needed an outside antenna. I have a Dell Inspiron 7000 laptop with a 14.5″ screen, 4 gig HD, 64 MB ram, and 300 MHz. It has two 4-hour batteries, but since I don't leave the computer on all the time, I've never needed the second battery. I use Fugawi mapping software with DRG 7.5 minute USGS maps.

I'm thinking about buying a Garmin III Plus GPS receiver in the future because you can download maps directly into the GPS unit. I'll certainly check out all the other brands before I buy, however.

Someday, I may decide to buy a stand to mount my computer in the car. In the meantime, I've been using a homemade desk that scts on the passenger seat. I took a plastic milk crate and turned it upside-down. I cut it on an angle so that the desktop is flat. The recessed bottom of the crate becomes the desktop. I covered the desktop with a layer of non-slip shelf liner. I bought nylon straps and quick release plastic clips like you use on a backpack. I strap the crate to the seat with one strap and the laptop to the crate with another. I can leave the laptop on while I'm moving over the roughest terrain although I close the lid so I can strap it down firmly. It also protects the computer from dust and the soft seat reduces the vibration.

How much did you spend on your GPS equipment? The Garmin II

Plus was about $250 plus a little more for the accessories. My laptop was about $3,000 with several upgrades but I use it for other things beside GPS. This was purchased directly from Dell. The Fugawi software costs about $90 purchased from 4x4*BOOKS*.com, and I've already mentioned I spent about $35 dollars for the DRG maps directly from Micropath. I spent less than $20 on my homemade desk. I also carry many folding maps that would be expensive to replace.

I don't want to spend that much but would still like to have a GPS unit. What can I do? You can buy quality GPS units for about $120 with basic features including 12 parallel channels. You don't need a computer, but you'll need to learn how to plot your position on a paper map. Use 1:100,000 scale USGS maps that cover a big area so you won't have to buy many maps. Check the maps you already own; they may be adequate.

If you have a home PC, I'd definitely spend a little more for a GPS unit that can download and upload data to your computer. The first time you try to key waypoints into your GPS unit, you'll know why a computer is important.

How can I learn more about GPS? The first thing I did was buy and read a book called *GPS Made Easy* by Lawrence Letham (see references and reading section). It explained GPS in easy-to-understand terms. Finding information about GPS units, different brands, etc., is more difficult. *4-Wheel Drive & Sport Utility Magazine* has been running a series of articles called GPS Notes by Michael Lawler. These articles have been very helpful because the information is up to date.

There's some good information on the Internet, too. Check out 4x4books.com, which sells GPS equipment and mapping products. They show and compare most GPS products and have the latest information on new products.

Most retail stores that sell GPS equipment don't seem to know much about it—at least the stores where I've shopped. I find it's better to contact the manufacturers directly. The three biggest brand names are Garmin, Magellan, and Lowrance. (See page 263 for addresses and telephone numbers.)

Note: The author is not sponsored by any manufacturer.

GPS Waypoint Coordinates

The following table lists waypoints for each trail. Waypoints are shown in Latitude/Longitude and UTM coordinates. All UTM coordinates are in Zone 12. Due to selective availability error, your readings will vary slightly from what is shown here. Not every intersection and turn is shown in these tables, just the turns at waypoints.

Wpt.	Mileage	Latitude North	Longitude West	UTM Easting	UTM Northing	Turn*

1. KLONDIKE BLUFFS

Wpt.	Mileage	Latitude North	Longitude West	UTM Easting	UTM Northing	Turn*
01	0	38° 44' 26.2"	109° 44' 01.0"	610064E	4288548N	R
02	1.1	38° 45' 14.0"	109° 43' 43.4"	610467E	4290025N	S
03	2.6	38° 46' 14.7"	109° 42' 55.3"	611601E	4291913N	L
04	3.7	38° 47' 00.7"	109° 43' 02.6"	611407E	4293329N	R
05	6.3	38° 48' 38.6"	109° 42' 13.7"	612542E	4296362N	R
06	6.9	38° 48' 15.5"	109° 41' 50.4"	613116E	4295660N	T

2. TOWER ARCH

Wpt.	Mileage	Latitude North	Longitude West	UTM Easting	UTM Northing	Turn*
01	0	38° 47' 43.1"	109° 39' 26.8"	616594E	4294710N	L
02	1.8	38° 46' 40.8"	109° 40' 41.3"	614824E	4292764N	S
03	3.3	38° 47' 14.0"	109° 41' 20.5"	613863E	4293773N	T
04	14.5	38° 42' 05.2"	109° 34' 46.6"	623515E	4284395N	L

3. TUSHER TUNNEL

Wpt.	Mileage	Latitude North	Longitude West	UTM Easting	UTM Northing	Turn*
01	0	38° 43' 37.1"	109° 43' 17.0"	611147E	4287048N	L
02	2.7	38° 43' 10.5"	109° 45' 42.4"	607646E	4286178N	R
03	3.6	38° 43' 39.9"	109° 46' 27.6"	606542E	4287072N	L
04	5.1	38° 42' 57.3"	109° 46' 47.5"	606079E	4285753N	T

4. HIDDEN CANYON OVERLOOK

Wpt.	Mileage	Latitude North	Longitude West	UTM Easting	UTM Northing	Turn*
01	0	38° 44' 53.7"	109° 44' 13.8"	609741E	4289391N	L
02	2.3	38° 44' 40.5"	109° 46' 45.1"	606096E	4288933N	L
03	3.9	38° 43' 29.1"	109° 47' 25.1"	605160E	4286719N	R
04	5.7	38° 43' 30.5"	109° 48' 36.8"	603426E	4286740N	S
05	6.9	38° 42' 59.7"	109° 49' 33.0"	602082E	4285772N	L
06	7.7	38° 42' 41.9"	109° 49' 13.2"	602568E	4285231N	T

5. HIDDEN CANYON

Wpt.	Mileage	Latitude North	Longitude West	UTM Easting	UTM Northing	Turn*
01	0	38° 44' 53.7"	109° 44' 13.8"	609741E	4289391N	L
02	2.3	38° 44' 40.5"	109° 46' 45.1"	606096E	4288933N	L
03	3.1	38° 44' 03.8"	109° 47' 04.3"	605648E	4287795N	L
04	3.8	38° 43' 40.4"	109° 46' 28.3"	606525E	4287086N	R
05	6.2	38° 42' 20.6"	109° 48' 10.7"	604084E	4284592N	R
06	7.8	38° 42' 23.8"	109° 49' 23.4"	602327E	4284668N	T

Wpt.	Mileage	Latitude North	Longitude West	UTM Easting	UTM Northing	Turn*

6. BARTLETT OVERLOOK

Wpt.	Mileage	Latitude North	Longitude West	UTM Easting	UTM Northing	Turn*
01	0	38° 37' 43.8"	109° 48' 03.8"	604362E	4276065N	R
02	1.5	38° 38' 33.4"	109° 49' 13.0"	602670E	4277572N	R
03	4.1	38° 40' 07.9"	109° 51' 09.7"	599812E	4280447N	R
04	6.7	38° 41' 45.9"	109° 49' 55.2"	601575E	4283490N	R
05	7.7	38° 42' 07.6"	109° 49' 10.0"	602658E	4284176N	T

7. SEVENMILE RIM

Wpt.	Mileage	Latitude North	Longitude West	UTM Easting	UTM Northing	Turn*
01	0	38° 40' 48.5"	109° 41' 29.1"	613827E	4281887N	L
02	2.0	38° 41' 59.6"	109° 42' 31.6"	612285E	4284056N	L
03	3.1	38° 41' 31.3"	109° 42' 48.4"	611892E	4283180N	L
04	3.9	38° 41' 00.6"	109° 42' 50.6"	611852E	4282232N	L
05	4.5	38° 41' 11.5"	109° 42' 33.5"	612260E	4282574N	R
06	5.6/ 0	38° 40' 35.3"	109° 42' 13.4"	612761E	4281464N	D
07	0.5	38° 40' 15.3"	109° 42' 05.7"	612957E	4280852N	R
08	0.9	38° 40' 04.4"	109° 42' 14.4"	612751E	4280511N	L
09	2.1	38° 39' 44.6"	109° 43' 07.9"	611467E	4279885N	S
10	2.6	38° 39' 29.2"	109° 43' 26.2"	611030E	4279404N	S
11	3.3/ 0	38° 39' 02.4"	109° 43' 40.7"	610692E	4278572N	T
12	1.1	38° 39' 47.8"	109° 43' 29.5"	610943E	4279974N	L
13	1.5	38° 39' 55.0"	109° 43' 55.3"	610315E	4280190N	L
14	2.2	38° 39' 42.9"	109° 44' 34.7"	609368E	4279804N	L
15	2.8/ 0	38° 39' 53.2"	109° 45' 04.4"	608648E	4280110N	R
16	0.8	38° 40' 31.6"	109° 44' 53.5"	608894E	4281296N	L
17	1.5	38° 41' 06.5"	109° 44' 57.9"	608772E	4282371N	L
18	2.7	38° 41' 46.4"	109° 45' 46.2"	607589E	4283586N	R
19	4.6	38° 43' 09.2"	109° 45' 43.2"	607628E	4286140N	R
20	7.2	38° 43' 36.8"	109° 43' 17.9"	611126E	4287038N	D

8. RAINBOW TERRACE

Wpt.	Mileage	Latitude North	Longitude West	UTM Easting	UTM Northing	Turn*
01	0	38° 41' 10.8"	109° 55' 07.8"	594037E	4282316N	R
02	0.2	38° 41' 20.3"	109° 55' 19.5"	593749E	4282607N	R
03	2.4	38° 42' 27.7"	109° 54' 36.7"	594760E	4284696N	R
04	6.3	38° 44' 55.5"	109° 56' 37.0"	591800E	4289219N	R
05	12.6	38° 47' 06.5"	109° 51' 02.0"	599837E	4293354N	R

9. SECRET SPIRE, DELLENBAUGH TUNNEL

Wpt.	Mileage	Latitude North	Longitude West	UTM Easting	UTM Northing	Turn*
01	0	38° 41' 04.3"	109° 54' 56.4"	594313E	4282120N	L
02	1.8	38° 40' 10.7"	109° 55' 44.5"	593171E	4280454N	T
01	0	38° 41' 04.3"	109° 54' 56.4"	594313E	4282120N	L
03	2.6	38° 41' 21.0"	109° 57' 30.0"	590597E	4282593N	L
04	3.0	38° 41' 02.8"	109° 57' 46.2"	590212E	4282027N	S

* R = Right   L = Left   S = Straight   D = Driver's Choice   T = Turnaround

Wpt.	Mileage	Latitude North	Longitude West	UTM Easting	UTM Northing	Turn*
10. SPRING CANYON POINT						
01	0	38° 41' 26.9"	109° 52' 53.2"	597281E	4282851N	L
02	10.6	38° 37' 47.8"	110° 01' 18.0"	585159E	4275959N	S
03	13.6	38° 36' 54.5"	110° 03' 37.3"	581806E	4274282N	T
04	1.7	38° 37' 43.3"	110° 02' 12.7"	583838E	4275806N	T
11. SPRING CANYON BOTTOM						
01	0	38° 38' 33.6"	109° 49' 12.7"	602677E	4277579N	S
02	9.4	38° 38' 39.3"	109° 58' 46.2"	588811E	4277586N	S
03	12.5	38° 37' 18.3"	110° 00' 10.7"	586797E	4275066N	T
12. HEY JOE CANYON						
01	0	38° 37' 17.9"	110° 00' 05.5"	586917E	4275057N	R
02	8.0	38° 38' 25.3"	110° 02' 38.4"	583203E	4277094N	R
03	8.6	38° 38' 32.7"	110° 02' 12.0"	583838E	4273330N	T
13. MINERAL POINT						
01	0	38° 35' 12.9"	109° 48' 18.3"	604073E	4271406N	R
02	6.9	38° 34' 27.0"	109° 54' 51.5"	594577E	4269874N	L
03	12.3	38° 32' 53.8"	109° 59' 06.8"	588431E	4266933N	T
14. MINERAL BOTTOM						
01	0	38° 34' 59.0"	109° 48' 01.7"	604480E	4270985N	R
02	14.5	38° 31' 01.9"	110° 00' 14.3"	586833E	4263466N	S
03	15.9	38° 31' 45.2"	109° 59' 24.7"	588020E	4264813N	T
15. GEMINI BRIDGES						
01	0	38° 39' 22.3"	109° 40' 35.1"	615169E	4279248N	L
02	4.7	38° 36' 00.2"	109° 40' 23.1"	615550E	4273025N	R
03	5.3	38° 35' 48.8"	109° 40' 49.3"	614919E	4272662N	R
04	6.1	38° 35' 46.6"	109° 41' 35.1"	613814E	4272578N	L
05	7.3	38° 35' 16.0"	109° 42' 22.7"	612675E	4271620N	L
06	7.7	38° 35' 08.2"	109° 42' 28.4"	612541E	4271378N	T
07	1.0	38° 35' 30.6"	109° 43' 25.5"	611150E	4272049N	R
08	1.7	38° 35' 45.2"	109° 44' 07.3"	610132E	4272485N	L
09	5.6	38° 34' 24.2"	109° 47' 29.8"	605265E	4269622N	D
16. METAL MASHER						
01	0	38° 39' 22.0"	109° 40' 34.3"	615190E	4279240N	L
02	4.7	38° 35' 59.4"	109° 40' 22.0"	615575E	4273000N	R
03	5.3	38° 35' 47.9"	109° 40' 49.2"	614923E	4272635N	R
04	6.1	38° 35' 46.5"	109° 41' 35.5"	613805E	4272576N	R
05	6.9	38° 36' 11.8"	109° 42' 01.4"	613166E	4273346N	R
06	7.3	38° 36' 31.4"	109° 42' 12.1"	612898E	4273946N	R
07	8.8	38° 37' 08.4"	109° 41' 20.9"	614122E	4275105N	L
08	9.3	38° 37' 20.2"	109° 41' 04.3"	614518E	4275475N	R
09	10.1	38° 37' 37.7"	109° 40' 35.4"	615209E	4276023N	S

Wpt.	Mileage	Latitude North	Longitude West	UTM Easting	UTM Northing	Turn*
10	10.5/ 0	38° 37' 55.3"	109° 40' 27.5"	615393E	4276570N	L
11	0.2	38° 37' 59.6"	109° 40' 32.7"	615263E	4276699N	R
12	1.9	38° 38' 30.2"	109° 41' 20.5"	614095E	4277628N	L
13	2.8	38° 38' 12.3"	109° 42' 02.1"	613098E	4277060N	R
14	3.9/ 0	38° 38' 13.9"	109° 42' 59.5"	611708E	4277091N	L
15	0.7	38° 37' 38.8"	109° 43' 02.7"	611645E	4276007N	S
16	1.6	38° 37' 05.5"	109° 43' 34.9"	610882E	4274971N	S
17	2.7	38° 36' 10.1"	109° 43' 59.9"	610301E	4273255N	S
18	3.8	38° 35' 40.2"	109° 44' 19.1"	609850E	4272327N	R

17. LONG CANYON

Wpt.	Mileage	Latitude North	Longitude West	UTM Easting	UTM Northing	Turn*
01	0	38° 32' 41.8"	109° 45' 48.9"	607751E	4266797N	L
02	3.3	38° 32' 30.7"	109° 42' 29.4"	612586E	4266524N	S
03	7.5	38° 32' 46.8"	109° 38' 50.5"	617877E	4267094N	D

18. BULL CANYON

Wpt.	Mileage	Latitude North	Longitude West	UTM Easting	UTM Northing	Turn*
01	0	38° 39' 22.3"	109° 40' 35.1"	615169E	4279248N	L
02	4.7	38° 36' 00.2"	109° 40' 23.1"	615550E	4273025N	R
03	5.3	38° 35' 48.8"	109° 40' 49.3"	614919E	4272662N	L
04	6.8	38° 34' 40.9"	109° 40' 37.2"	615244E	4270574N	R
05	8.7	38° 35' 04.2"	109° 42' 16.8"	612824E	4271257N	T

19. GOLD BAR RIM

Wpt.	Mileage	Latitude North	Longitude West	UTM Easting	UTM Northing	Turn*
01	0	38° 35' 59.2"	109° 44' 22.7"	615559E	4272992N	L
02	1.0	38° 35' 51.9"	109° 39' 42.5"	616535E	4272783N	L
03	1.5	38° 36' 05.8"	109° 39' 16.9"	617149E	4273219N	L
04	2.1	38° 36' 23.3"	109° 39' 14.3"	617204E	4273761N	L
05	2.8	38° 36' 24.1"	109° 38' 50.6"	617777E	4273794N	S
06	3.3	38° 36' 44.9"	109° 38' 44.5"	617914E	4274436N	L
07	3.8	38° 36' 51.3"	109° 38' 30.4"	618253E	4274638N	T

20. POISON SPIDER MESA

Wpt.	Mileage	Latitude North	Longitude West	UTM Easting	UTM Northing	Turn*
01	0	38° 32' 00.9"	109° 36' 24.8"	621426E	4265733N	R
02	1.1	38° 32' 05.1"	109° 36' 43.9"	620960E	4265855N	S
03	1.6	38° 32' 10.0"	109° 37' 09.6"	620336E	4265997N	S
04	2.5	38° 32' 37.3"	109° 37' 14.7"	620200E	4266836N	S
05	2.8	38° 32' 38.5"	109° 36' 59.3"	620574E	4266878N	S
06	2.9	38° 32' 40.9"	109° 36' 56.0"	620651E	4266954N	S
07	3.2	38° 32' 50.3"	109° 37' 02.0"	620503E	4267242N	S
08	3.4	38° 32' 58.6"	109° 36' 57.4"	620609E	4267499N	S
09	4.0	38° 33' 17.7"	109° 36' 39.6"	621033E	4268093N	S
10	5.0	38° 33' 33.6"	109° 35' 46.4"	622311E	4268604N	L
11	5.2	38° 33' 37.8"	109° 35' 42.1"	622413E	4268736N	L
12	5.3/ 0	38° 33' 42.9"	109° 35' 44.2"	622360E	4268892N	R

* R = Right   L = Left   S = Straight   D = Driver's Choice   T = Turnaround

Wpt.	Mileage	Latitude North	Longitude West	UTM Easting	UTM Northing	Turn*
13	0.2	38° 33' 45.3"	109° 35' 35.7"	622565E	4268970N	R
14	0.3	38° 33' 48.0"	109° 35' 27.7"	622757E	4269054N	R
15	0.5	38° 33' 49.3"	109° 35' 16.5"	623028E	4269100N	S
16	0.6	38° 33' 52.1"	109° 35' 12.7"	623120E	4269188N	S
17	0.9	38° 34' 02.6"	109° 35' 20.8"	622917E	4269509N	S
18	1.1	38° 34' 10.4"	109° 35' 28.1"	622738E	4269746N	R
19	1.3	38° 34' 15.8"	109° 35' 29.8"	622693E	4269910N	L
20	1.6	38° 34' 25.7"	109° 35' 37.6"	622499E	4270213N	L
21	2.1/ 0	38° 34' 41.2"	109° 35' 55.9"	622050E	4270686N	L
22	0.3	38° 34' 34.7"	109° 36' 11.2"	621683E	4270478N	L
23	0.7	38° 34' 15.7"	109° 36' 02.2"	621909E	4269897N	D
13	1.5	38° 33' 45.3"	109° 35' 35.7"	622565E	4268970N	R
24	—	38° 35' 07.2"	109° 35' 40.4"	622414E	4271490N	T

21. GOLDEN SPIKE

Wpt.	Mileage	Latitude North	Longitude West	UTM Easting	UTM Northing	Turn*
01	0	38° 33' 44.2"	109° 35' 43.9"	622367E	4268932N	S
02	0.4	38° 33' 59.3"	109° 35' 58.1"	622018E	4269391N	L
03	0.6	38° 34' 06.2"	109° 36' 08.6"	621760E	4269601N	S
04	0.9/ 0	38° 34' 15.2"	109° 36' 17.6"	621537E	4269876N	S
05	0.3	38° 34' 26.0"	109° 36' 24.5"	621364E	4270204N	S
06	0.5	38° 34' 38.4"	109° 36' 18.4"	621508E	4270589N	R
07	0.6	38° 34' 42.0."	109° 36' 15.4"	621577E	4270703N	L
08	1.1	38° 34' 51.5"	109° 36' 15.1"	621508E	4270955N	S
09	1.8	38° 35' 19.1"	109° 36' 23.5"	621364E	4271842N	R
10	1.9	38° 35' 27.6"	109° 36' 29.0"	621226E	4272102N	R
11	2.3	38° 35' 47.4"	109° 36' 23.6"	621348E	4272715N	L
12	2.6/ 0	38° 35' 54.9"	109° 36' 29.4"	621205E	4272944N	L
13	0.3	38° 35' 52.9"	109° 36' 46.8"	620784E	4272875N	R
14	0.7	38° 36' 09.6"	109° 36' 54.4"	620594E	4273389N	R
15	0.9	38° 36' 15.2"	109° 36' 55.2"	620572E	4273559N	L
16	1.1	38° 36' 21.1"	109° 37' 01.1"	620425E	4273739N	L
17	1.4	38° 36' 24.6"	109° 37' 14.2"	620108E	4273842N	L
18	1.5	38° 36' 25.2"	109° 37' 20.3"	619959E	4273859N	R
19	1.7	38° 36' 31.0"	109° 37' 27.6"	619781E	4273037N	S
20	1.9	38° 36' 32.3"	109° 37' 41.2"	619452E	4274071N	R
21	2.2	38° 36' 36.7"	109° 37' 56.8"	619072E	4274200N	L
22	2.4/ 0	38° 36' 30.8"	109° 38' 05.1"	618874E	4274017N	L
23	0.3	38° 36' 29.7"	109° 38' 13.7"	618667E	4273980N	R
24	0.5	38° 36' 35.3"	109° 38' 22.3"	618455E	4274149N	L
25	0.9	38° 36' 42.7"	109° 38' 30.9"	618245E	4274373N	S
26	1.2	38° 36' 50.3"	109° 38' 29.0"	618288E	4274607N	L

22. CLIFF HANGER

Wpt.	Mileage	Latitude North	Longitude West	UTM Easting	UTM Northing	Turn*
01	0	38° 31' 26.9"	109° 36' 04.9"	621924E	4264692N	R
02	2.2	38° 31' 09.9"	109° 37' 06.1"	620448E	4264146N	L
03	2.6	38° 31' 24.7"	109° 37' 13.4"	620267E	4264599N	S

Wpt.	Mileage	Latitude North	Longitude West	UTM Easting	UTM Northing	Turn*
04	3.6	38° 31' 46.3"	109° 38' 08.9"	618911E	4265246N	R
05	4.3	38° 31' 37.6"	109° 38' 31.0"	618381E	4264968N	T
06	—	38° 31' 35.9"	109° 36' 45.6"	620934E	4264954N	T

23. HURRAH PASS
01	0	38° 32' 00.1"	109° 35' 59.6"	622036E	4265719N	S
02	6.6	38° 27' 58.7"	109° 36' 01.2"	622110E	4258277N	R
03	9.7	38° 28' 54.5"	109° 37' 28.5"	619970E	4259965N	T

24. MOAB RIM
01	0	38° 33' 34.7"	109° 34' 56.4"	623521E	4268658N	L
02	1.1	38° 33' 59.0"	109° 34' 13.3"	624552E	4269422N	S
03	1.8	38° 33' 26.6"	109° 34' 13.8"	624558E	4268423N	R
04	2.4	38° 33' 03.8"	109° 34' 16.1"	624511E	4267721N	S
05	3.5	38° 32' 43.2"	109° 33' 29.6"	625648E	4267103N	L
06	4.3	38° 32' 54.0"	109° 32' 52.9"	626530E	4267449N	T
07	5.3	38° 32' 54.3"	109° 33' 41.7"	625350E	4267439N	R
08	5.6	38° 33' 01.6"	109° 33' 52.2"	625090E	4267660N	S
09	5.9	38° 33' 06.6"	109° 34' 08.2"	624702E	4267808N	L

25. PRITCHETT CANYON
01	0	38° 32' 08.2"	109° 35' 55.7"	622128E	4268969N	L
02	0.3	38° 32' 10.0"	109° 35' 42.5"	622446E	4266027N	S
03	1.7	38° 31' 39.2"	109° 34' 36.8"	624050E	4265103N	R
04	2.5	38° 31' 21.5"	109° 34' 01.8"	624906E	4264663N	S
05	3.6	38° 30' 54.2"	109° 33' 22.8"	625865E	4263744N	R
06	4.2	38° 30' 41.5"	109° 33' 07.9"	626232E	4263360N	S
07	4.4	38° 30' 43.8"	109° 32' 56.1"	626517E	4263433N	R
08	5.7	38° 29' 56.9"	109° 33' 25.5"	625826E	4261976N	S
09	6.1	38° 28' 41.7"	109° 33' 41.4"	625479E	4259655N	S

26. PRITCHETT ARCH
01	0	38° 25' 15.8"	109° 25' 55.4"	636878E	4253492N	R
02	3.0	38° 24' 59.5"	109° 28' 38.6"	632928E	4252922N	R
03	6.7	38° 26' 43.8"	109° 30' 56.5"	629533E	4256083N	L
04	10.5	38° 26' 51.1"	109° 33' 29.2"	625827E	4256249N	S
05	12.3	38° 28' 12.6"	109° 33' 37.9"	625577E	4258757N	S
06	14.5	38° 29' 38.9"	109° 33' 43.9"	625390E	4261416N	S
07	15.0	38° 29' 55.8"	109° 33' 25.1"	625838E	4261943N	L
08	15.2	38° 30' 01.0"	109° 33' 33.7"	625627E	4262101N	T

27. KANE CREEK CANYON
01	0	38° 27' 58.0"	109° 36' 02.4"	622081E	4258254N	L
02	3.7	38° 25' 59.2"	109° 33' 33.0"	625760E	4254649N	S
03	4.5	38° 25' 26.7"	109° 33' 07.5"	626394E	4253655N	S

* R = Right   L = Left   S = Straight   D = Driver's Choice   T = Turnaround

253

Wpt.	Mileage	Latitude North	Longitude West	UTM Easting	UTM Northing	Turn*
04	6.6	38° 23' 58.2"	109° 32' 16.2"	627681E	4250948N	S
05	10.7	38° 22' 57.9"	109° 29' 02.4"	632412E	4249164N	S
06	12.8	38° 23' 10.9"	109° 27' 33.8"	634555E	4249600N	L
07	13.3	38° 22' 54.2"	109° 27' 19.3"	634917E	4249091N	L

28. BEHIND THE ROCKS

Wpt.	Mileage	Latitude North	Longitude West	UTM Easting	UTM Northing	Turn*
01	0	38° 26' 24.0"	109° 25' 44.2"	637113E	4255599N	R
02	0.9	38° 26' 09.6"	109° 26' 21.3"	636222E	4255138N	R
03	1.3	38° 26' 25.3"	109° 26' 32.8"	635934E	4255617N	L
04	2.3	38° 26' 25.7"	109° 27' 24.7"	634677E	4255609N	S
05	3.0	38° 26' 32.8"	109° 27' 58.0"	633865E	4255814N	S
06	3.6/ 0	38° 26' 52.4"	109° 28' 27.5"	633140E	4256405N	L
07	1.1	38° 26' 25.7"	109° 29' 20.2"	631877E	4255562N	S
08	2.0	38° 26' 00.7"	109° 30' 07.6"	630739E	4254774N	R
09	2.5	38° 26' 18.5"	109° 30' 04.7"	630801E	4255324N	R
10	3.7	38° 27' 09.5"	109° 29' 41.4"	631341E	4256903N	L
11	5.0	38° 26' 43.9"	109° 30' 52.7"	629626E	4256086N	R
12	5.4	38° 26' 58.8"	109° 31' 03.8"	629348E	4256542N	S
13	5.7	38° 27' 09.9"	109° 31' 13.1"	629117E	4256880N	L
14	6.1	38° 27' 21.4"	109° 31' 29.4"	628716E	4257230N	L
15	6.7	38° 27' 41.2"	109° 32' 06.4"	627810E	4257826N	S
16	6.9/ 0	38° 27' 39.6"	109° 32' 26.5"	627323E	4257766N	R
17	1.0	38° 28' 25.9"	109° 32' 36.0"	627069E	4259192N	L
18	3.6	38° 29' 38.0"	109° 33' 44.2"	625384E	4261389N	L

29. PICTURE FRAME ARCH

Wpt.	Mileage	Latitude North	Longitude West	UTM Easting	UTM Northing	Turn*
01	0	38° 25' 15.8"	109° 25' 55.4"	636878E	4253492N	R
02	3.0	38° 24' 59.5"	109° 28' 38.6"	632928E	4252922N	R
03	5.4	38° 26' 18.5"	109° 30' 04.7"	630801E	4255324N	T
04	11.0	38° 26' 18.2"	109° 33' 16.8"	626144E	4255240N	T

30. FLAT IRON MESA

Wpt.	Mileage	Latitude North	Longitude West	UTM Easting	UTM Northing	Turn*
01	0	38° 21' 26.0"	109° 26' 02.4"	636827E	4246403N	R
02	0.3	38° 21' 26.9"	109° 26' 16.4"	636488E	4246426N	R
03	0.6	38° 21' 38.7"	109° 26' 25.4"	636264E	4246786N	R
04	1.5	38° 22' 01.0"	109° 26' 54.1"	635555E	4247463N	R
05	1.8	38° 22' 07.6"	109° 27' 05.7"	635271E	4247662N	L
06	2.2	38° 21' 47.4"	109° 26' 54.9"	635544E	4247042N	R
07	2.4	38° 21' 41.0"	109° 26' 59.3"	635441E	4246843N	S
08	3.1	38° 21' 25.8"	109° 27' 24.4"	634839E	4246366N	S
09	3.2	38° 21' 23.8"	109° 27' 21.9"	634901E	4246305N	L
10	3.5	38° 21' 11.6"	109° 27' 15.6"	635060E	4245932N	S
11	4.2	38° 20' 38.3"	109° 27' 45.3"	634355E	4244894N	R
12	4.8	38° 20' 53.8"	109° 28' 15.4"	633616E	4245358N	S
13	6.5	38° 21' 21.2"	109° 29' 38.2"	631593E	4246169N	L
14	7.3/ 0	38° 20' 54.5"	109° 29' 40.2"	631557E	4245346N	R

Wpt.	Mileage	Latitude North	Longitude West	UTM Easting	UTM Northing	Turn*
15	0.4	38° 20' 39.4"	109° 29' 34.8"	631698E	4244883N	S
16	1.3	38° 20' 08.2"	109° 29' 03.8"	632464E	4243935N	L
17	1.7	38° 19' 58.7"	109° 28' 53.5"	632719E	4243644N	R
18	2.4	38° 19' 30.5"	109° 29' 00.9"	632554E	4242773N	L
19	2.7/ 0	38° 19' 24.9"	109° 29' 12.9"	632266E	4242593N	T
20	0.2	38° 19' 27.7"	109° 29' 03.7"	632487E	4242686N	R
21	0.6	38° 19' 28.5"	109° 28' 36.5"	633148E	4242722N	R
22	0.9	38° 19' 21.5"	109° 28' 24.9"	633434E	4242510N	R
23	1.2	38° 19' 09.2"	109° 28' 26.2"	633407E	4242130N	S
24	1.5	38° 19' 08.0"	109° 28' 12.2"	633748E	4242097N	L
25	1.7	38° 19' 20.0"	109° 28' 14.1"	633695E	4242466N	R
26	2.4	38° 19' 22.4"	109° 27' 44.4"	634416E	4242553N	R
27	3.2	38° 19' 57.9"	109° 27' 15.8"	635092E	4243659N	R
28	5.0	38° 19' 26.4"	109° 25' 33.7"	637588E	4242730N	L

31. HELL'S REVENGE

Wpt.	Mileage	Latitude North	Longitude West	UTM Easting	UTM Northing	Turn*
01	0	38° 34' 31.2"	109° 31' 19.2"	628751E	4270481N	L
02	0.4	38° 34' 46.5"	109° 31' 35.0"	628360E	4270946N	L
03	0.7	38° 34' 53.1"	109° 31' 42.1"	628187E	4271148N	L
04	1.0	38° 35' 05.1"	109° 31' 56.1"	627841E	4271513N	S
05	1.2	38° 35' 10.3"	109° 32' 02.4"	627685E	4271671N	R
06	1.4	38° 35' 16.0"	109° 32' 00.3"	627734E	4271846N	R
07	1.5	38° 35' 20.5"	109° 31' 58.1"	627786E	4271987N	R
08	1.6	38° 35' 23.5"	109° 31' 58.0"	627787E	4272079N	S
09	1.9	38° 35' 40.1"	109° 31' 53.4"	627889E	4272592N	S
10	2.1	38° 35' 48.3"	109° 31' 50.3"	627960E	4272844N	L
11	2.5	38° 36' 02.3"	109° 31' 59.3"	627736E	4273274N	R
12	3.1/ 0	38° 36' 26.1"	109° 32' 05.7"	627568E	4274006N	T
13	0.8	38° 36' 04.2"	109° 32' 05.6"	627582E	4273329N	R
14	0.9	38° 35' 58.7"	109° 32' 09.9"	627482E	4273160N	S
15	1.2	38° 35' 49.7"	109° 32' 22.0"	627193E	4272878N	S
16	1.7	38° 35' 38.7"	109° 32' 35.8"	626864E	4272532N	S
17	1.8	38° 35' 34.5"	109° 32' 36.2"	626857E	4272403N	L
18	2.2	38° 35' 37.4"	109° 32' 18.8"	627276E	4272499N	R
19	2.6	38° 35' 24.6"	109° 32' 15.3"	627366E	4272106N	R
20	2.7	38° 35' 22.9"	109° 32' 21.0"	627231E	4272050N	S
21	2.9/ 0	38° 35' 13.3"	109° 32' 24.4"	627152E	4271755N	R
22	0.2	38° 35' 17.8"	109° 32' 32.6"	626953E	4271889N	L
23	0.4	38° 35' 15.4"	109° 32' 40.8"	626755E	4271811N	R
24	0.6	38° 35' 19.1"	109° 32' 50.0"	626531E	4271923N	L
25	0.8	38° 35' 09.6"	109° 32' 38.8"	626806E	4271635N	S
26	1.0	38° 35' 04.6"	109° 32' 26.7"	627101E	4271484N	S
27	1.5	38° 34' 52.2"	109° 32' 01.4"	627720E	4271112N	S
28	1.6	38° 34' 46.6"	109° 31' 56.6"	627838E	4270942N	R
29	2.5	38° 34' 11.7"	109° 31' 31.8"	628457E	4269874N	R

* R = Right   L = Left   S = Straight   D = Driver's Choice   T = Turnaround

Wpt.	Mileage	Latitude North	Longitude West	UTM Easting	UTM Northing	Turn*

32. FINS & THINGS

Wpt.	Mileage	Latitude North	Longitude West	UTM Easting	UTM Northing	Turn*
01	0	38° 34' 47.7"	109° 29' 55.1"	630777E	4271023N	R
02	0.5	38° 34' 36.6"	109° 29' 37.4"	631211E	4270689N	R
03	0.8	38° 34' 41.0"	109° 29' 32.9"	631317E	4270825N	R
04	1.5	38° 34' 46.0"	109° 29' 20.9"	631607E	4270983N	R
05	1.8	38° 34' 55.6"	109° 29' 16.8"	631700E	4271280N	R
06	2.1	38° 34' 57.3"	109° 29' 14.1"	631765E	4271336N	R
07	2.5	38° 34' 53.6"	109° 28' 52.2"	632296E	4271230N	R
08	3.0/ 0	38° 34' 37.5"	109° 28' 32.9"	632772E	4270742N	L
09	0.1	38° 34' 42.5"	109° 28' 31.8"	632795E	4270895N	R
10	0.5	38° 34' 38.8"	109° 28' 15.1"	633201E	4270788N	L
11	0.6	38° 34' 44.9"	109° 28' 10.4"	633312E	4270978N	R
12	1.1	38° 35' 03.9"	109° 28' 09.0"	633336E	4271565N	L
13	1.6	38° 34' 59.9"	109° 28' 37.1"	632659E	4271429N	L
14	2.6	38° 35' 20.9"	109° 29' 28.2"	631411E	4272058N	R
15	3.0	38° 35' 33.4"	109° 29' 43.1"	631044E	4272437N	R
16	3.7	38° 35' 31.8"	109° 30' 17.1"	630223E	4272374N	S
17	4.0	38° 35' 24.1"	109° 30' 05.7"	630504E	4272141N	R
18	4.1	38° 35' 19.9"	109° 30' 03.3"	630562E	4272013N	R
19	4.4	38° 35' 14.5"	109° 30' 13.9"	630309E	4271842N	R
20	4.7	38° 35' 17.9"	109° 30' 27.0"	629991E	4271941N	R
21	5.1	38° 35' 26.5"	109° 30' 47.7"	629485E	4272198N	R
22	5.3	38° 35' 34.3"	109° 30' 52.1"	629375E	4272436N	D
23	5.5	38° 35' 29.2"	109° 30' 53.4"	629347E	4272279N	L
21	5.6	38° 35' 26.5"	109° 30' 47.7"	629485E	4272198N	R
20	6.0	38° 35' 17.9"	109° 30' 27.0"	629991E	4271941N	S
24	6.4	38° 34' 57.0"	109° 30' 23.8"	630079E	4271299N	D

33. PORCUPINE RIM

Wpt.	Mileage	Latitude North	Longitude West	UTM Easting	UTM Northing	Turn*
01	0	38° 34' 54.7"	109° 24' 55.8"	638015E	4271359N	L
02	0.3	38° 35' 02.4"	109° 24' 42.8"	638327E	4271603N	S
03	1.9	38° 35' 10.8"	109° 23' 11.8"	640524E	4271900N	S
04	3.1	38° 35' 39.2"	109° 22' 35.7"	641381E	4272791N	S
05	3.7	38° 35' 56.8"	109° 23' 05.0"	640664E	4273321N	S
06	4.2/ 0	38° 36' 11.9"	109° 23' 22.3"	640236E	4273780N	T
07	2.6	38° 35' 05.6"	109° 23' 11.2"	640541E	4271739N	R

34. SAND FLATS ROAD

Wpt.	Mileage	Latitude North	Longitude West	UTM Easting	UTM Northing	Turn*
01	0	38° 34' 31.3"	109° 31' 21.4"	628698E	4270484N	S
02	7.1	38° 34' 54.9"	109° 24' 57.0"	637986E	4271365N	S
03	12.4	38° 33' 53.4"	109° 21' 04.6"	643644E	4269568N	S
04	19.8	38° 31' 22.0"	109° 20' 16.2"	644900E	4264922N	D

35. STEEL BENDER

Wpt.	Mileage	Latitude North	Longitude West	UTM Easting	UTM Northing	Turn*
01	0	38° 32' 16.5"	109° 28' 23.6"	633070E	4266399N	R
02	0.7	38° 32' 19.6"	109° 27' 59.2"	633658E	4266504N	L

Wpt.	Mileage	Latitude North	Longitude West	UTM Easting	UTM Northing	Turn*
03	1.4	38° 31' 53.8"	109° 27' 32.8"	634311E	4265719N	S
04	2.5	38° 31' 52.1"	109° 26' 35.5"	635699E	4265691N	R
05	3.1	38° 31' 42.6"	109° 26' 05.6"	636429E	4265411N	R
06	3.6	38° 31' 29.2"	109° 25' 31.5"	637261E	4265010N	S
07	4.7	38° 30' 55.0"	109° 24' 58.1"	638087E	4263970N	R
08	5.0	38° 30' 43.5"	109° 25' 01.0"	638022E	4263615N	L
09	6.1	38° 30' 09.0"	109° 24' 17.3"	639100E	4262570N	D
10	6.5	38° 30' 15.3"	109° 23' 53.6"	639670E	4262775N	S
11	6.9	38° 29' 40.7"	109° 23' 36.5"	640103E	4261714N	L
12	8.5	38° 28' 55.7"	109° 23' 58.0"	639606E	4260318N	S
13	8.7	38° 28' 51.6"	109° 24' 08.9"	639346E	4260188N	R
14	9.1	38° 28' 58.8"	109° 24' 25.1"	638948E	4260403N	L

36. ONION CREEK, FISHER TOWERS

Wpt.	Mileage	Latitude North	Longitude West	UTM Easting	UTM Northing	Turn*
01	0	38° 43' 27.0"	109° 21' 17.8"	643008E	4287244N	R
02	9.4	38° 41' 19.7"	109° 13' 11.4"	654829E	4283541N	S
03	10.4	38° 40' 37.5"	109° 12' 40.5"	655602E	4282254N	T

37. TOP OF THE WORLD

Wpt.	Mileage	Latitude North	Longitude West	UTM Easting	UTM Northing	Turn*
01	0	38° 48' 37.9"	109° 18' 16.0"	647219E	4296910N	R
02	5.3	38° 46' 14.8"	109° 14' 57.2"	652099E	4292587N	R
03	8.6	38° 43' 57.6"	109° 15' 39.4"	651161E	4288340N	R
04	9.6	38° 43' 15.2"	109° 15' 55.7"	650792E	4287025N	T

38. ROSE GARDEN HILL

Wpt.	Mileage	Latitude North	Longitude West	UTM Easting	UTM Northing	Turn*
01	0	38° 41' 20.6"	109° 13' 12.4"	654806E	4283567N	L
02	3.1	38° 43' 09.9"	109° 11' 06.8"	657773E	4286995N	S
03	5.2	38° 43' 46.6"	109° 10' 34.6"	658529E	4288145N	S
04	5.9	38° 43' 41.9"	109° 11' 10.1"	657674E	4287981N	S
05	6.7	38° 43' 35.9"	109° 12' 02.9"	656404E	4287770N	S
06	12.6	38° 47' 12.4"	109° 13' 20.0"	654411E	4294409N	L
07	14.8	38° 46' 15.4"	109° 14' 57.4"	652096E	4292606N	S

39. THOMPSON CANYON

Wpt.	Mileage	Latitude North	Longitude West	UTM Easting	UTM Northing	Turn*
01	0	38° 38' 41.9"	109° 09' 24.6"	660409E	4278784N	L
02	9.2	38° 41' 34.4"	109° 11' 25.3"	657385E	4284042N	S
03	10.2	38° 41' 02.8"	109° 12' 13.5"	656240E	4283046N	S
04	10.9	38° 40' 37.6"	109° 12' 39.7"	655622E	4282257N	R

40. GEYSER PASS

Wpt.	Mileage	Latitude North	Longitude West	UTM Easting	UTM Northing	Turn*
01	0	38° 29' 11.9"	109° 18' 58.8"	646849E	4260948N	R
02	4.5	38° 28' 38.7"	109° 16' 36.8"	650307E	4259988N	S
03	7.8	38° 29' 07.8"	109° 13' 53.9"	654238E	4260961N	R
04	13.3	38° 27' 18.0"	109° 11' 53.4"	657223E	4257630N	R
05	16.7	38° 25' 45.3"	109° 11' 14.5"	658222E	4254791N	S

* R = Right   L = Left   S = Straight   D = Driver's Choice   T = Turnaround

Wpt.	Mileage	Latitude North	Longitude West	UTM Easting	UTM Northing	Turn*
06	20.6	38° 23' 23.2"	109° 09' 41.4"	660568E	4250456N	R
07	25.1	38° 20' 35.4"	109° 12' 24.1"	656720E	4245205N	R

41. LA SAL PASS

Wpt.	Mileage	Latitude North	Longitude West	UTM Easting	UTM Northing	Turn*
01	0	38° 26' 02.1"	109° 20' 17.8"	645040E	4255063N	S
02	6.1	38° 25' 58.2"	109° 16' 54.9"	649960E	4255032N	L
03	7.6	38° 25' 38.7"	109° 16' 32.4"	650518E	4254439N	L
04	9.4	38° 25' 08.9"	109° 15' 02.6"	652714E	4253564N	S
05	10.6	38° 25' 16.9"	109° 13' 59.4"	654241E	4253839N	R
06	16.5	38° 21' 51.9"	109° 11' 08.2"	658517E	4247600N	R
07	18.4	38° 20' 35.4"	109° 12' 24.1"	656720E	4245205N	R

42. SHAFER TRAIL

Wpt.	Mileage	Latitude North	Longitude West	UTM Easting	UTM Northing	Turn*
01	0	38° 30' 26.8"	109° 39' 38.2"	616786E	4262764N	S
02	2.2	38° 29' 27.0"	109° 40' 20.7"	615783E	4260904N	S
03	5.8	38° 28' 20.4"	109° 41' 48.5"	613686E	4258821N	S
04	11.2	38° 27' 46.6"	109° 46' 16.6"	607201E	4257691N	S
05	13.0	38° 27' 35.6"	109° 47' 37.4"	605247E	4257324N	R
06	18.2	38° 28' 18.8"	109° 48' 36.8"	603791E	4258637N	D

43. LATHROP CANYON

Wpt.	Mileage	Latitude North	Longitude West	UTM Easting	UTM Northing	Turn*
01	0	38° 28' 18.8"	109° 48' 36.8"	603791E	4258637N	L
02	5.3	38° 27' 35.6"	109° 47' 37.4"	605247E	4257324N	S
03	8.2	38° 26' 17.9"	109° 45' 57.0"	607714E	4254963N	R
04	16.6	38° 24' 01.8"	109° 47' 37.3"	605337E	4250734N	L
05	20.1	38° 22' 12.5"	109° 46' 20.9"	607235E	4247391N	T

44. WHITE RIM

Wpt.	Mileage	Latitude North	Longitude West	UTM Easting	UTM Northing	Turn*
01	0	38° 28' 19.2"	109° 48' 36.7"	603793E	4258651N	L
02	17.4	38° 23' 26.4"	109° 47' 34.5"	605419E	4249645N	S
03	28.1	38° 19' 51.9"	109° 49' 37.1"	602529E	4242994N	S
04	36.1	38° 16' 29.2"	109° 51' 45.0"	599499E	4236708N	R
05	42.9	38° 19' 25.1"	109° 54' 33.8"	595334E	4242079N	S
06	53.2	38° 22' 26.2"	109° 57' 52.9"	590437E	4247608N	S
07	64.2	38° 25' 48.0"	110° 00' 29.3"	586576E	4253784N	S
08	68.2	38° 27' 11.6"	110° 00' 23.9"	586679E	4256364N	R
09	70.4	38° 28' 32.0"	109° 59' 52.9"	587403E	4258849N	L
10	76.9	38° 31' 01.9"	110° 00' 14.3"	586833E	4263466N	R
11	91.3	38° 34' 59.0"	109° 48' 01.7"	604480E	4270985N	L

45. CHICKEN CORNERS

Wpt.	Mileage	Latitude North	Longitude West	UTM Easting	UTM Northing	Turn*
01	0	38° 28' 54.5"	109° 37' 28.5"	619970E	4259965N	S
02	2.5	38° 28' 14.0"	109° 38' 52.2"	617960E	4258686N	L
03	4.4	38° 27' 10.9"	109° 40' 03.2"	616268E	4256714N	R
04	6.8	38° 25' 45.6"	109° 41' 18.6"	614476E	4254060N	R
05	10.0	38° 27' 03.4"	109° 42' 54.6"	612115E	4256426N	S
06	11.5	38° 26' 29.2"	109° 44' 09.9"	610305E	4255346N	T

Wpt.	Mileage	Latitude North	Longitude West	UTM Easting	UTM Northing	Turn*

46. LOCKHART BASIN

Wpt.	Mileage	Latitude North	Longitude West	UTM Easting	UTM Northing	Turn*
01	0	38° 25' 45.6"	109° 41' 18.6"	614476E	4254060N	L
02	4.7	38° 25' 31.2"	109° 43' 00.4"	612014E	4253583N	S
03	13.9	38° 22' 14.2"	109° 41' 45.1"	613926E	4247530N	L
04	21.8	38° 19' 43.4"	109° 40' 38.5"	615608E	4242908N	S
05	28.0	38° 16' 13.6"	109° 42' 52.0"	612457E	4236399N	S
06	34.2	38° 12' 49.3"	109° 40' 37.1"	615825E	4230147N	S
07	37.1	38° 10' 32.9"	109° 39' 55.2"	616906E	4225957N	D

47. COLORADO RIVER OVERLOOK

Wpt.	Mileage	Latitude North	Longitude West	UTM Easting	UTM Northing	Turn*
01	0	38° 10' 01.4"	109° 45' 32.2"	608719E	4224873N	R
02	4.5	38° 12' 46.3"	109° 47' 19.2"	606047E	4229919N	L
03	7.3	38° 12' 57.5"	109° 49' 41.0"	602595E	4230220N	T

48. ELEPHANT HILL

Wpt.	Mileage	Latitude North	Longitude West	UTM Easting	UTM Northing	Turn*
01	0	38° 08' 31.5"	109° 49' 34.9"	602847E	4222024N	R
02	1.5	38° 09' 07.2"	109° 50' 30.9"	601472E	4223108N	L
03	3.4	38° 08' 14.5"	109° 51' 38.9"	599835E	4221464N	R
04	3.9	38° 08' 28.6"	109° 52' 02.2"	599262E	4221889N	R
05	5.3	38° 09' 31.0"	109° 51' 41.4"	599745E	4223819N	L
06	8.5	38° 10' 55.5"	109° 52' 30.6"	598516E	4226410N	T

49. SALT CREEK/ HORSE CANYON

Wpt.	Mileage	Latitude North	Longitude West	UTM Easting	UTM Northing	Turn*
01	0	38° 09' 00.4"	109° 45' 15.9"	609141E	4222997N	S
02	2.2	38° 07' 33.8"	109° 44' 52.4"	609749E	4220336N	R
03	3.3	38° 06' 52.0"	109° 45' 14.1"	609238E	4219039N	T
04	5.5	38° 07' 07.1"	109° 44' 19.1"	610571E	4219524N	S
05	6.5	38° 06' 38.4"	109° 43' 50.1"	611289E	4218649N	L
06	12.4	38° 03' 49.9"	109° 43' 52.7"	611296E	4213454N	T

50. LAVENDER CANYON

Wpt.	Mileage	Latitude North	Longitude West	UTM Easting	UTM Northing	Turn*
01	0	38° 09' 10.6"	109° 37' 37.2"	620301E	4223468N	S
02	1.8	38° 08' 06.0"	109° 37' 51.8"	619976E	4221471N	R
03	3.5	38° 06' 49.4"	109° 38' 13.3"	619486E	4219104N	L
04	5.0	38° 06' 26.4"	109° 36' 51.0"	621501E	4218426N	R
05	12.9	38° 01' 37.8"	109° 39' 07.3"	618309E	4209481N	R
06	14.5	38° 01' 04.8"	109° 39' 48.4"	617324E	4208449N	S
07	18.4	37° 58' 58.8"	109° 41' 41.7"	614616E	4204525N	T

* R = Right   L = Left   S = Straight   D = Driver's Choice   T = Turnaround

Glossary

Airing down - Letting air out of your tires to improve traction.

ARB lockers - A brand of differential locker that can be quickly activated when needed but turned off when not in use. (See differential locker.)

Articulation - The flexibility of your suspension system. Greater articulation means your wheels will go up and down more to better accommodate ground undulation.

BLM - Bureau of Land Management.

Cairn - A stack of rocks that marks an obscure trail. (See photo page 27.)

Clevis - A U-shaped device with a pin at one end that is used to connect tow straps.

Come-along - A hand-operated ratchet that functions as a winch.

Cryptobiotic crust - A brown or black, jagged crust that slowly forms on loose desert soils. Nature's first step to controlling erosion. (See photo page 23.)

Desert Varnish - A dark coating on hard rock surfaces created by a natural chemical/oxidation process. Takes thousands of years to form. (See page 16.)

Differential locker - Optional gearing installed inside your differential that equalizes power to wheels on both sides of an axle. Eliminates loss of power when climbing steep undulating hills. Not the same as locking-in your hubs.

Fin - Any smooth, round, elongated rock formation.

High centered - When your undercarriage gets stuck on a rock, mound, log, or ridge. Usually requires you to jack up your vehicle to get free.

High-lift jack - A tool that allows you to quickly lift your vehicle high off the ground. Considered a necessity on hard-core trails. Also substitutes for a winch.

Lift - A vehicle modification that raises the suspension or body of a vehicle to provide greater ground clearance.

Locker - (See differential locker.)

Low range - A second range of gears that increases the power of your vehicle. Used for climbing steep grades, especially at higher altitude.

Petroglyphs - Indian motifs abraded into rock surfaces and desert varnish.

Pictographs - Indian motifs painted on rock surfaces using pigments and dyes.

Safari - Easter Jeep Safari. Moab's annual major four-wheel-drive event held the week prior to Easter.

Skid plates - Plates that protect vulnerable parts of your undercarriage.

Slickrock - Any smooth, rounded rock formation. Slippery for horses and wooden wagon wheels. Provides excellent traction for rubber tires.

Snatch block - A pulley that opens so it can be slipped over your winch cable.

Spur road - A side road that dead ends, often rougher than the main road.

Switchback - A zig-zag road for climbing a steep grade.

Talus - Loose fragmented rock formed by freezing and thawing above timberline.

Tow point, tow hook - A point on your vehicle that enables you to quickly and safely attach a tow strap. Considered a basic necessity for four-wheeling.

USGS - United States Geological Survey.

Whoop-ti-do - Undulating terrain that's fun to drive. Often occurs in sandy areas, although some areas of slickrock create the same effect.

W.S.A. - Wilderness Study Area.

References & Reading

Above and Beyond Slickrock, by Todd Campbell, Wasatch Publishers, Salt Lake City, UT. Moab's premiere mountain biking guide. (revised 1995)

Canyon Rims Recreation Area, by F.A. & M.M. Barnes, Canyon Country Publications, Moab, UT. An illustrated, comprehensive guide to the Canyon Rims Recreation Area. Covers range of topics including geography, natural and human history, roads and trails, and recreational opportunities. (1991)

Coyote's History of Moab, by Jose Knighton, Compost Press, Moab, UT. A concise, entertaining history of Moab. (1994)

Desert Survival Handbook, by Charles A. Lehman, Primer Publishers, Phoenix, AZ. A basic guide to desert survival. (1996)

Exploring Canyonlands & Arches National Parks, by Bill Schneider, Falcon Publishing, Inc., Helena, MT. A hiking and backroad guide to Canyonlands and Arches National Park. (1997)

A History of Grand County, by Richard A. Firmage, published by Grand County and the Utah State Historical Society. A complete textbook history of Grand County including the town of Moab. (1996)

GPS Made Easy, by Lawrence Letham, published by The Mountaineers, Seattle, WA. Hundred-page handbook covers the basics of GPS. (1998)

Hiking, Biking and Exploring Canyonlands National Park and Vicinity, by Michael R. Kelsey, Kelsey Publishing, Provo, UT. Comprehensive guide to Canyonlands National Park. (1992)

Moab Country Day Hikes, by Fran & Terby Barnes, Canyon Country Publications, Moab, UT. Forty day hikes in the Moab Area. (1996)

Mountain Biking Moab, by David Crowell, Falcon Publishing Co., Inc., Helena, MT. Pocket-size mountain biking guide of Moab. (1997)

Utah Byways, by Toni Huegel, Post Company, Idaho Falls, ID. Backcountry guide to Utah featuring 60 drives for Sport Utility Vehicles. Includes quality maps and photographs. (1996)

40 Grand Trails From Deadhorse Point Road, by Jack Bickers, 4-WD Trailguide Publications, Moab, UT. Hiking and backroad guide featuring areas along Highway 313—Deadhorse Point Road. (1991)

Addresses & Phone Numbers

Arches National Park
P. O. Box 907
Moab, UT 84532
(435) 719-2299
www.nps.gov/arch

Bureau of Land Management
82 East Dogwood
Moab, UT 84532
(435) 259-2100

Canyonlands National Park Reservation Office
2282 S. West Resource Blvd.
Moab, UT 84532
(435) 259-4351 Fax: 259-4285
www.nps.gov/cany

Canyonlands N.P. Ranger Districts:
Island in the Sky (435) 259-4712
Needles (435) 259-4711
Maze (435) 259-2652

Chamber of Commerce
805 North Main
Moab, UT 84532
(435) 259-7814

Dan Mick's Guided Tours
600 Millcreek Drive
P. O. Box 1234
Moab, UT 84532-1234
(435) 259-4567
www.danmick.com

Dead Horse Point State Park
P. O. Box 609
Moab, UT 84532
(435) 259-2614

Farabee Jeep Rentals (stock Jeeps)
401 North Main
Moab, UT 84532
(435) 259-7494

Grand County Travel Council
P. O. Box 550
Moab, UT 84532
(435) 259-1370
(800) 635-6622

Manti-La Sal National Forest Moab Ranger District
62 East 100 North
Moab, UT 84532
(435) 259-7155

Moab Information Center
Main & Center Street
Moab, UT 84532
(800) 635-6622

Moab Offroad
(4x4 service and hard-core
Jeep rentals)
2251 South Highway 191
Moab, UT 84532
(435) 259-5678

Museum, Dan O'Laurie Memorial
118 Center Street
Moab, UT 84532
(435) 259-7985

Needles Outpost (call ahead)
(now offering Jeep rentals)
P. O. Box 1107
Monticello, UT 84535
(435) 979-4007

LOCAL MAP SOURCES & BOOKSTORES

Back of Beyond Bookstore
83 North Main Street
Moab, UT 84532
(435) 259-5154

Canyon Country Publications
P. O. Box 963
Moab, UT 84532
(435) 259-6700

Canyonlands Natural History Association
3031 South Hwy. 191
Moab, UT 84532
(435) 259-6003 or
1-800-840-8978
www.cnha.org

T. I. Maps, etc.
29 East Center Street
Moab, UT 84532
(435) 259-5529
www.moab.net/timaps

GPS EQUIPMENT & COMPUTER MAPS

4X4*BOOKS*.com
(308) 381-4410,
Fax: (308) 384-4497
www.4x4books.com

All Topo Maps
P.O. Box 58596
Salt Lake City, UT 84108-0596
(888) 450-4922
www.alltopo.com

Delorme Mapping
P. O. Box 298
Yarmouth, ME 04096
(207) 846-7000
www.delorme.com

Fugawi
Northport Systems, Inc.
1246 Yonge Street, Suite 302
Toronto, Ontario
M4T 1W5 Canada
(416) 920-0447
www.fugawi.com

Garmin International
1200 E. 151st Street
Olathe, KS 66062
(800) 800-1020
www.garmin.com

Lowrance Electronics, Inc.
12000 E. Skelly Drive
Tulsa, OK 74128-1703
(800) 324-1356
www.lowrance.com

Magellan Corporation
960 Overland Court
San Dimas, CA 91773
(909) 394-5000
www.magellangps.com

Map Tech
655 Portsmouth Ave.
Greenland, NH 03840
(800) 627-7236
www.maptech.com

Micropath
2023 Montane Drive East
Golden, CO 80401-8099
(303) 526-5454
www.micropath.com

OziExplorer
www.powerup.com.au/~lornew/
oziexp.html (in Australia)

Wildflower Productions
375 Alabama Street, Suite 400
San Francisco, CA 94110
(415) 558-8700
www.topo.com

Index

About the Author

Charles A. Wells graduated from Ohio State University in 1969 with a degree in graphic design. After practicing design in Ohio, he moved to Colorado Springs, CO, in 1980 and worked 18 years in the printing business. Over the years, he and his family enjoyed a wide array of recreational activities including hiking, biking, rafting, and skiing. He bought his first SUV in 1994 and began exploring places he was previously not able to reach in the family sedan. He later joined a four-wheel-drive club and began visiting Moab where he quickly fell in love with the area. This book follows two successful Colorado backroad guidebooks.

All of the trails in this book were driven by the author in the vehicles described below. He wrote the trail descriptions based on his own observations, shot most of the photographs, and created all the maps. No sponsors were involved. The result of this hands-on approach is a valuable and unbiased reference for both novices and hard-core four-wheeling enthusiasts.

Author with Jeep Grand Cherokee above Long Canyon. Equipped with automatic transmission, factory skid plates, tow points, CB radio, and LT235-75R15 BFG all-terrain tires.

Jeep is a registered trademark of Chrysler Corporation.

Jeep Cherokee on Cliff Hanger. Equipped with Tomken 5″ lift, bumpers, rocker skids, tire carrier, and brush guard; 8,000 lb. Warn winch; Dana 44 rear axle; 410 gears; ARBs front & rear; Tera Low 4 to 1 transfer case; skid plates; stock 4-liter engine with 5-speed; K&N air filter; full interior roll cage; 32 x 11.50 BFG A/T tires; tow points; fold-in mirrors; and CB radio.

Order Form

Order 4 ways: (We accept Visa, Mastercard, Discover, American Express)
1. Call toll-free **1-877-222-7623**
2. Online at www.funtreks.com (secure site)
3. By Mail: Send this completed order form to:
   FunTreks, Inc, P. O. Box 3127, Monument, CO 80132
4. Fax this completed order form to 719-277-7411.

Please send me the following book(s): (I understand that if I am not completely satisfied, I may return the book(s) for a full refund, no questions asked.)

Qty.

Guide to Colorado Backroads & 4-Wheel Drive Trails (2nd Edition)
        ISBN 0-9664976-6-X, 286 pages, Price $24.95   _____

Guide to Northern Colorado Backroads & 4-Wheel Drive Trails
        ISBN 0-9664976-8-6, 194 pages, Price $19.95   _____

Guide to Moab, UT Backroads & 4-Wheel Drive Trails
        ISBN 0-9664976-2-7, 268 pages, Price $24.95   _____

Guide to Arizona Backroads & 4-Wheel Drive Trails
        ISBN 0-9664976-3-5, 286 pages, Price $24.95   _____

Guide to Southern California Backroads & 4-Wheel Drive Trails
        ISBN 0-9664976-4-3, 286 pages, Price $24.95   _____

Guide to Northern California Backroads & 4-Wheel Drive Trails
        ISBN 0-9664976-5-1, 286 pages, Price $24.95   _____

ATV Trails Guide, Moab, UT (full color)
        ISBN 0-9664976-7-8, 160 pages, Price $18.95   _____

Name: (please print)_____

Address:_____

City:_____ State:____ Zip:_____

Telephone: (_____) _____-_____

Sales Tax: Colorado residents add 2.9%. (Subject to change without notice.)
Shipping: $4.00 for first book and $1.00 for each additional book.

Payment Method: Check one:
_____ Check
_____ Visa
_____ Mastercard   Card number:_____
_____ Discover   Expiration Date:_____
_____ American Express   Name on card:_____

Thanks for your order!

Order Form

Order 4 ways: (We accept Visa, Mastercard, Discover, American Express)
1. Call toll-free **1-877-222-7623**
2. Online at www.funtreks.com (secure site)
3. By Mail: Send this completed order form to:
   FunTreks, Inc, P. O. Box 3127, Monument, CO 80132
4. Fax this completed order form to 719-277-7411.

Please send me the following book(s): (I understand that if I am not completely satisfied, I may return the book(s) for a full refund, no questions asked.)

Qty.

Guide to Colorado Backroads & 4-Wheel Drive Trails (2nd Edition)
ISBN 0-9664976-6-X, 286 pages, Price $24.95   _____

Guide to Northern Colorado Backroads & 4-Wheel Drive Trails
ISBN 0-9664976-8-6, 194 pages, Price $19.95   _____

Guide to Moab, UT Backroads & 4-Wheel Drive Trails
ISBN 0-9664976-2-7, 268 pages, Price $24.95   _____

Guide to Arizona Backroads & 4-Wheel Drive Trails
ISBN 0-9664976-3-5, 286 pages, Price $24.95   _____

Guide to Southern California Backroads & 4-Wheel Drive Trails
ISBN 0-9664976-4-3, 286 pages, Price $24.95   _____

Guide to Northern California Backroads & 4-Wheel Drive Trails
ISBN 0-9664976-5-1, 286 pages, Price $24.95   _____

ATV Trails Guide, Moab, UT (full color)
ISBN 0-9664976-7-8, 160 pages, Price $18.95   _____

Name: (please print)_____
Address:_____
City:_____ State:_____ Zip:_____
Telephone: (_____) _____-_____

Sales Tax: Colorado residents add 2.9%. (Subject to change without notice.)
Shipping: $4.00 for first book and $1.00 for each additional book.

Payment Method: Check one:
_____ Check
_____ Visa
_____ Mastercard   Card number:_____
_____ Discover   Expiration Date:_____
_____ American Express   Name on card:_____

Thanks for your order!